The Handbook of Children's Rights: Comparative Policy and Practice is the first comprehensive and radical appraisal of developments in children's rights in British and international settings. It brings together contributions from academics, social welfare practitioners, educationalists, child psychologists and politicians. This clearly structured and engaging book examines children's claims for rights in the social, welfare, judicial, educational and other settings. The various chapters consider the divergent responses of governments, the voluntary sector and other agencies to young people's rights claims by exploring and assessing the range of policy proposals designed to meet them.

The book has four broad objectives:

- to explore the various strands to the debate concerning children's rights and review developments in rights provision across the 1980s and 1990s;
- to evaluate the impact of recent British legislation on children's rights in key areas such as education, social services, criminal justice and the UN Convention on The Rights Of The Child;
- to examine recent policy proposals and initiatives in the British setting intended to secure rights for children and young people;
- and finally, to offer a comparative perspective on children's rights by examining issues and developments in a number of countries including America, Scandinavia, Australia and Russia.

The Handbook of Children's Rights will be invaluable to students of education, social work, social policy, sociology, youth and community work, law, politics, philosophy and policy studies as well as those studying postgraduate courses in social work, juvenile justice and education.

Bob Franklin is Reader and Director of Studies in the Department of Journalism Studies at the University of Sheffield.

Thomas Hammarberg is a member of the UN Committee on the Rights of the Child. He was formerly Secretary General of Amnesty International (1980–86) and Director of Rädda Barnen, Swedish Save the Children (1986–92).

The Handbook of Children's Rights

Comparative Policy and Practice

Edited by Bob Franklin
Preface by Thomas Hammarberg

London and New York

First published 1995
by Routledge
11 New Fetter Lane, London EC4P 4EE

Simultaneously published in the USA and Canada
by Routledge
29 West 35th Street, New York, NY 10001

Typeset in Times by LaserScript, Mitcham, Surrey
Printed and bound in Great Britain by
Mackays of Chatham PLC, Chatham, Kent

British Library Cataloguing in Publication Data
A catalogue record for this book is available from the British Library

Library of Congress Cataloguing in Publication Data
A catalogue record for this book has been requested

ISBN 0-415-11059-9 (hbk)
ISBN 0-415-11060-2 (pbk)

Contents

Contributors

Jo Aldridge is a Research Associate in the Department of Social Sciences, Loughborough University and a former journalist.

Gillian Alexander is Head of Kirklees Early Years Service (KEYS).

Barry Anderson is Head of the Youth Crime Section at the National Association for the Care and Resettlement of Offenders (NACRO).

Saul Becker is Director of the Young Carers Research Project in the Department of Social Sciences, Loughborough University and Director of Studies for the interdisciplinary Masters Degree programme in Policy, Organisation and Change in Professional Care, Loughborough University.

Shane Ellis is employed by Save The Children Fund as Leeds Children's Rights Officer.

Judith Ennew is a freelance writer and researcher, and co-founder of Streetwise International.

Målfrid Grude Flekkøy is a clinical psychologist. She was Norwegian Ombudsman for Children 1981–89. She has also been a Senior Fellow, UNICEF, International Child Development Centre.

Annie Franklin is Deputy Divisional Director for Save The Children Fund (North and East Division).

Bob Franklin is Reader in Journalism Studies at the University of Sheffield. He has taught previously at the Universities of Keele, Leeds, Northumbria at Newcastle-upon-Tyne and York.

Michael Freeman is Professor of Law at University College London.

Thomas Hammarberg is a member of the UN Committee on the Rights of the Child. He was formerly Secretary General of Amnesty International (1980–86) and Director of Rädda Barnen, Swedish Save the Children (1986–92).

Judith Harwin is a Lecturer in the Department of Social Administration at the London School of Economics.

Tony Jeffs is Reader in Social Policy, University of Northumbria at Newcastle-upon-Tyne. He is the author of several books on youth policy and is co-founder of the journal *Youth and Policy*.

Margaret Kennedy is National Co-ordinator of the 'Keep Deaf Children Safe' Child Abuse Project.

Gerison Lansdown is Director of the Children's Rights Development Unit.

Joan Lestor is Labour Member of Parliament for Eccles and Labour Party Shadow Minister for Overseas Development.

Christina Lyon is Professor of Law at Liverpool University.

Peter Newell is Director of End Physical Punishment of Children (EPOCH).

Nigel Parton is Professor of Child Care at Huddersfield University.

Cynthia Price Cohen is Director of ChildRights International Research Institute.

Moira Rayner is the Chairperson of the Board of the National Children's and Youth Law Centre, funded by the Australian Youth Foundation and based in Sydney, NSW. She is a barrister with particular interest in children's rights. She was the Commissioner for Equal Opportunities for the State of Victoria, in Australia, between 1990 and 1994.

Preface

The United Nations Convention on the Rights of the Child is a unique document. Since its adoption in November 1989 it has had a response dwarfing all previous international human rights treaties. The rate of ratification has been unprecedented, and the Convention could enter into force within less than a year. A monitoring committee could thereby be appointed and start functioning.

One explanation for this progress is that the Convention itself is more than a dry document with some rules on how to behave. It has a *vision*. It expresses some basic values about the treatment of children, their protection and participation in society. These can be found in Articles 2, 3, 6 and 12 of the Convention.

The choice of these Articles as 'general principles' was made by the UN Committee on the Rights of the Child during its first session in September–October 1991, when it agreed guidelines on how the initial reports by governments should be written and structured. These Articles were put under a special heading in the guidelines – before norms on civil rights, family aspects, health, education and the other more substantive provisions. It was made clear that the Committee wanted governments to report on the application of these principles separately, but also when reporting on the realisation of all other Articles.

A major aspect of the philosophy behind the Convention is that children, too, are equals; as human beings they have the same inherent value as grown-ups. The affirmation of the right to play underlines that childhood is valuable in itself; these years are not merely a training period for adult life. The idea that children have equal value may sound like a truism but is, in fact, a radical thought – not at all respected today.

Children – especially when very young – are vulnerable, and need special support to be able to enjoy their rights in full. How can children be granted equal value and at the same time the necessary protection? Part of the answer lies in the principle of 'the best interests of the child':

> *In all actions concerning children, whether undertaken by public or private social welfare institutions, courts of law, administrative authorities or legislative bodies, the best interests of the child shall be a primary consideration.*

(Art. 3, 1)

Whenever official decisions are taken which affect children, their interests should be seen as important. The interests of the parents or the state should not be the all-important consideration. This is indeed one of the major messages of the Convention.

This principle gives by its very nature importance to another principle, the one about respecting the views of the child. In order to know what actually is in the interests of the child it is only logical to listen to him or her:

> *States Parties shall assure to the child who is capable of forming his or her own views freely in all matters affecting the child, the views of the child be given due weight, in accordance with the age and maturity of the child.*

(Art. 12, 1)

Somewhat simplistically, this has been termed by some commentators as the 'participation element' in the Convention. The idea is that the child has the right to be heard, and have his/her ideas taken seriously. The reports by State Parties so far have been vague on this article; some have stated that children of, for instance, twelve years of age have the right to reject an adoption or a change of name or nationality. Few have displayed a comprehensive approach to this principle – which ought to affect life in schools, families and politics. The point is put on the agenda however.

The principle most directly related to children's economic and social rights is formulated in the right-to-life article. The article goes further than just granting children the right not to be killed; it includes the right to survival and to development:

> *States Parties shall ensure to the maximum extent possible the survival and development of the child.*

(Art. 6, 2)

The word 'survival' is unusual in human rights treaties; it is borrowed from the terminology used in development discussions. Its use in this connection was proposed by UNICEF during the drafting process. The purpose was to introduce a dynamic aspect to the right to life, including the need for preventive action such as immunisation.

The term 'development' relates to the individual child and should be interpreted in a broad sense. It adds a qualitative dimension to the article. Not only physical health is intended but also mental, emotional, cognitive, social and cultural development.

Modern child psychology has made clear how important the first days, weeks and months are for the future development of the child. This should also be considered in serious efforts to implement Article 6. It is essential that from the very beginning the child has the opportunity to relate to and communicate fully with the mother and/or another adult.

The Article could be seen as the platform for all other Articles in the Convention dealing with economic, social and cultural rights for children. Its wording about 'the maximum extent possible' implies a recognition that implementation requires resources and that certain measures may not be possible for poorer countries. At the same time, the formulation indicates that priority should be given to the implementation of this requirement in every country.

The fourth general principle of the Convention, as identified by the Committee on the Rights of the Child, is that *all* children should enjoy their rights, that no child should suffer discrimination:

> *States Parties shall respect and ensure the rights set forth in the present Convention to each child within their jurisdiction without discrimination of any kind, irrespective of the child's or his or her parent's or legal guardian's race, colour, sex, language, religion, political or other opinion, national, ethnic or social origin, property, disability, birth or other status.*
>
> (Art. 2, 1)

The message is about equality of rights. Girls should be given the same opportunities as boys. Refugee children, children of indigenous or minority groups should have the same rights as all others. Children who are disabled should be given the same opportunity to lead a decent life as others.

These are the principles of the Convention. But are they anything more than well-intended rhetoric?

That question formulates the challenge. We know that few areas have been so riddled by political hypocrisy as children's rights and welfare. It is obvious that the implementation of the Convention will depend to a large extent on political will.

When drafting the reporting guidelines, the UN Committee chose that governments should put heavy emphasis on this very aspect: on political measures to make reality of the principles and provisions of the Convention. It had in mind a comprehensive approach to reform, not least the establishment of procedures which would encourage constant scrutiny of what is actually done in this domain. Of particular interest here is Article 4:

> *States Parties shall undertake all appropriate legislative, administrative and other measures for the implementation of the rights recognized in this Convention. With regard to economic, social and cultural rights, States Parties shall undertake such measures to the maximum extent of their available resources and, where needed, within the framework of international co-operation.*

The Article describes obligations of conduct rather than of result; the emphasis is on what efforts the State Party makes in promoting the implementation of the Convention. A State Party should review its legislation and ensure that the laws are consistent with the Convention. The 'administrative and other measures' could include a range of steps in order to make the implementation effective. Mechanisms should exist on national and local levels to co-ordinate policies and to monitor the implementation of the Convention. In some countries there is nowadays an *Ombudsman*, or a similar institution for ombudswork for the rights of the child; the intention in most such cases is to ensure a system of independent monitoring.

Other mechanisms could be created for watching the rights of the child, including the establishment of complaints procedures. National commissions with non-governmental organisations have been established in a number of countries. The political decision-making itself is of course crucial. What procedures are there to ensure that child matters are taken seriously in both the Parliament and in local assemblies? What opportunities do children and their representatives have to make themselves heard? A major objective of the procedures is to encourage free public discussion on the rights of the child.

One important means towards genuine realisation of the Convention is education and training of personnel working with children: nursery school teachers, other teachers, child psychologists, paediatricians and other health personnel, the police, social workers and others. A deep understanding among these professionals about the rights of the child could be immensely important, and the UN Committee does ask questions about this aspect.

Let us look closer at Article 4. What precisely is meant by the formulation 'to the maximum extent of their available resources'? The intention is not to offer an escape clause for the less resourced countries; the Convention asks *all* State Parties to give priority, within their means, to the implementation of the Convention.

This has interesting implications. One is that countries with more resources should offer services to children on a higher absolute level than is possible for poor countries. The Convention should not only be seen as a list of minimum requirements. Richer countries should ask more from themselves, and should also put in 'the maximum extent' of their resources. This makes the Convention more relevant in the affluent societies.

Resources should not be seen as static. For the long-range perspective the dynamic dimension is politically interesting: the *mobilisation* of resources. Although the authorities are directly responsible for the implementation of the Convention, the resources of the whole society matter, including those in the so-called civil society. This ought to be a spur for governments to encourage and be open to initiatives by non-governmental groups.

The issue of privatisation of public services is part of this discussion. One argument for such moves has been precisely that more resources may be mobilised; private activities have also been regarded as more cost-effective. The Convention does not take a position on whether, for example, health clinics and schools should be run in the private or public sector. What is important, however, is that the rights of the child are respected. In that regard the government will always be responsible and that responsibility cannot be privatised. This, in turn, raises a question about steps taken by a government to ascertain that private services for children achieve the standards specified in Convention. A related discussion concerns what resources are made available for child-related services: *how* budgets can or cannot be trimmed during a period of recession. Programmes of structural adjustment have been enforced in most countries during recent years; this has been an economic necessity. How do these policies relate to the rights of the child?

A responsible – and future-oriented – economic policy is naturally in the interest of children. It is desirable for them that space is created for necessary investments and that foreign debts are reduced. The problem relates to the present priorities, to how the cuts and savings are made.

UNICEF and others have discussed structural reform *with a human face*, the intention being to create safeguards against cuts with severe social consequences. The World Summit for Children in September 1990 called for reforms to promote world economic growth 'while ensuring the well-being of the most vulnerable sectors of the populations, in particular the children'. That is in the spirit of the Convention on the Rights of the Child.

June 1994

Part I

Children's rights: an overview

Chapter 1

The case for children's rights: a progress report

Bob Franklin

It seems barely credible that it is only a decade since the Director of Research for a major children's charity reviewed *The Rights of Children* (Franklin, 1986) in a cynical and disparaging way, deriding what seemed to him to be the evidently absurd assumption which informed the book; namely that children possess rights and that adults should respect them. His concluding query signalled much of the overall flavour of the review; 'Whatever next? Will Neil, the hippy in the television series "The Young Ones", start campaigning for rights for lentils?' Thankfully, such ill-informed jibes now smack of anachronism. During the 1980s, children's rights seemed to come of age in a number of respects.

Intellectually, the discussion of children's rights was no longer confined to the allegedly more eccentric sections of the 'chattering classes' but achieved respectability. The legitimacy of children's claims to enjoy the possession of rights has been acknowledged, and informs government policy and legislation as well as the practice of welfare professionals. Politically, children's rights became contested territory for the major political parties. The Labour party's manifesto for the 1992 general election contained proposals for a Minister for Children and a Children's Rights Commissioner (see chapter 7), while the Liberal Democrats advocated lowering the age of suffrage to 16.

Legally, the notion of the 'best interests of the child' increasingly came to be supplemented, if not superseded, by the principle that where appropriate the wishes of the child should inform legal decisions. In an early essay, Hilary Rodham (subsequently Hilary Rodham Clinton) had argued that judicial and legal systems should presume children's competence and entitlement to rights (Rodham, 1974). The Children Act 1989 is an obvious example of legislation intended to acknowledge and concede children's abilities as autonomous decision-makers (see chapters 3 and 5).

Institutionally, the development of organisations such as End Physical Punishment of Children (EPOCH) and the Children's Legal Centre, but particularly the appointment of Children's Rights Officers in more than a dozen local authorities, attest to society's growing commitment to children's rights (see chapters 6 and 16). In Israel, New Zealand, Costa Rica and Norway ombudswork with children acknowledges, protects and promotes their rights (see chapter 13). Internationally, the United Nations Convention on the Rights of the Child has established a minimum set of rights for children. Governments which ratify the Convention accept a binding commitment to meet its standards and provisions for children (see chapters 5 and 8).

This growing acknowledgement of children's rights during the 1980s derived from a fortuitous combination of circumstances and events which provided particularly fertile terrain in which children's rights, both as concept and practice, could be nurtured. The International Year of the Child (IYC) in 1979 focused attention on children's rights issues, but triggered two further significant events. On the eve of IYC, the Polish government proposed the drafting of a United Nations Convention on the Rights of the Child, to establish an internationally agreed minimum set of rights for children and secure individual governments' compliance with them (see chapter 8). In the UK, the International Year of the Child prompted the establishment of the Children's Legal Centre which began campaigning and advising children about their rights. The Centre's lobbying and educational work has been significant in restructuring the discourse about children's rights by advocating children's rights to participate in the decision-making processes and institutions which influence and affect their lives (Children's Legal Centre, 1993). Other pressure groups, such as Justice for Children and the Family Rights Group, devoted to the promotion of the rights of children and their families, raised the public profile of children's rights issues. The media reflected and heightened the significance of rights issues in the public agenda. Esther Rantzen's *Childwatch* television programme attracted substantial audiences and led to the establishment of ChildLine in 1986.

Other, less happy circumstances provided additional impetus to the emergence of a nascent, albeit loosely-structured, informal and occasionally contradictory, movement for children's rights. The tragic deaths of Jasmine Beckford, Kimberley Carlile and Tyra Henry, reported in an explosion of sensationalist media coverage, served to demonstrate dramatically children's claims for protection rights. Paradoxically, when social workers placed more than 100 children in care because of alleged sexual abuse – in what came to be dubbed by the media as 'the Cleveland affair' – it was children's rights to autonomy and independence from an overly interventionist state which seemed to have been abrogated and to require assertion (Franklin and Parton, 1991).

These high profile cases also exploded the myth of the family as an institution which offered its members security and safety; for children, and also for women, the family was a potentially dangerous arena. The perception of the family as a place of quiet sanctity increasingly became disrupted by a reluctant acknowledgement that children's interests and rights could not be presumed to be identical with those of their parents; indeed children's and parents' rights might be antipathetic.

The 1990s have witnessed a reaction against children's rights, however – in the spheres of ideology, policy and practice. Ideologically, children have become the focus of a moral panic, in which the media have played a crucial role. Media presentations of children have metamorphosed them from the innocent 'sugar and spice' angels, reminiscent of the iconography of "Bubbles" in the Pears' soap advertisement, into inherently evil demons who, typifying Britain's declining moral standards, seem incapable of distinguishing right from wrong. This tendency reached its nadir in press reports of the Bulger case. The headline in the *Today* newspaper, under pictures of the two accused boys, described them as 'Born to Murder'. The day after they had been sentenced, the *Daily Star* headline asked, 'How Do You Feel Now You Little Bastards?' (25 November 1993). Ideologically, the reaction against children has perhaps been all the greater precisely because it is a reaction to an earlier mythical, cultural construct of the child as the personification of innocence and purity.

The media-inspired demonising of children has prompted a predictable retreat in some areas from policies intended to promote and protect children's rights. There has been, for example, a government retreat from recent criminal justice policy attempting to rehabilitate young offenders and divert them from custody (chapter 4); a retreat by the courts from considering seriously the voice of the child in family proceedings (chapter 3), and from moves to limit the use of parental physical punishment (chapters 5 and 16). Showing respect for children is 'soft' in 'Back to Basics Britain'. On 16 March 1994, a High Court judge ruled in favour of the childminder who insisted on hitting the children in her care, despite Article 19 of the UN Convention and the Department of Health guidelines, which many observers believed were intended to outlaw such barbarism. One journalist suggested that Sutton Council's case against the childminder was foolish and amounted to little more than 'parents being accused of mental cruelty for failing to buy Jaffa cakes for tea' (Bradley, 1993: 15). The ideology of children as inherently evil feeds – and is sustained by – this policy retreat. Society constructs the children it needs. Instead of policies to protect children in the community, the government and media have preferred to promote policies to protect the community from children.

Some practitioners have also become increasingly sceptical about children's rights. Claims that 'it has all gone too far' are perhaps too commonplace. A popular misconception seems to prevail which believes that rights for children can only be won at the expense of denying rights to others; whether parents or the practitioners and people who work with children.

It should be clear from these initial remarks, that recent progress in achieving rights for children has been faltering and uneven, but it has also been structured by important landmarks. Cruelty to children became a criminal offence in Britain in 1889, some sixty years after similar legislation outlawed cruelty to animals. It was 25 years later that Eglantyne Jebb and her Save the Children Fund International Union drafted the Geneva Convention. In 1959, the United Nations issued its first Declaration of the Rights of Children, announcing young peoples' entitlements to adequate nutrition, free education and medical care, as well as rights against exploitation and discriminatory practices. The 1980s were characterised by an increasing interest and concern with children's moral and political status, as well as their social and welfare needs. 1989 witnessed the signing of a redrafted, but considerably strengthened, Convention on the Rights of the Child. Thirty years after the original Declaration and four years after International Youth Year, the Convention marked the tenth anniversary of the UN International Year of the Child. In the early 1990s, individual nation signatories must report to the UN on their progress in implementing the Convention. Consequently, it seems an appropriate time to reassess some of the central arguments concerning children's rights and to take stock of the achievements of recent years in securing and promoting rights for children.

Much of the initial discussion concerning children's rights has been philosophical and conceptual in character. It has been concerned to establish the case for children's rights (Worsfold, 1974; Watson, 1980; Eekelaar, 1992 and Freeman, 1985, 1992); to construct elaborate schemes of classification for rights (Wald, 1979; Rogers and Wrightsman, 1978); to argue the case for extending children's political rights (Harris, 1982; Holt, 1975; Hoyles and Evans, 1989; Franklin, 1986, 1989, 1992); to suggest a 'compromise' which would offer a limited extension of rights to specific children (Archard, 1993); to reconcile potential clashes between acting in a child's best interests and conceding children's autonomy rights (Eekelaar, 1994); to suggest that advocacy of children's rights is simply a device for diminishing the 'real' freedoms of adults (Heartfield, 1993) or, alternatively, to dismiss children's rights claims (Scarre, 1980, 1989; Purdy, 1994).

But in the effort to address these general and theoretical considerations, practical suggestions for change have often been overlooked. In the British setting there has been, until quite recently and with honourable exceptions, little detailed elaboration of the sorts of institutional innovations which might facilitate the empowerment of children. This book explores both conceptual and policy aspects of children's rights by bringing together contributions from academics and researchers, social and welfare practitioners working in both the voluntary and statutory sectors, educationalists, child psychologists, politicians and professionals working in pressure groups promoting children's rights in specific spheres. The various chapters consider the divergent responses of governments, the voluntary sector and other agencies, to young people's rights claims by exploring and assessing the range of policy proposals designed to meet them. The intention is to offer a radical appraisal, by academics and practitioners, of recent developments in children's rights.

The book has four broad objectives. First, to examine and assess the various strands in the debate concerning children's rights and to review developments in rights provision throughout the 1980s and 1990s. Second, to evaluate the impact of recent British legislation on children's rights in key areas such as education, social and welfare services and criminal justice, as well as looking at some of the key provisions of the UN Convention and measuring English law against them. Third, to examine recent policy proposals and initiatives in the British setting intended to establish and promote rights for children and young people.

Finally, to offer a comparative perspective on children's rights by exploring issues and developments in America, Australia, Scandinavia and Russia, by considering the specific rights claims of street children and by examining the claims of children everywhere to have their rights to physical integrity respected.

This brief introduction attempts to contextualise the subsequent chapters by clarifying some of the ambiguities inherent in the phrase 'children's rights', by assessing the various strands in the debate about children's rights and, finally, by providing an overview of some of the major institutional reforms implemented to secure rights for children.

PROBLEMATIC DEFINITIONS; 'CHILDREN' AND 'RIGHTS'

Societies tend to divide their members' life cycles into two broad age states; childhood and adulthood. The transfer from one to the other is often associated with the acquisition of distinctive rights, privileges and obligations and is usually celebrated to confirm the significance of this *rite de passage*. In Britain, the age of 18 signals the age of majority, when individuals become formally adult, but this age boundary creates a number of anomalies. It means, for example, that a nurse, a soldier on active service as well as a parent with two children of her own, may legally be defined as 'a child'.

In truth, definitions of children, as well as the varied childhoods which children experience, are social constructs formed by a range of social, historical and cultural factors. Being a child is not a universal experience of any fixed duration, but is differently constructed expressing the divergent gender, class, ethnic or historical locations of particular individuals. Distinctive cultures, as well as histories, construct different worlds of childhood. Louisa Alcott's 'Little Women' would share few of the childhood experiences of Frank Richard's 'Billy Bunter' at Greyfriars school, or the children at Grange Hill comprehensive.

But while childhood may be difficult to define in an unproblematic way, it has often been mythologised as a 'golden age' in which children, untroubled by the adult concerns of work and economic life, are free to enjoy themselves. Adult platitudes seek constantly to persuade children that childhood years are the 'best years of their lives' (Holt, 1975; Franklin, 1986). But even cocoons can stifle and oppress as well as comfort. The modern conception of childhood – which dates from the sixteenth century and stresses the innocence and frailty of children – forcefully ejected children from the worlds of work, sexuality and politics, and designated the classroom as the major focus of children's lives (Plumb, 1972; Aries, 1962; Laslett, 1965; Holt, 1975). Children were no longer allowed to earn money or to decide how to spend their time; they were forced into dependency on adults and obliged to study or play (Pinchbeck and Hewitt, 1973). The 'golden age' mythology is difficult to sustain, however, when schools are excluding a growing number of their pupils (see chapter 2) and when a culture of high-rise architecture combined with the modern dependency on cars and limited local authority play provision, means that suitable play spaces for children are rare

(Titman, 1993). Cute, contented and dependent, but without autonomy in important decisions concerning their lives, children 'should be seen and not heard'.

Three other factors underscore the complexity of the notion of children and childhood. First, the age boundary between childhood and adulthood is established at different ages in different spheres of activity. In the UK, a child reaches the age of criminal responsibility at 10 but is not politically an adult until 18. These boundaries, moreover, are constantly shifting. The age of political suffrage was lowered from 21 to 18 in 1969; in February 1994 the age of homosexual consent was similarly reduced. In different countries other boundaries and limits prevail. In some states of Australia, for example, a child as young as seven can be considered criminally responsible and adult (see chapter 14). This variation of age limits across different societal histories and cultures, means that the numerous boundaries demarcating childhood can regress into an arbitrary and inconsistent relativism.

Second, the definition of everyone under 18 years as a child, or more accurately as a 'non-adult', obscures the inherent diversity of childhood and attempts to establish a false uniformity of needs and rights for an evidently heterogenous group. The age range from zero to eighteen embraces the most rapid and extensive period of an individual's physical, emotional and intellectual growth, in which they develop a wide range of skills and competencies and express a divergent range of needs. Consequently, the period between birth and adulthood is usually divided into four distinct periods; infancy, childhood, adolescence and early adulthood, with different needs, rights and responsibilities being judged appropriate for the different age groups. It seems absurd, for example, to suggest that a 17-year-old might enjoy greater empathy with a two-year-old than a near-age mate of 19 years, but it is the two-year-old and 17-year-old who are children. But children are not an homogeneous group with uniform needs. Children in their early years and disabled children, for example, have particular needs which must be met and may confront particular difficulties in prosecuting their rights claims (see chapters 10 and 11).

Third, the experiences of children in other countries, as well as some children in Britain, can radically subvert this mythologised and modern understanding of childhood. Ennew, for example, argues that the conception of childhood which stresses domesticity and dependency, is largely a Western definition which places certain children – especially street children – 'outside childhood'. The place for childhood to take place is 'inside'; 'inside society, inside a family, inside a private dwelling'. Consequently street children are society's 'ultimate outlaws' placed 'outside childhood' (see chapter 15).

In Britain, children who care for a terminally ill parent illustrate the tensions which can exist between the realities of childhood and its socially constructed image. Child carers are not dependent but depended upon; perhaps even to toilet an incontinent or profoundly ill parent. Aldridge and Becker suggest that caring for an adult may, 'deny child carers the experience of childhood' (see chapter 9).

While precise definition is evidently problematic, it seems apparent that childhood is a condition or circumstance characterised by powerlessness. It is important to recall that the term 'child' was used initially to describe anyone of low status, without regard for their age (Hoyles, 1979). Being a child continues to express more about power relationships than chronology, although the two are intimately intertwined. Children's powerlessness reflects their limited access to economic resources, their exclusion from political participation and the corresponding cultural image of childhood as a state of weakness, dependency and incompetence. Definitions of 'a child' and 'childhood' entail more than a specification of an age of majority; they articulate society's values and attitudes towards children. These are typically disdaining and ageist (Franklin and Franklin, 1990).

The definition of rights is a good deal less problematic, although it has not always been so. In the early 1970s, children's rights were described as 'a slogan in search of a definition' (Rodham, 1973: 487) but in the subsequent two decades theoretical discussion and the UN Convention as well as other children's rights charters, have mapped out much of the rights terrain. A wide range of rights have been claimed by and for children including the basic human rights to life, health services, education and a reasonable standard of living (UN Convention Articles 1, 24, 28, 27) as well as more radical claims for the right to vote, work and own property (Holt, 1975; Farson, 1977; Franklin, 1986). It is important that discussions of children's rights should keep two broad distinctions in mind; between legal and moral rights, and between welfare and liberty rights.

The distinction between legal and moral rights is easy to establish. A legal right is an entitlement which is acknowledged and enforced by an existing law. Legal rights are rights which children possess. A moral right, however, enjoys no legal endorsement (Feinberg, 1973). A moral right is a claim for a right which it is believed children should possess. Children's right to education is a legal right since every child has a statutory entitlement to receive education up to their sixteenth birthday. But children's right to vote is not established in law. It is a claim for an additional right and signals the need to reform existing legal entitlements.

The distinction between welfare and liberty rights corresponds to Rogers and Wrightsman's division of rights into the 'nurturance' versus 'self determination orientations' (Rogers and Wrightsman, 1978: 61). More recently the distinction has been expressed in terms of rights to protection versus rights to participation. These are, of course, very different kinds of rights – both in terms of the type of claims which rights holders are making, as well as the 'qualifications' necessary to exercise them. The possession of welfare rights – to education, health, to a minimum standard of living – require only that the right holder possesses '*interests* which can be preserved, protected and promoted' (Archard, 1993: 65). But claims for liberty rights – to participate in decision-making, to vote – require that the right holder, 'must be capable of making and exercising choices' (Archard, 1993: 65). Children's claims to protection rights have rarely been contested. Indeed, a number of philosophers including Jeremy Bentham have argued that animals deserve such rights since their possession requires only that the animal (human or non-human) is sensual and capable of suffering (Harris, 1982). Children's claims for liberty rights, however, have been hotly contested by philosophers like John Stuart Mill who argue that such rights require the capacities for reason, rationality and autonomy and that therefore children are excluded from their possession – along with people who are mentally ill or brain damaged (Scarre, 1980; Mill, 1969).

CHILDREN'S RIGHTS: THE DEBATE

Children in all societies are denied the right to make decisions about their affairs which as adults we take for granted. This denial of rights occurs both in the public realm of children's involvement in education and the care arrangements of the state and the private realm of the family. Children's lack of decision-making rights includes relatively unimportant matters such as decisions about which clothes to wear or what time to go to bed, to more significant concerns about the right to help structure the educational curriculum at school and the right to vote. But any society wishing to deny children, or any other group, rights which are the common property of other groups, should be able to offer clear and sustainable reasons for doing so. The burden of proof always rests with those who wish to exclude others from participation; children should not be obliged to argue their case for possessing the same rights as everyone else.

The argument for denying participation rights to children has two interrelated strands. First, it is alleged that children are not rational or capable of making reasoned and informed decisions. Rights to autonomy in decision-making grow with maturity. Locke stated the matter unequivocally. 'We are born free as we are born rational' he claimed, 'not that we have actually the exercise of either; age that brings one brings with it the other too' (Locke, 1964: 326).

Second, children lack the wisdom born of experience and consequently they are prone to make mistakes. By denying them the right to participate and make decision for themselves, society is attempting nothing more heinous than protecting children from their own incompetence. These two strands were cogently interwoven into a classic statement and defence of paternalism by the Master of the Rolls in *Re S* [1993], where he claimed '. . . a child is, after all, a child':

> The reason why the law is particularly solicitous in protecting the interests of children is because they are liable to be vulnerable and impressionable, lacking the maturity to weigh the longer term against the shorter, lacking the insight to know how they will react and the imagination to know how others will react in certain situations, lacking the experience to measure the probable against the possible.

This case is discussed further in chapter 3.

Both objections to children's rights claims can be met either positively or negatively; i.e., by asserting that children do possess the qualities which critics allege that they do not, or by conceding that if children do lack the skills and qualities necessary for participating in decision-making, they lack them to no greater degree than adults who are not, on this ground, disqualified from participation. Libertarians offer a number of arguments.

First, children do reveal a competence for rational thought and do make informed choices – from decisions about which television programmes to watch or which football teams to support, to more important issues such as developing strategies for dealing with a bully at school or an abusing parent at home. Children who have been sexually abused have to make a very complex assessment of the consequences for their family of disclosing that abuse. In these circumstances children display remarkably sophisticated skills in decision-making and evaluating outcomes.

Second, the argument which suggests that children are likely to make mistaken choices, because they lack experience of decision-making, rests on tautology and a confusion. The tautology is evident. If children are not allowed to make decisions because they have no experience of decision-making, how do they ever get started? This is catch 22. 'Even children, after a certain point, had better not be "treated as children" ', Feinberg remarks, 'else they will never acquire the outlook and capability of responsible adults' (Feinberg, 1980: 110). There is, moreover, nothing wrong with making mistakes; we all do it. Mistakes are not necessarily negative, but can provide positive opportunities to learn from our experiences. Why not allow children, like adults, the possibility to learn from their mistakes and grow in knowledge and experience as a consequence?

The confusion in the argument is also clear. It does not follow that children should not make decisions simply because they might make the wrong ones. It is important not to confuse the right to do something with doing the right thing. As Dworkin argues, we often accept that adults have the right to do something which is wrong for them (Dworkin, 1977: 188). Smoking offers an obvious example.

But even if it was conceded that children are not competent decision-makers, it could still be argued that they lack these competencies to no greater degree than adults. Since adults are not excluded from participation in decision-making on this ground, the exclusion of children represents a case of double standards. History offers convincing illustrations of the inadequacy of adult decision-making; it is little more than a catalogue of blunders. War, inequality, famine, racism and injustice are some of the fruits of adult deliberation and choice. It is hard to imagine a worse track record. To deny children the right to make mistakes would deprive them of a right which adults have exercised extensively. It would be hypocritical.

But if paternalists wish to insist that the possession of certain competencies is the criterion for participation, then it is a criterion which argues for the exclusion of adults as well as children. Presumably the paternalist intention is not to exclude children from decision-making merely because they are children, since this is not an argument but simply another tautology. Their argument about age-related rights regresses eventually to a debate concerning competence and, on this reasoning, it is not children who should be denied rights but all incompetent people – without regard to their age. Argued consistently, the paternalist position risks excluding adults as well as children and leads to unacceptably elitist conclusions. It is predictable that the exclusion of children has rarely raised the issue of elitism. There are other problems. Who, for example, would decide who is competent to participate? University professors? Educational psychologists? Political parties, local magistrates or Plato's philosophers? Nor do the difficulties end here. What might serve as criteria of competence and how might we test to establish them?

Finally, the denial of participation rights to children is unfair because children can do nothing to change or ameliorate the conditions which exclude them. If the grounds for exclusion were ignorance or lack of education, then the ignorant might endeavour to become wise and uneducated people might be motivated to read and learn. But young people cannot prematurely grow to the age of majority even if foolish enough to entertain such an ambition. Nor is the allegation of inequity met by the suggestion that the denial is temporary since children eventually become adults and acquire the appropriate status and rights. The argument here rests on a confusion between particular children and children as a social group. An individual child matures to adulthood, but this does not alter the status of children as a social group; the 13 million people in the UK who are denied the right to participate in making decisions about important matters in their lives.

In summary, the argument for denying participation rights to children on the grounds that they are not rational and lack experience has been strongly contested by libertarians. Under pressure, those opposed to children's rights have offered three additional arguments.

First, it is argued that children should not possess participation rights because they are incapable of what the German philosopher Kant called 'self maintenance'; what might now be described as self sufficiency. Kant believed that, 'the children of the house . . . attain majority and become masters of themselves . . . by their actually attaining to the capability of self maintenance' (Kant, 1887: 118). But the criterion of self maintenance fails to distinguish adults from children; it merely distinguishes between those who are capable of self maintenance and those who are not. It might, however, be used to justify excluding disabled people, sick and older people, as well as people who are unemployed, from participating in decision-making. Each of these groups could be judged to be incapable of self maintenance. But it is surely a dubious moral claim to suggest that anyone who lacks self sufficiency should be subject to the intervention of others in their affairs and denied autonomy rights?

A second argument suggests that the advocacy of children's rights is antipathetic to adult rights and diminishes adults' 'genuine' rights claims (Heartfield, 1993: 13); children's rights are bogus – a trojan horse. Children's rights are demands for protection either by parents or by the state in the guise of 'super parent'. But for adults, democratic rights are, above all else, the 'right to independence from the state . . . . Whenever the spurious notion of children's rights is invoked we can be sure that an attack on the real freedoms of adults is not far behind' (Heartfield, 1993: 14). But this argument is wrong-headed on two counts. First, children's rights have never been reducible to claims for protection, but have always embraced claims for participation rights. Children want the same autonomy rights that adults enjoy. Second, the argument blames the victim. If children's claims for rights were being used to undermine adult rights, the appropriate strategy would be to criticise the state which was seeking to reduce adult rights, rather than to attack children whose rights entitlements are already considerably less than those of adults.

A third argument is based on what might be termed 'future oriented consent' or what Archard calls the 'caretaker argument' (Archard, 1993: 51–7). The argument suggests that a parent (or some other rational adult) has a right to restrict a child's freedom and to make decisions in a child's best interest, on the understanding that the child must eventually come to acknowledge the correctness of the decision made on their behalf. A child, for example, may not wish to attend school, but education is essential if that child is to develop into a rational and autonomous adult. A parent is therefore entitled to override the child's current wishes to guarantee their future independence. It is precisely because the caretaker argument places such a high value on individual autonomy and critical rationality in decision-making that intervention in children's affairs is judged permissible. As Archard notes with an evident sense of irony, 'the caretaker thesis thinks self determination too important to be left to children' (Archard, 1993: 52).

Dworkin suggests that these parental interventions constitute 'a wager by the parent on the child's subsequent recognition of the wisdom of restrictions. There is an emphasis on . . . what the child will come to welcome, rather than on what he does welcome' (Dworkin, 1977: 119). This is no mean trick. As Archard points out, the caretaker must not only choose what the child would choose if competent to make the choice autonomously, but also have regard for the interests of the adult which the child will become. 'The caretaker' Archard claims, 'chooses for the child in the person of the adult which the child is not yet but will eventually be' (Archard, 1993: 53). There are two difficulties here. If the justifiability of the intervention depends on future consent, there is no way of judging at the time of the intervention whether it is appropriate. But the more serious objection is that the intervention by the adult might generate 'self justifying' rather than 'future oriented' consent. The consent of the child at some future date may simply be a product of the very process of intervention. The benchmark of successful brainwashing is that the person violated in this way is happy and confirmed in their new beliefs. If Freud was correct to suggest that the child is father to the man, then on this account the man may be substantially fashioned by the caretaker. The caretaker argument may amount to little more than a vicious circle of self justifying adult intervention in children's lives.

Libertarians like Holt have little time for caretakers. They argue that children possess the competencies necessary to make decisions about important matters in their lives and should be allowed to participate in making those decisions. The UN Convention offers some endorsement for this view. More recently the debate has tended to move away from questions about whether children have a right to participate in decision-making, to consider and attempt to construct analytical models for children's participation.

Hart has developed an eight level 'ladder' to represent children's participation (Hart, 1992). The various 'rungs' of the ladder are not incremental, deterministic or sequential stages through which participation must progress but, to adopt a different metaphor, yardsticks against which to measure the extent and quality of children's participation.

The first three rungs of the ladder – manipulation, decoration and tokenism – more accurately express children's *involvement* rather than *participation* in a particular enterprise. 'Manipulation', for example, may reflect the involvement of children as consultants in a project where they are not given any feedback. Flekkoy offers the example of opinion polls which use children as their respondents (Flekkoy, 1992: 124). 'Decoration' expresses those involvements of children which stress their 'decorative character'. The parading of children in T-shirts bearing slogans which the children may not have chosen is an obvious example here; arranging for children to sing or dance at conferences is similarly 'decorative' (see chapter 15). 'Tokenism' describes children's notional involvement in conferences or other events, when there has been no attempt to consult the group whose composition the child 'representatives' are intended to reflect.

In truth there are only five rungs of genuine, but graded, participation. The bottom of the ladder, described as 'assigned but informed' is when a project is chosen, designed and planned by adults but where the participating children are well informed, understand the objectives of the enterprise and fulfil a meaningful role. The subsequent rungs – 'consulted and informed', 'adult designed with shared decisions with children', 'child designed and directed', and 'child designed with shared decisions with adults' – reflect the increasing possibilities for children's participation. It is instructive of children's limited participation in decision-making – even in institutions such as schools where children are crucially significant and should be centrally involved – to lean the ladder against the institution and see how few rungs children are able to climb.

Holt believes that given the opportunity children will be keen to participate in decision-making in their families and their communities. There is not of course, nor can there be, any obligation to participate. But Holt argues that children, without regard to age, should participate when their interest and knowledge of affairs motivates them to do so. As their interest develops, so their participation will increase in a benign spiral; if their interest wanes they will remove themselves from involvement. This does not imply that all children will want to participate and it seems probable that very young children would abstain (Holt, 1975).

CHILDREN'S RIGHTS; DEVELOPING EMPOWERING POLICIES AND INSTITUTIONS

Children have been excluded from participation in formal decision-making for so long, that it seems unlikely that they could enter this arena without the initial support and advocacy of adults. A number of proposals detailing policies and institutional reforms to facilitate children's participation have been suggested including: Ombudswork with children; the appointment of Children's Rights Officers; the establishment of a Minister for Children and the UN Convention on the Rights of the Child.

The idea of Ombudswork with children was first suggested in the British setting by the National Council for Civil Liberties' (NCCL) Committee on the Rights of Children in 1969. It was envisaged that a children's ombudsman would initiate child-centred legislation; guarantee compliance with existing child protection laws; distribute information to central and local government to inform the policy process; publicise and campaign for enhanced rights for children; consider particular cases; act as a mediator in disputes between children and parents and represent young people in court (Brimblecombe, 1981).

Recently, a related proposal to create a post of Children's Rights Commissioner has generated considerable interest – prompted, in part, by the Norwegian experience of ombudswork with children recorded in Flekkoy's various accounts (Flekkoy, 1989, 1991). The study by Rosenbaum and Newell (1991) offers the most thorough exploration of the idea of a Commissioner, and examines in close detail a possible organisational structure for such an office, paying particular attention to the important issue of the various ways in which children and young people themselves might become involved in the enterprise.

The Commissioner should: organise local or national discussion forums for young people; establish advisory groups of children to discuss policy and set priorities for the Commissioner's work; establish a network of regional advisory groups; develop specialist advisory groups – for example children in care and adopted children – to advise the Commissioner about those issues; maintain close contacts with national and local organisations of children and young people; request feedback from children via media; establish children's opinions on particular issues via survey research; take note of children's opinions contained in letters and telephone calls to the Commissioner (Rosenbaum and Newell, 1991). Organisationally, the Commissioner would report to the relevant Minister (the Minister for Children when the portfolio is established – see chapter 7), while a Commons Select Committee would support the Commissioner's work in order to give the office some influence in dealings with Ministers.

Britain has witnessed a development similar to the proposal for a Children's Rights Commissioner, but at the local level – a Children's Rights Officer (CRO). In 1988, Leicestershire County Council appointed a CRO whose role included the processing of complaints from children in the local authority's care, but also embraced an underlying brief to assist, 'all children in care by developing and promoting an awareness, sensitivity and respect of, and for, their rights and interests' (Lindsay, 1988: 19). More specifically, that 'duty' might involve arbitrating in cases where the rights of children clash with the plans of social workers or the policies of the local authority (Jervis, 1988). More than a dozen local

authorities have followed Leicestershire's lead although the range and scope of
the Officers' briefs may vary. Ellis and Franklin claim that CROs have achieved
greater success in protecting the rights of individual children than in promoting
the rights of children as a social group (chapter 6).

United Nations International Youth Year in 1985, prompted the resurrection
of a different proposal to guarantee children's rights; a Minister for Children. In
1992, the Labour Party became the first national party to be committed to the
proposal. Children are the 'largest minority in Britain's democracy without a
political voice'. The Minister will be their 'national political champion' (Lestor,
chapter 7).

The Minister's major function would be to 'argue children's case within
government, . . . to make Britain more child friendly and to counter the fragmentation of services' which currently characterises so much service provision
for young people (chapter 7). Such a 'cross departmental' Minister will have an
opportunity to 'see the whole child' and ensure provision of their needs. In
addition, the Minister will initiate legislation beneficial to young people, as well
as fighting to secure the resources necessary to implement such measures. The
Minister should scrutinise all legislation to assess its impact on young people,
campaign, agitate and publicise the cause of young people and, finally, become a
political focus for young people, their problems and the promotion of their
interests (Jackson, 1976).

But the task of coordinating, initiating and keeping a watchful eye on all
legislation relating to young people might prove a challenging brief (Deakin,
1982). Joan Lestor acknowledges it will be 'a very daunting enterprise' not least
because in the past, 'governments have fought shy of innovations which might
unsettle the status quo' and the 'Whitehall machine . . . lacks enthusiasm for
change' (chapter 7).

The UN Convention on the Rights of the Child is undoubtedly the most
significant recent policy development intended to promote and protect children's
rights. The Convention incorporates civil, economic, social and cultural rights,
including the most basic right to life, the right to adequate health care, food, clean
water and shelter, rights to protection against sexual abuse, neglect and exploitation, rights to education, privacy and freedom of association, expression and
thought. The 54 Articles of the Convention constitute a mixed but highly desirable
bag of rights which have been grouped into three broad categories and labelled
the 'three Ps'; rights to provision, protection and participation. The centrality of
the Convention is reflected in the fact that every contributor to this book discusses and evaluates its provisions. Substantial claims are made concerning the
Convention's significance. Joan Lestor, for example, believes that it has established for the first time a 'universally agreed set of rights for children' and also
'stimulated debate within the developed world about a meaningful interpretation
and implementation of those rights' (see chapter 7). Lansdown claims, that 'if
implemented fully it would dramatically improve the status of children in society'
(chapter 8).

But the British government's commitment to the Convention continues to be equivocal. When the idea for the Convention was initially mooted in 1979, the British government opposed the proposal as unnecessary. The government eventually ratified the Convention on 18 December 1991, but entered the maximum three reservations expressing an unwillingness to provide special protection for 16-year-olds in the labour market, to amend immigration and nationality legislation and to discontinue placing young people with adults in custody. Subsequently, the government has failed to consult appropriate children's organisations when producing its report to the UN Committee on the Rights of the Child, intended to monitor implementation of the Convention (chapter 8).

The UK's First Report to the UN Committee on the Rights of the Child claimed that the government's accession to the Convention requirements had been achieved without the need for any additional resources, any improvements in legislation or any changes in attitudes or practices towards children. Such government claims seem at best optimistic and naive; the Director of the Children's Rights Development Unit described them as 'misleading and dishonest by omission'. Such reasoning has led Freeman to argue for the incorporation of the Convention into English law, so that breach of the Convention would be, 'an infringement of English law with all the implications this would have' (see chapter 5).

The British government is not alone in displaying a reluctance to meet its Convention commitments. America has yet to ratify the Convention (chapter 12), while the introduction in 1992, by the state of Western Australia of indeterminate sentencing for certain juvenile offences constituted, 'a deliberate breach of the Convention' (chapter 14).

Government indifference poses a significant difficulty for those concerned with children's rights, but three other aspects of the Convention are problematic. First, the Convention's definition of a child as 'every human being up to the age of 18 years', conforms to legal specifications of the age of majority in Britain, but generates many of the anomalies and difficulties in establishing an agreed understanding of childhood discussed earlier. A young person of 17, for example, can hold a pilot's licence but cannot drive a road passenger vehicle; in some countries the age of majority is 21 while in Nicaragua and Brazil, young people can vote at 16 (Newell, 1991). But if the Convention decrees that childhood ends at 18, it deliberately chooses to avoid designating the point at which it begins. Involvement in contentious debates about abortion and embryo research might have threatened its adoption. Margaret Kennedy is convinced that childhood and the need to protect children begins at conception (see chapter 11).

Second, Ennew argues that the 'child' in the Convention is not a universal, but a Northern child, exported inappropriately and with damaging consequences to the context of the South. The cultural imagery of the child reflected in the Convention excludes some children from childhood. 'The Convention in drafting process, the resulting text and its implementation, takes as its starting point Western, modern childhood which has been "globalised", first through colonialism and then through the imperialism of international aid' (see chapter 15). Ennew drafts a distinctive charter of rights for street children. Other contributors support the view that particular groups of children require distinctive provision. Kennedy, for example, enumerates a list of rights necessary for disabled children (chapter 11) while Becker and Aldridge draw up an inventory of rights claims for children who are carers (chapter 9).

Third, government policy and legislation may not only fail to comply with Convention requirements, but may directly subvert them. In Britain, the High Court decision of February 1994 to uphold the right of a childminder to hit children in her 'care' directly breaches Article 19 of the Convention which requires State Parties to

> take all appropriate legislative, administrative, social and educational measures to protect the child from physical or mental violence, injury or abuse, neglect . . . maltreatment . . . while in the care of parent(s), legal guardian(s) or any other parent who has care of the child.

The Criminal Justice and Public Order Act 1994 offers another obvious example; Rayner's discussion of legislation in certain Australian states testifies to other government's willingness to breach the Convention. The Convention, moreover, may serve to offer cynical politicians and governments an excuse when challenged about their commitments to the needs of children or the adverse impact of government policy on children in areas like housing, education and the economy. Governments can now claim 'we have ratified the Convention'. Signing international Conventions is no substitute for effective government legislation intended to promote children's rights. Nor can rights be bought on the cheap. The issue of children's rights is fundamentally an issue about resources and their distribution. Securing rights for children will require governments to reallocate resources in their favour.

SUMMARY AND PROSPECTS

The proposals for improving children's rights listed above, along with the many others which have been suggested – a children's congess (Deakin, 1982), a youth charter (Wallace, 1985, see also chapter 4), Youth Councils (Franklin, 1989), a commission for children (Powley, 1981) or the establishment of self advocacy groups such as the National Association of Young People in Care (NAYPIC) or Who Cares? (Page and Clarke, 1977; Gardner, 1987) – should not be considered as alternatives. The best strategy for improving children's rights is not to select from among these 'competitor' recommendations but to employ a number of complementary proposals. Establishing a Minister for Children and appointing a Commissioner for Children is the crucial starting point. Their work should be complemented by CROs, appointed in every major local authority to deal with all aspects of service provision for children, and be involved in drafting child impact statements for local policy matters. Adults, however, must assume an enabling role which necessarily carries the germs of its own destruction. Children must be allowed and encouraged to participate in decision-making especially in policy areas such as education where they constitute the significant consumer group. Similarly a range of issues about young people in care could be addressed and resolved if a framework for decision-making existed which allowed young people themselves a more determinant voice.

Three obstacles which continue to block children's access to rights emerge repeatedly in the various chapters in this book. The first, is the growing number of children who are obliged to live in poverty (see chapters 2, 7, 8, 9, 12, 13, 14 and 17). Since 1979, the UK has witnessed a threefold increase in child poverty with 30 per cent of children now living in poverty and a further 10 per cent living on the margins of poverty (Kumar, 1993; Bradshaw, 1990). Poverty has serious implications for rights. Children's access to rights will not be achieved merely by theorising and advocating institutional reforms; it will require resources. The value of formal rights and freedoms, moreover, is undermined and eventually denied by poverty. An old adage captures the reliance of rights on resources rather neatly by the observation that 'We all have the right to eat in the grill bar of the Ritz, so long as we can afford to pay the bill'. But the adage requires updating to accommodate the circumstances of child poverty in Britain. A study by NCH Action for Children revealed that the one in four children who live on social security benefit in Britain in 1994 could not afford the diet of bread, gruel, soup, cabbage and suet pudding served up in a Victorian workhouse in 1876 (see Brindle, 1994). Beyond the developed world, poverty imposes much greater privations on children and is growing rapidly (Durning, 1992).

Second, a number of contributors highlight the fragmentation in the provision of services for children and the deleterious implications of failing to see the 'whole' child for meeting children's needs and rights. Lestor identifies this fragmentation in provision at national level (chapter 7) while Alexander is concerned with the local arena and the implications for services for children in their early years (chapter 10). In America (chapter 12) and Australia (chapter 14) it is the federal structure of governments which allows for differences in children's access to rights and services, while in the UK the 'informal' federalism of the juvenile justice system prompts a regime of 'justice by geography'.

Finally, the various chapters illustrate quite clearly the extent to which governments ignore children; if governments are culpable they must be held responsible for their child neglect. Lestor acknowledges that because children 'do not have a vote . . . because they do not lobby decision-makers, . . . they are all too often the statistically unrecognised victims of bad policies' (chapter 7). The chapters on Scandinavia, America and Australia confirm that governments display little concern for the needs and rights of communities that lack electoral clout. If children's rights are to be protected and promoted, it is essential that, 'children – the one quarter of the population who do not vote – are inked in on the political agenda' (Jackson and Jackson, 1981: 256). Lestor believes this can be achieved by establishing a Minister for Children. It may be time, however, to consider lowering the age of majority to 16. Newell calculates this would give voting rights to about 1,800,000 young people (Newell, 1991: 3). Giving more young people the right to vote would not resolve the many difficulties which they confront, but it would place the responsibility for protecting children's rights where it properly belongs. Not in the hands of well meaning but potentially paternalistic adults, but with those who have the greatest interest in ensuring that those rights are not infringed; children themselves.

CASES CITED

Re S [1993] 2 FLR 437.

REFERENCES

Archard, D. (1993) *Children; Rights and Childhood* Routledge: London.
Aries, P. (1962) *Centuries of Childhood* Jonathan Cape: London.
Bradley, A. (1993) 'Smacking Kids' *Living Marxism* October, p. 15.
Bradshaw, J. (1990) *Child Poverty and Deprivation in the UK* National Children's Bureau: London.
Brimblecombe, F. (1981) *The Children's Committee, The Final Report* HMSO: London.
Brindle, D (1994) 'Basic Benefit Will Not Buy Children a Workhouse Diet' *Guardian* 1 February, p. 5.
Children's Legal Centre (1993) *The Children's Legal Centre Annual Report 1993* Children's Legal Centre: London.
Deakin, N. (1982) *A Voice For All Children* Bedford Square Press, NCVO: London.
Durning, A. (1992) 'Life On The Brink' in G. Albee, A. Bond and T. Cook Monsey (eds) *Improving Children's Lives: Global Perspectives on Prevention* Sage, London pp. 37–49.
Dworkin, R. (1977) *Taking Rights Seriously* Duckworth: London.
Eekelaar, J. (1992) 'The Importance of Thinking that Children Have Rights' *International Journal of Law and the Family* Vol. 6 pp. 221–35.
—— (1994) 'The Interests of the Child and the Child's Wishes; the role of dynamic self determination' *International Journal of Law and the Family* Vol. 8 pp. 42–61.
Farson, R. (1977) 'Birthrights' in B. Gross and R. Gross (eds) *The Children's Rights Movement* Andover Press, NY: USA.
Feinberg, J. (1980) 'Legal Paternalism' *Rights, Justice and the Bounds of Liberty: Essays in Social Philosophy* Princeton University Press: USA.
Feinberg, J. (1973) *Social Philosophy* Prentice Hall: USA.
Flekkøy, M. (1989) 'Child Advocacy In Norway' *Children and Society* Vol. 2 (4).
—— (1991) *A Voice For Children; Speaking Out As Their Ombudsman* UNICEF / Kingsley.
—— (1992) 'Closing Address' in M. de Langen and M. Drouglaever Fortuyn (eds) *Towards the Realisation of Human Rights of Children* Defence of Children International: Holland.
Franklin, A. and Franklin, B. (1990) 'Age and Power; A Political Economy of Ageism' in T. Jeffs and M. Smith (eds) *Youth Work In a Divided Society* pp. 1–28, Macmillan.
Franklin, B. (ed.) (1986) *The Rights of Children* Blackwells: Oxford.
Franklin, B. (1989) 'Children's Rights: Developments and Prospects' *Children and Society* Vol. 3 pp. 50–67.
—— (1992) 'Votes for Children' *Childright* April no. 85 pp. 10–15.

Franklin, B. and Parton, N. (1991) 'Media Reporting of Social Work; a framework for analysis' in B. Franklin and N. Parton (eds) *Social Work, the Media and Public Relations* Routledge: London.

Freeman, M.D.A. (1985) *The Rights and the Wrongs of Children* Pinter: London.

—— (1992) 'Taking Children's Rights More Seriously' *International Journal of Law and the Family* Vol. 6 pp. 52–71.

Gardner, R (1987) *Who Says? Choice and Control In Care* London National Children's Bureau: London.

Harris, J. (1982) 'The Political Status Of Children' in K. Graham (ed.) *Contemporary Political Philosophy: Radical Studies* Cambridge University Press: Cambridge, pp. 35–59.

Hart, R. (1992) *Children's Participation from Tokenism to Citizenship* Innocenti Essays No. 4 UNICEF: London.

Heartfield, J. (1993) 'Why Children's Rights are Wrong' *Living Marxism* October, pp. 13–15.

Holt, J. (1975) *Escape From Childhood* Penguin: Harmondsworth.

Hoyles, M. (1979) *Changing Childhood* Writers and Readers: London.

Hoyles, M. and Evans, P. (1989) *The Politics of Childhood* Journeyman: London.

Jackson, B. (1976) 'A Minister For Children' *New Society* 15 January, pp. 94–7.

Jackson, B. and Jackson, S. (1981) *Childminder* Penguin: London.

James, G. and Wadcock, G. (1986) *Signpost; A Guide to Setting Up Complaints Procedures For Children In Care* National Children's Bureau: London.

Jervis, M. (1988) 'Crossing The Boundaries In Social Work' *Social Work Today* 5 May, pp. 12–13.

Kant, I. (1887) *The Philosophy of Law* T. & T. Clark: London.

Kumar, V. (1993) *Poverty and Inequality in the UK: the effects on children* National Children's Bureau: London.

Laslett, P. (1965) *The World We Have Lost* Methuen: London.

Lindsay, M. (1988) 'Child's Rights Officer By Appointment' *Childright* Vol. 49 July–August, pp. 16–19.

Locke, J. (1964) *Two Treatises of Government* P. Laslett (ed.) Cambridge University Press: Cambridge.

Newell, P. (1991) *The UN Convention and Children's Rights In The UK* National Children's Bureau: London.

Mill, J.S. (1969) *Utilitarianism* M. Warnock (ed.) Fontana: London.

Page, R. and Clarke, G. (1977) *Who Cares?* National Children's Bureau: London.

Pinchbeck, I. and Hewitt, M. (1973) *Children in English Society* 2 Vols Routledge & Kegan Paul: London.

Plumb, J.H. (1972) *In The Light of History* Penguin: London.

Powley, T. (1981) *The Representation of Children's Rights and Interests* The Children Committee, DHSS: London.

Purdy, L. (1994) 'Why Children Should Not have Equal Rights' *International Journal of Children's Rights* Vol. 2, pp. 1–17.

Rodham, H. (1973) 'Children Under the Law' *Harvard Educational Review* Vol. 43 pp. 479–93.

—— (1974) 'Children's Rights; A Legal Perspective' in P. Vardin and I. Brody (eds) *Children's Rights; Contemporary Perspectives 1979* Teachers College Press Harvard, MA: USA.

Rogers, C. M. and Wrightsman, L.S. (1978) 'Attitudes Towards Children's Rights: Nurturance or Self Determination' *Journal of Social Issues* Vol. 34 (2).

Rosenbaum, M. and Newell, P. (1991) *Taking Children's Rights Seriously: A Proposal For a Children's Rights Commissioner* Calouste Gulbenkian Foundation: London.

Scarre, G. (1980) 'Children and Paternalism' *Philosophy* Vol. 55.

—— (1989) *Children, Parents and Politics* Cambridge University Press: Cambridge.

Titman, W. (1993) *Special People, Special Places* available from Learning Through Landscapes, the Law Courts, Winchester.

Wald, M. (1979) 'Children's Rights; A Framework For Analysis' *University of California Davis Law Review* Vol. 12 pp. 255–82.

Wallace, J. (1985) *Youth Charter* Bill no. 55 9 January, HMSO: London.

Watson, D. (1980) *Caring For Strangers* Routledge: London.

Worsfold, V. (1974) 'A Philosophical Justification for Children's Rights' *Harvard Educational Review* Vol. 44, pp. 142–57.

Part II

Children's rights:
The changing legal framework

Chapter 2

Children's educational rights in a new ERA?

Tony Jeffs

British schools remain depressing places for those sympathetic to the rights of young people and committed to their extension. During a decade and a half in which a torrent of legislation has sought to re-shape the administrative structure, ethos and content of our education system, it is impossible to isolate a single reform, clause within an Act, or ministerial directive designed to extend the capacity of young people to influence or exercise some measure of control over their own education. It is noteworthy that all educational legislation has chosen to disregard the 'Gillick Judgement' set out by Woolf (1985) and endorsed by Scarman, that 'a child under 16 can give a true consent depending on her maturity and understanding and the nature of the consent required'. Guidelines for those working in child protection have stressed that professionals must recognise that children 'have a right to be consulted and their views taken into account' (Department of Health, 1988: 9). The Children Act 1989 (see chapter 3) intends that account be taken of the views of young people concerning their future well-being. But this guidance stands in stark contrast to the norm within the education sector where pupils excluded from school are denied the right even to 'make representations' to the body deciding whether or not they may be re-admitted to school. Educational legislation has always cast young people in the mould of powerless subjects within the system. It is an approach that is rarely questioned by educationalists or parents and it appears that whatever else may change within education, those with the power intend to keep it so.

The United Nations Convention on the Rights of the Child stressed the right of young people to free education. It also requested that the education provided should respect the values of the young person (Article 29). In Britain, although many hidden costs do exist, the right to a free education to the age of 16 is guaranteed by law. The major challenge is that schools continue to treat children and young people in ways that would be unthinkable and intolerable for adults. Successive governments and many parents encourage schools to operate in ways that 'express contempt for the values of a free society' (Strike, 1982: 147). Disrespect for young people is nowhere more evident than in the continued use of physical punishment in some private schools, despite its long overdue abolition in public sector schools since the 1993 Education Act.

THE NEW LAWS; ESTABLISHING CENTRALISED CONTROL

Establishing central control over local decision-making

The fifteen years following the election of a Conservative government in 1979 saw the introduction of more Education Acts than the preceeding eighty. The legislation emerged without extensive consultation and only minimal parliamentary debate (Armstrong, 1988; Brown, 1993). Some initiatives, like the Technical and Vocational Educational Initiative (TVEI) appeared without public debate or notification (Dale *et al.*, 1990) while others were rushed through when parliament and schools were on vacation. The reforms and their mode of implementation have been justified by reference to an urgent need to counter falling standards, reduce ill-discipline, extend choice and inject an enterprise culture into education. A more covert agenda, however, has been a determination to deny locally elected representatives the capacity to shape policy, to weaken the teacher unions and to neutralise the influence of progressive educationalists (Simon, 1988; Bates, 1992). To secure these ends, control over policy has increasingly been transferred to Ministers and their appointees who can operate without effective scrutiny by parliament (Pring, 1994). Consequently, either by design or over-sight we have acquired an administrative structure that both opens 'the way for the eventual privatisation of state education' and enables central government to dictate what is taught in the schools, in ways that 'could potentially be used for any political end whatsoever' (O'Connor, 1990: 21).

These reforms have produced a corrupt and corrupting educational system dominated by patronage, that allows the executive to marginalise the ideologically 'unsound' and 'disloyal'. Mildly oppositional LEAs are placed on public hit-lists; liberal Education Officers who criticise government policy are branded as mad and dangerous; and Inspectors are instructed to compile secret dossiers on headteachers' attitudes to the National Curriculum. It is a centralised system that according to one of Her Majesty's Inspectors is 'driven by ideological malice' (interview with the author). Another described the educational system as 'permeated by an atmosphere of fear and distrust in which hardly anyone dare give voice to oppositional thoughts' (interview) and where 'civil servants who give unwelcome advice on the efficient implementation of policy are removed' (Pring, 1994). Resistance at grass-roots level, amongst teachers, parents and students, often seems to be the only constraint upon the writ of the government (Meighan, 1993). In Scotland, for example, more than half of all parents withdrew their children from assessment tests while in England and Wales a teacher boycott achieved a similar end. School students played little part in these conflicts except as cyphers; none of the parties considered they might have an opinion or have required consultation. It often appears that the only point of agreement among teachers, government and parents is that children should remain 'ghosts at every meeting' (Acton, 1989).

Establishing control of teachers and governors

For all its awesome powers to control the education system, central government continues to appear in the majority of students' perceptions as remote and distant. For most students, control appears to reside largely with teachers, heads and that hazy, ill-defined group – school governors. The analysis flows not from juvenile naivety but lived experience. Despite the increasing centralised control over funding and curricula, responsibility for implementation of a number of key aspects has been passed 'down the line'. Denied control over what is taught for all but a small proportion of the school day, governors and headteachers have by way of compensation been granted a budget to spend. They have also acquired: an unprecedented freedom to hire and fire teachers; control over the use of the school building; the ability to decide which pupils should be admitted; powers to suspend and expel students; the ability to award contracts for such matters as school dinners and cleaning services; increased powers to impose discipline and create rules. Although teaching staff are represented on governing bodies, neither heads nor governors are obliged to consult them – or students – about any of these matters.

Many teachers have come to believe that their newly found 'freedom' is little more than a chimera. Three reasons undermine claims about enhanced teacher autonomy. First, somewhere between 70 and 80 per cent of the typical school budget is consumed by historic staff costs leaving little scope for teacher involvement in financial decision-making. Second, the overall size of the budget is linked predominantly to pupil numbers at a time when demographic trends are reducing the number of young people in many localities by as much as a third. Again, this demography militates against any teacher autonomy in budgetary concerns. Finally, the national curriculum allows little scope for teachers to influence important matters such as the timetable or even lesson content.

Governors and headteachers must often see themselves as catspaws obliged to balance impossible budgets and police a system they can barely influence. Perhaps unsuprisingly in such circumstances, many schools find it difficult to recruit and retain governors (West, 1993). Serving governors, however, cannot augment their number from amongst those who might, given the chance, be most willing to serve; the students themselves.

Securing the exclusion of children

The exclusion of children is a tragedy not least because we know that students of all ages would welcome the opportunity to be consulted and share in policy formulation (Kitzinger, 1987; Harber, 1989; Cullingford, 1992). The reason is that the 1986 Education Act (Section 15(14)) excludes anyone under 18 from membership. By so doing, it reversed a discernible trend of increased student involvement and led to the sacking of many hundreds of serving student governors (Children's Legal Centre, 1987). Until that Section of the Act is repealed, all substantive progress regarding the involvement of young people in the decision-making process in their schools is effectively blocked. This denial of meaningful student representation guarantees that even on those few occasions when school councils or other consultative exercises have been established, they will attract little sustained enthusiasm amongst students or commitment from staff. Worse, they may reinforce the scepticism encountered amongst primary school students regarding the ability of individuals to bring about change and exercise influence (Cullingford, 1992). The reasons for this are evident. First, student members of school councils lack access to the next tier of decision-making. They are unable, therefore, to gauge how seriously their views are treated or discover which issues are being decided by senior management or governors. Second, until such councils are given a legal or quasi-legal status they can only exist as a grace-and-favour concession. As long as headteachers can close them down without being held accountable for that decision the ability of the student to speak freely on controversial issues will be severely constrained. Finally the presence of student representatives on governing bodies – there by right not indulgence – able freely to question and assess the reports presented by staff, will enable laymembers to judge the validity of what they are told about school-life.

At a national level the power of the executive is now such that everything is 'subject to political control, from the school timetable to the teaching of the apostrophe' (Fisher, 1993: 17). Until the headlong rush towards centralisation is reversed, hopes of extending children's rights within education will be severely constrained. Devolution of decision-making regarding such matters as curriculum content, testing and funding is a prerequisite for the involvement of staff, parents, the community and young people (Ranson, 1993). Such decisions must, in the words of de Tocqueville be 'put within the people's reach' (quoted in Rendell and Ward, 1989: 51), otherwise fewer and fewer will consider it either worthwhile or dignified to take responsiblity for the trivia which central government currently leaves within their perview. This applies to young people as much as adults.

AUTHORITARIANISM AND DEMOCRACY INSIDE THE SCHOOL

According to Harber (1992), schools predominately operate management structures which do nothing to induct young people into a democratic political culture. What exists fails the test applied by Gutman (1987) since it does nothing to prepare young people to participate effectively in the democratic process. Attempts to promote 'citizenship' and 'political literacy' therefore inevitably achieve little because as the Schools Council pointed out, schools do not 'practice what they seek to promote' (1981: 14). Even teachers, who are adults and professionals, find their 'rights of participation are a political ritual which lends support to what is in reality a system of autocracy' (Ball, 1987: 125–6).

Legal constraints impose limitations on the extent to which young people may be involved in the decision-making process, but these do not present insurmountable obstacles for schools seeking to establish regimes characterised by informal democracy. Creating an atmosphere where a relaxed, friendly, non-authoritarian ethos prevails, is possible within schools. An atmosphere that eschews those features that discriminate against students on the basis of age – such as uniforms, formal deference (use of 'sir' and 'miss'), separate staffrooms, entrances and toilets – along with a predictable host of petty rules applied only to the young.

The resilience of the traditional management model which replicates so many features of the Fordist factory is, according to Torrington and Weightman, an anachronism. Headteachers now enjoy a dominance almost 'unknown in our experience of studying management in a wide range of undertakings' (Torrington and Weightman, 1988: 8). It has become fashionable to talk of the need to empower young people and create markets that expand 'consumer' choice, but schools continue to operate in ways designed to 'turn out a mass, standardized product' (Best, 1993: 125). Almost all head teachers remain predominately 'control driven' (Sergiovanni, 1992); obsessed with rules and good order, surveillance and monitoring – and locked into inspection systems designed to control teachers and ensure they replicate that relationship in their 'management' of students. Paradoxically, as factory employment declines in a de-industrialised Britain, schools seem ever more eager to embrace many of the least attractive attributes of the sweat-shop. To institute clocking-in for sessions and even lessons; bells to signal the start and end of lessons; employment of the gate-keeper-cum-receptionist to scrutinise every visitor; imposition of uniforms to supress individuality amongst staff and students; erection of high perimeter-fences to keep the students in and the community out; and crude payment-by-result schemes, offering (for example) greasy hamburgers for full attendance or 'good work'. Factory culture now thrives in many schools, spelling out that the 'nurturance of educational autonomy' has been set aside in favour of imposed discipline and control (Cremin, 1990: 14).

Increasing control of teachers has implications for the rights claims of children. Recent legislation has eroded the control of classroom teachers over the content of what they teach and the methods they deploy. Teachers' loss of autonomy has resulted in students being denied opportunities to negotiate behaviourial norms and lesson content. A centrally determined curriculum has curtailed the right of students, especially older ones, to choose 'options'. Compulsory testing from the age of seven has also led to undue concentration upon what is to be tested. With professional survival and salary determined directly, or indirectly by test scores, it is inevitable that all but the most independent-minded teacher will focus on what is assessed and jettison anything which is not. As a member of the National Curriculum Council explained, this narrowing down is no accident (Clanchy, 1992). The right of children to a broad-based, intellectually stimulating education has been sacrificed on the high altar of competition. Refusal to offer young people choice and a measure of control over what they are taught produces conflict and disenchantment. By far the most common cause for truancy is dissatisfaction with the content and quality of individual lessons (O'Keefe, 1993). Until young people are given a genuine opportunity to influence curriculum content, indifference, disruption and absenteeism will remain intractable problems.

COMPETITION

Marketing schools

Recent legislative reforms have sought to locate competition at the core of the educational experience. Parents must compete to secure their child a place in the 'best' school; staff must compete for merit money; schools are obliged to compete to recruit a diminishing number of pupils and to rise up league tables based on test scores, examination results and truancy rates. A crude 'Gradgrind' model now determines the educational experience of many young people. Competition erodes the sense of community and collegiate endeavour within classroom and school, eradicating – according to a senior education officer – 'any sense of a wider educational community' (interview with author). Headteachers begin to distrust colleagues in neighbouring schools who are viewed increasingly as 'competitors'. It has become commonplace and depressing for headteachers to regale visitors with tales of how their rivals fiddle test scores, concoct false truancy returns and mislead parents and feeder schools to attract students. Students have no choice but to join in these educational game shows while diminishing attention is paid to their rights or needs. According to a popular guide on how to market your school, it is essential to 'persuade' staff and students to display total commitment, (rather like the employees of a hamburger chain or Disney World) to the school's Mission Statement; every contact with outsiders is judged to constitute a marketing activity and opportunity (Gray, 1991). For many heads, image takes precedence over content as they struggle for success, survival or even a privately negotiated performance-related bonus 'at the expense of a concern with current pupil experience' (Wallace, 1993).

Establishing parentocracy

Brown (1990) has coined the term 'parentocracy' to help describe the new structure in which parents have acquired considerable power. Their representatives form a sizeable proportion of the governing body and their votes decide whether a school remains under LEA control – thus they can effectively block closure and prevent reorganisation. Those who have the income and time, and live in urban areas, can also exercise real choice regarding where to send their child. Consequently schools are obliged to listen carefully to the views of parents. Young people can benefit from this. The vast majority of parents, for example, choose a school following consultation with their child and 80 per cent of children appear to attend a school for which they opted (West et al., 1993).

Parent power, however, cannot be welcomed uncritically by those concerned with extending the rights of children. Parent's wishes must be considered but they should not – as at present – automatically override those of young people. The right of young people to be consulted and, where applicable, for their views to be given precedence must be enshrined in future legislation. They should, for example, be protected from the desire of parents to impose beliefs, values and behavioural norms which they do not share. Nor should a young person who does or does not wish to attend a school of a particular religious denomination, be obliged to because their parent(s) wish it. Also parents should not have an absolute right to place children in boarding schools against the wishes of a young person. A child's wish to retain regular contact with friends, siblings, relatives and community should take precedence over a parent's desire to send their child away in order to enjoy an unencumbered social life. In many households the views of young people regarding educational matters are respected and can prevail, but where this is not so the law must ensure that young people have a 'right of appeal'. Unrestrained parental power over other areas of a young person's life are not tolerated by the law. The government's desire to create an educational market economy is hardly sufficient grounds for setting aside the principle of self-determination in respect of decisions regarding an individual's educational experiences.

The growth of competition has been exploited by many parents for the benefit of their children. But while some young people have undoubtedly benefited, others – who may already be disadvantaged by poverty or handicap – have suffered further discrimination. Their right of access to resources, knowledge and institutions has often been curtailed unfairly by recent changes. Five examples will illustrate the detrimental impact of recent changes.

First, there has been an unprecedented increase in the number of pupils statemented under the 1981 Education Act as having special educational needs. The deluge has resulted less from a concern for the needs of these pupils, than a desire to remove 'academically weak' pupils from the National Curriculum testing process to protect school ratings. The fact that this proceedure can stigmatise young people or be wholly inappropiate is rarely, if ever, a consideration.

Second, schools are increasingly deploying public relations techniques and agencies to attract pupils and 'massage' the school's image (Passmore, 1993). Like much advertising, content can border on the dishonest. For schools with spare capacity the motive is to acquire 'bums for seats'; elsewhere it is to attract high rather than middle or low 'academic achievers'.

Third, external examination results are the ultimate 'indicator of success' for secondary schools. Many schools are trying to deter or prevent marginal students from entering examinations in order to inflate pass rates. The new system only backs sure-fire winners; it offers little support to mere hopefuls.

Fourth, students seeking entry into sixth forms are increasingly being denied impartial careers advice. Fear of losing students has led to information concerning programmes of study available in other schools, Sixth Form and Further Education colleges being withheld. Careers officers are carefully monitored, and where they fail to put the interests of the school first, it may cost them the contract to 'supply careers advice' in the future. So serious has the problem become that the 1993 Education Act (para. 263–265) *obliges* schools to supply information regarding programmes of study elswhere.

Finally, suspensions of pupils increased between 1988–1991 by 66 per cent (Advisory Centre for Education, 1993) and the Department for Education (DFE) recorded an additional 31 per cent growth in the following year as schools have sought to off-load troublesome students. In some schools up to 15 per cent of the students are suspended at any given time (Office for Standards in Education (OFSTED), 1993). One police force found over 25 per cent of 'truants' stopped by their officers had been suspended or expelled (Pyke *et al.*, 1993).

Competition is encouraging schools to discriminate against certain young people via denial of entry, exclusion or suspension. All schools, and especially the over-subscribed, have a positive incentive to keep out those with expensive special needs, those who might damage their league tables scores and individuals from backgrounds and localities with a 'history' of disruptive behaviour and truancy. Competition, unchecked, must inevitably produce what the *Financial Times* (1992) described as 'schools of last resort'. The *FT*'s solution was to offer successful schools a bribe to take the hard-to-place. The DFE came up with a cheaper alternative and in the 1993 Act gave itself powers to take over 'failing schools' and appoint a team of trouble-shooters to run them. The negative impact of competition is experienced not solely by the disadvantaged. It sets parent against parent, school against school and student against student in a way that leaves little space for young people to exercise their rights as individuals, to exercise a measure of control over what they learn and how they are treated. The young person is not seen as the customer; that role is assigned to parents. What the young person has to learn in addition to the national curriculum is to survive in a system that more and more 'rewards shrewdness rather than principles, and encourages commercial rather than educational decision-making. Concern for social justice is replaced by concern for institutional survival, collectivism with indi- vidualism, cooperation with suspicion and need with expediency' (Gerwitz *et al.*, 1994). A system which encourages those operating it to dehumanise the young people it claims to serve. As one headteacher explained, with regret rather than enthusiasm, 'I know it is wrong but I am beginning to see them more and more as little bundles of income and less as children' (interview with author).

The commercialisation of education

Viewing students as a source of income rather than as individuals with a right to the best possible education reflects the growing commercialisation of much education provision. The determination of the government to insert the business ethic into every corner of education is symbolised by the appointment of sup- posed entrepreneurs to chair the quangos that are responsonsible for managing the curriculum, testing and funding; the legal requirement that governing bodies must contain representatives from the local business community; and that inspector's reports on schools are circulated to local employers but not, for example, to community groups. Schools are also being pressured to develop links with industry and secure sponsorship (Miller, 1993). Many of these links are relatively harmless but some are not. The involvement of some firms is designed to corrupt the educational process. McDonalds and Burger King, for example, are conscious of the increasing number of young people who find factory farming and the slaughter of animals for food unacceptable, and are actively seeking sponsorship to guarantee their views on these issues appear on the agenda. Major pollutants, such as oil companies and British Nuclear Fuels, energetically court schools. Banks which are equally eager to capture young clients seek to place advertising materials in schools; one examination board has already allowed a bank to 'sponsor' their certificates, thus reducing them to the level of a coupon. In the USA where it is estimated that children aged four to twelve spent $8.6 billion in 1991, over 20 million students are now using corporate sponsored teaching materials. The independent Consumers Union rightly accuses schools of 'selling the kids entrusted to them to any bidder' (quoted in Norris, 1993: 15). Cable television has also moved into American schools providing free 'educational programmes' in order to broadcast advertising material during breaks to a captive audience (Apple, 1990). Since students are legally obliged to attend, and teachers are placed in a position of intellectual authority over them, it is totally unacceptable for schools to exploit that situation either for their own or other's profit. This is of course not a wholly new situation, as McClure noted, 'strong pressure is being brought to bear to commercialise our education, to make it a paying proposition, to make it subservient to the God of Wealth and thus convert us into a money-making mob' (McCLure, 1917: 214).

What undoubtedly has changed is the determination of the government to push aside those values that have been put in place to protect young people from indoctrination by employers and producers. To assist in opening up schools – as the media has been – to allow the manipulation of young people as future consumers and employees. All young people have the right to a free education that develops their talents and abilities to the full. Implicit within that right is an expectation that those who deliver it will seek to place truth before indoctrination. That expectation places on teachers and schools a duty to seek to protect young people from authoritarian governments that wish to shape education to their ends, and employers and producers who seek to restrict access to knowledge that does not serve their interests. The national curriculum is wrong because it places boundaries around what young people may learn and curtails the ability of both teachers and students jointly to develop programmes of study that reflect the needs of the young person. Now the growing power and influence of large multi-national corporations threatens the right of young people to an education worthy of the name. What is required is that both young people and their teachers are protected from those financial and managerial pressures which seek to force them to use tainted source material, and that young people are given equal access to those critical and questioning ideas, which those with wealth, power and influence will always seek to stifle.

DISCIPLINE AND TRUANCY

Many agencies are involved in the education of young people – families, the media, religious bodies, providers of commercial leisure, communities, youth groups and schools. Of these only schools are government controlled. Therefore when significant segments of the population express concern about a 'social problem' schools are often perceived as the medium via which the problem can be tackled. Economic decline, unemployment, military weakness and crime have each been blamed on our schools and have in turn stimulated reforms. Less discipline in schools and families, alongside a diminution of respect for authority, have recently been cited by the Home Secretary as the causes for increased crime (Lawson, 1993). This view is apparently shared by over 80 per cent of the public (NOP, 1993). Such simplistic and glib explanations have encouraged ministers to insist that 'schools be firm on discipline' (Forth, 1993: 12) and teach core values 'deliberately, fearlessly and explicitly' placing at the top of the list 'regard for proper authority' (Patten, 1993). Inspectors' reports reflect this emphasis, with a good school apparently being one where military discipline reigns, managers manage and pupils know their place. Within the literature on school discipline considerable emphasis is placed on the need for 'whole school policies' (Jones and Jones, 1992; MacBeath, 1992). It is difficult to envisage a more dishonest term, for any notion that 'whole school' might involve young people in a debate regarding what values could or should reside at the heart of the community is always absent. Whole school policy does not entail staff and students creating a system of shared rules and regulations in the collaborative way described by White (1988). Rather the term adds a spurious aura of collaboration to what is normally a top-down model, symbolised by ludicrous Mission Statements pinned to classroom walls and rules written by senior teachers or heads then rubber-stamped by governors. Teachers and students who digress find themselves isolated – both for failing to enforce or obey rules they did not agree to, and for being poor team members. Within a fundamentally undemocratic structure, whole school policies amount to nothing more than the portrayal of coercion as collaboration in a way that justifies subjecting students who disagree to suspension and behaviour modification programmes (OFSTED, 1993). Although exceptions do exist, most schools enforce discipline in ways that coincide with the government's desire that servility and proper regard for authority should have precedence over a commitment to helping young people 'learn not just to *behave* in accordance with authority but to *think* critically about authority, if they are to live up to the democratic ideal of sharing political sovereignty as citizens' (Gutman, 1987: 51, emphasis in original).

Entwined with the obsession with discipline is a fixation with truancy. Lack of longtitudinal research makes it impossible to discern if it is increasing, but policy is founded upon a blithe assumption that it is. Even those who hold high office can be tempted to bizarre and unwarranted speculation. According to John Patten, the truant is 'at risk of becoming one of the malingering employees of tomorrow, or worse still of drifting into a life of crime. Show me a persistent young truant, and there is a potential young criminal' (Patten, 1993). Fighting truancy is therefore equated with fighting crime, yet research fails to provide substantive evidence to sustain this linkage (O'Keefe, 1993).

The sole solution offered by the government for dealing with truancy appears to be the installation of technology to monitor attendance and the internal movement of students. Schools have also tried closing exits to minimise slippage, abandoning breaks and reducing lunch periods, and fitting closed circuit television to scan the school perimeter. Fortress schools designed to keep students in and the public out are become more and more commonplace. Aesthetically offensive, they also transmit a crude message of social control informing young people that they have few rights and minimal power. Beyond the gates a disturbing development has been the introduction of joint police and Educational Welfare Officer patrols in city centres and shopping malls checking out those who might be of school age. Elsewhere shopkeepers have been recruited to watch for truants (Welsh Office, 1985) and schools have been told to enforce school uniforms to enable concerned citizens to recognise and apprehend truants (Patten, 1993). This harassment of young people in public places and the encouragement of adults to monitor their movements, to stop and question them when they are going about their lawful business, is unacceptable. It transforms being young into a crime and gives concrete expression to a misguided belief that all young people are a threat to good order. If such measures are truly the price required for keeping some young people in schools, the question must surely be raised whether is it a price worth paying?

CONCLUSION

We know that the overwhelming majority of young people, even a majority of those who truant and miss occasional lessons, view education as a worthwhile and enjoyable experience (O'Keefe, 1993; Cullingford, 1992). Parents, with very few exceptions, are similarly anxious to support the school and encourage their children to take every advantage of the educational opportunities offered (Jowett et al., 1991). Finally the decision of over 80 per cent of young people to continue in full-time education beyond the statutory leaving age, despite the absence of mandatory grants for those aged 16 to 18, provides overwhelming proof of the commitment of parents and young people to education. A great reservoir of goodwill exists towards schools, but many schools continue to perceive the community, parents and young people as hostile. Worse, many schools continue to operate as if their very survival depends on keeping the first two groups at bay and the latter incarcerated.

The root cause of this problem and so many others is that schools are expected simultaneously to act as educational institutions and as warehouses. The two roles are not compatible. Until we begin to reassess the place of compulsion within education it is difficult to see how real progress can be made with respect to extending children's rights in the context of the school. Compulsion ensures that young people are axiomatically viewed as second-class members of the school community. The bottom line being that they, unlike the adults, have no option but 'to put up and shut up' about the way they are treated. Compulsion demands that schools find ways of keeping some young people within the building against their will. It corrupts the whole education process, forcing teachers to behave in ways that contradict their prime role as educators; 'there are only two jobs where you are holding people against their will – prison wardens and teachers' (White and Johnson, 1993: 111). It leads to the imposition of rules and the adoption of management styles that undermine the rights, freedoms and dignity of the majority of young people. It demeans teachers and brings schools into disrepute. All in order to lock in the system a handful of persistent truants and the many who might, when they have something better to do, miss the odd lesson.

Compulsion also allows parents to abuse the education system. Schools can be used as a warehouse where children can be dumped. Parents can enjoy the freedom to work or play while deluding themselves that they are giving their children an educational opportunity; in truth they merely serve their own self-interest. It also enables cynical governments to use schools to hide youth unemployment. Young people are now being kept in schools and other edu- cational settings for an increasing number of years with some starting as early as three. The length of the school day is also expanding for many. In America some schools have young people delivered at 07.30 for breakfast club and keep them until they are collected ten hours later. Many British schools are following suit, having discovered that summer play programmes and pre- and post-school pro- vision are profitable and attractive to parents. Little if any evidence exists that this expansion in the hours spent on school premises is beneficial to young people. Nor is it asked if such transactions might infringe the rights of the young person, be counter-productive or whether using schools for such purposes devalues their role and standing as educational institutions.

Until compulsion is abandoned the slow process of developing new demo- cratic management structures for our schools – a process that has been stalled for over a century – will not begin in earnest. Compulsion has been defended for too long by an unholy alliance of self-serving educationalists and concerned social reformers who believe it is essential to ensure that irresponsible parents send their children to school. To construct a whole system around the need to deal with the tiny proportion of parents who might behave in that way is an obvious nonsense however, especially when we know that schools, the courts and welfare agencies have patently failed to do so (Carlen et al., 1992). The right of those children to an education must be secured, but doing so should not be allowed to serve as an excuse for the maintenance of the present repressive structure.

We are already half-way to a preferable alternative. The state recognises that it has a duty to provide free education for all up to the age of 16. Now we merely have to accept that some young people, a tiny proportion, may not wish to partake of it. Some may only wish to withdraw from a small segment – say physical education – others for a short period of time. All that is required is a mechanism to allow that to happen while ensuring that withdrawal is not the result of coercion or factors such as poverty. The appointment of a children's Ombudsman, operating along similar lines to the office in Norway would help enormously (see chapter 13). Such a child's advocate, supported by Children's Rights Officers could monitor withdrawals and, where complaints are made by young people against schools, investigate and adjudicate.

If we were to go further and establish mechanisms in schools to enable young people to contribute to the school's management and decision-making procedures, then many of the administrative and behavioural problems that presently obsess those managing the system would evaporate. Creating such structures cannot be left to chance. The right of young people to be consulted should be legally established and protected. A number of Australian federal education programmes made funding conditional upon the creation of decision-making structures within the recipient schools based on genuine teacher involvement (White and Johnson, 1993). A similar approach could well be adopted here with state funding linked to the establisment of administrative structures that guarantee the right of parents, teachers and young people to make a full contribution. It seems desirable to make funding conditional, at least in part, on the existence of structures that embody democratic rather than authoritarian values and which recognise the right of young people to participate in the exercise, or control, of power. Students must be allowed to make collective and individual decisions about their own educational experience in a way that currently they are denied. The prospects for such a sea-change taking place in the near future are not good but that must not deter those concerned with children's rights from trying. No institution impinges upon the daily lives of children more than the school and none is so contemptuous of their opinions or the concept of democracy. That situation cannot remain unchallenged.

REFERENCES

Abrams, F. (1993) 'Schools Return to Classical Mode' *Independent* 5 September.
Advisory Centre for Education (ACE) (1993) 'Fair Play' *ACE Bulletin* (53) pp. 7–9.
Acton, A. (1989) 'Democratic Practice in a Primary School' in C. Harber and R. Meighan (eds) *The Democratic School: Educational Management and the Practice of Democracy* Ticknall, Derbyshire: Education Now Publishers.
Apple, M. (1990) *Constructing the Captive Audience* Maddison, Wisconsin: University of Wisconsin.
Armstrong, H. (1988) 'Women and children first' *Times Educational Supplement* 8 April.
Ball, C. (1987) *The Micro-Politics of the School* London: Methuen.
Bates, S. (1992) 'Major Targets Left Ideas in Schools' *Independent* 29 June.
Best, J. H. (1993) 'Perspectives on Deregulation of Schooling in America' *British Journal of Educational Studies* 41(2) pp. 122–33.
Brown, P. (1990) 'The "third wave": education and the ideology of parentocracy' *British Journal of Sociology of Education* Vol. 11.

Carlen, P., Gleeson, D. and Wardhaugh, J. (1992) *Truancy: The Politics of Compulsory Schooling* Buckingham: Open University Press.

Children's Legal Centre (1987) *Education Rights Handbook* London: Children's Legal Centre.

Clanchy, J. (1993) 'Terse but not to the point' *Times Educational Supplement* 5 March.

Cremin, L. A. (1990) *Popular Education and Its Discontents* New York: Harper Row.

Cullingford, C. (1991) *The Inner World of the School* London: Cassell.

—— (1992) *Children and Society: Children's Attitudes to Politics and Power* London: Cassell.

Dale, R. *et al.* (1990) *The TVEI Story* Buckingham: Open University Press.

Department for Education (1993) *Statistical Bulletin on Women in Post-Compulsory Education 26/93*.

Department of Health (1988) *Protecting Children: A guide for social workers undertaking a comprehensive assessment* London: HMSO.

Financial Times (1992) 'The future of school education' Editorial, 25 June.

Fisher, T. (1993) 'Locked into a destructive Patten' *New Statesman* 5 November.

Flekkoy, M. G. (1991) *A Voice for Children: Speaking Out as Their Ombudsman* London: Jessica Kingsley.

Forth, E. (1993) 'Eric Forth Announces Most Ambitious Assault on Truancy' *DFE News* June.

Gerwitz, S., Ball, S. and Bowe, R. (1994) 'Values and Ethics in the Education Market Place: the case of Northwark park' *International Studies in the Sociology of Education* Vol. 3 (2) pp. 232–53.

Gray, L. (1991) *Marketing Education* Buckingham: Open University Press.

Gutman, A (1987) *Democratic Education* Princeton: Princeton University Press.

Harber, C. (1989) 'Political Education and Democratic Schools' in C. Harber and R. Meighan (eds) *The Democratic School: Educational Management and the Practice of Democracy* Ticknall, Derbyshire: Education Now Publishers.

—— (1992) *Democratic Learning and Learning Democracy: Education for Active Citizenship* Ticknall, Derbyshire: Education Now Publishers.

Haigh, G. (1993) 'Early Morning Calls – Lend Them Your Ears' *Times Educational Supplement* 5 November pp. 16–17.

Johnson, D. (1990) *Parental Choice in Education* London: Unwin Hyman.

Jones, N. and Jones, E. B. (1992) *Learning To Behave: Curriculum and Whole School Management Approaches to Discipline* London: Kogan Page.

Jowett, S., Baginsky, M. and McNeil, M. M. (1991) *Building Bridges: Parental Involvement in Schools* Windsor: NFER-Nelson.

Judd, J. (1994) 'Patten Reveals His Schoolday Beatings' *Independent* 5 January.

Kitzinger, J. (1987) 'Unfairness in Schools' *Values* 2(2).

Lawson, M. (1993) 'Whose Fault Is It Anyway' *Independent on Sunday* 7 November.

MacBeath, J. (1992) *Education In and Out of School: The Issues and the Practice in Inner-cities and Outer Estates* Edinburgh: Scottish Office.

McClure, J. D. (1917) 'Preparation for practical life' in A. C. Benson (ed.) *Cambridge Essays on Education* London: Cambridge University Press.

Meighan, R. (1993) *Theory and Practice of Regressive Education* Nottingham: Educational Heretics Press.

Miller, A. (1993) *Building Effective School–Business Links* London: Department for Education.

Morgan, R. (1993) *School Life: Pupils' Views on Boarding* London: Department of Health.

National Curriculum Council (1993) *Spiritual and Moral Development – A Discussion Paper* York: NCC.

NOP (National Opinion Poll) (1993) 'The Way We Live Survey' *Independent* 30 November.

Norris, B. (1993) 'Beware dubious gifts' *Times Educational Supplement* 21 May.

O' Connor, M. (1990) *Secondary Education* London: Cassell.

Office for Standards in Education (OFSTED) (1993) *Access and Achievement in Urban Education* London: HMSO.

O' Keefe (1993) *Truancy in English Secondary Schools* London: Truancy Research Project University of North London.

Passmore, B. (1993) 'Survival of the slickest' *Times Educational Supplement* 12 November.

Patten, J. (1993) 'Truancy – Time for the Responsible Citizen to Strike Back' *DFE press release* 26 November.

Pring, R. (1994) *Speech to North of England Conference on Education* Chester, January.

Pyke, N., Prestage, M. and Dean, C. (1993) 'Police fear growing tide of exclusions' *Times Educational Supplement* 19 November.

Ranson, S. (1993) *Local Democracy for the Learning Society* London: National Commission for Education.

Rendell, R. and Ward, C. (1989) *Undermining the Central Line* London: Chatto & Windus.

Schools Council (1981) *The Practical Curriculum* London: HMSO.

Schools Council (1981) *The Practical Curriculum* London: Methuen.

Sergiovanni, T. (1992) 'Why we should seek substitutes for leadership' *Educational Leadership* 49 (5) pp. 41–5.

Simon, B. (1988) *Bending the Rules* London: Lawrence & Wishart.

Strike, K. (1982) *Learning and Liberty* Oxford: Martin Robertson.

Torrington, D. and Weightman, J. (1988) *The Management and Organization of Secondary Schools* Manchester: University of Manchester Institute of Science and Technology.

Wallace, G. (1993) 'Across the great divide' *Times Educational Supplement* 22 October.

Welsh Office (1985) *Attendance and Achievement in Secondary Schools* Cardiff: HMI (Wales) Occasional Paper.

West, A. and David (1993) *Choosing a Secondary School: the Parents' and Pupils' Stories* London: Centre for Educational Research.

West, S. (1993) *Educational values for School Leadership* London: Kogan Page

White, P. (1988) 'The Playground Project: A democratic learning experience' in H. Lauder and P. Brown (eds) *Education in Search of a Future* Lewes: Falmer.

White, V. and Johnson, K. (1993) 'Inside the Disadvantaged Schools Programme: The Politics of Practical Policy-making' in L. Angus (ed.) *Education, Inequality and Social Identity* London: Falmer Press.

Chapter 3

Children's rights and the Children Act 1989

Christina Lyon and Nigel Parton

INTRODUCTION

According to the Lord Chancellor, the Children Act 1989 'represents the most comprehensive and far reaching reform of child care law in living memory' (Hansard, 6 December 1988, col. 488). The Act attempts to strike a new balance between the role of the state, the responsibilities of parents, and the rights of children. This chapter summarises the main Sections of the Act which have implications for children's rights, and examines the way in which these rights are framed and constituted. The chapter outlines the particular influences at play in the period prior to the enactment of the legislation which were crucial to its construction. Finally the chapter analyses the implementation of the Act, focusing on a number of legal cases in order to determine whether the rights which appear to have been given to children under the Act have actually been translated into action – in the form of legal and social work decisions made in relation to them. Our central question throughout is whether children's rights have been advanced by the Children Act 1989 both in theory and in practice.

In answering that question we will argue that these rights can only be understood and assessed in the context of the overall Act and other policy developments and pieces of legislation. A central theme will be that the way children's rights are framed in the legislation is not primarily concerned with improving the rights of children *per se*, but in providing a legal mechanism for opening up the private household, and parental behaviour in particular, to new forms of surveillance and thereby making the family more visible to social regulation (Alan Prout, personal communication). At the same time the practices of welfare professionals are themselves made more visible and subject to new forms of monitoring and accountability. The emergence of notions of children's rights in the context of the Children Act has proved a contradictory manoeuvre by which the family is distanced from state interventions, while the arbitrary powers of both family members and state agents are monitored and partly assessed through the words and actions of children, but nevertheless interpreted through a reconstituted legal discourse (Bell, 1993).

CHILDREN'S RIGHTS AND THE CHILDREN ACT

A major criticism of English law before the Children Act 1989 was that it was too reliant on notions of welfare paternalism which viewed children as defenceless and in need of protection by state agents – primarily social workers – who knew what was in children's interests. As a result, welfare professionals had far too much arbitrary power to intervene in the family and did not need to take into account the views and wishes of family members, whether parents or children and young people. The role of the state, and thereby the policies and practices of welfare professionals, were assumed to be inherently benevolent. Further the primary focus was the welfare of the family, with little recognition that the interests of family members might be different and that these should be dis-aggregated, so that children and young people might make distinctive rights claims. The Act is the first serious legislative attempt to redress this imbalance and may be considered to be the first English legislation in which children's rights are taken seriously and are not simply identified with a unified notion of 'welfare'.

A central element of the Act is the reconstitution of the parent's position as one of 'parental responsibility' rather than 'parental rights' (Sections 2 and 3) (Eekelaar, 1991; Edwards and Halpern, 1992). This move implies a reconceptualisation of children as persons to whom duties are owed, rather than as possessions over which power is exercised. This reconstitutes children as persons in their own right and thereby requires a greater effort to be made to involve children in decisions affecting them by any organisation or person having legal responsibility for them whether this be parents, a local authority or a voluntary organisation. In summarising the new measures in the Act which attempt to bring this about, we have (following Bainham, 1990), divided the provisions into three groups: those which try to accommodate children's views; those which recognise children's capacity for independent action; and those which affect older teenagers aged 16 and 17.

The Act introduces a statutory checklist which the court is required to consider when making decisions regarding 'the welfare of the child'. The first factor on the checklist is to have regard to the 'ascertainable wishes and feelings of the child concerned (considered in the light of his age and understanding)' (Section 1(3)(a)). A similar duty is placed on local authorities (Sections 22(4) and (5)), voluntary organisations (Section 61(2) and (3)) and persons running registered children's homes in relation to children looked after by them (Section 64(2) and (3)). Those concerned must also take steps to ascertain the wishes and feelings of the child before taking any decision with respect to him/her, and in making the decision must give due consideration to the child's views – again bearing in mind his/her age and understanding. No clarification is offered, however, concerning what constitutes 'due consideration' or what weight should be attached to the views of the child in the context of the views of the adults involved, whether family or welfare professionals.

Similarly, the Act imposes more rigorous requirements on local authorities making them more accountable for the decisions relating to children in their care (Section 26). The views of children should be ascertained before their case is reviewed and children should be informed subsequently of any decision. Although it is not a requirement, wherever possible the child or young person should be present and a full participant in the review. Another innovative feature is the requirement to establish complaints procedures, with an independent element, in relation to children looked after or 'in need' (Section 26(3)). Again however, these requirements in relation to reviews and complaints are available to parents and those with parental responsibility and others whom the authority considers to have an interest in the child. The child's view is just one amongst numerous parties and it is left open as to how the various views and interests are weighed.

The Act also contains provisions intended to facilitate the presentation of children's views to the court. The evidence of children who are not capable of understanding the nature of an oath may be heard if, in the court's opinion, they understand the duty to be truthful and have sufficient understanding to justify the evidence being heard (Section 96(1) and (3)). Apart from welfare reports however, the principal way in which children's views are to be put before the court is via the guardian ad litem. In certain proceedings, essentially 'public law' proceedings, the court is now under a duty to appoint a guardian ad litem unless satisfied that it is not necessary in order to safeguard the child's interests (Section 41(1)). Proceedings in which guardians ad litem are appointed are now more extensive than previously and include those relating to the new child assessment and emergency protection orders. The main function of a guardian ad litem is to safeguard the interests of the child – and they have a duty to ascertain the child's views and to ensure these are clearly presented to the court.

The net effect of these new provisions is to enhance the legal relevance of the child's views. In theory it should be more difficult for the court and welfare professionals to regard the child as essentially an *object* of welfare. Children must be allowed to make an independent input to decisions concerning them although their views may be superseded by the views of others and/or overtaken by other considerations. Children are entitled to have a say in matters affecting them but not the final say. The provisions offer children qualified autonomy but stop well short of allowing children full consequence of action.

A number of provisions, however, appear to create the possibility of a more absolute autonomy. The concept of autonomy is regarded as the most controversial of three types of children's interests (Eekelaar, 1986). The other two, according to Eekelaar are 'basic' and 'developmental' interests. The 'basic' refers to general physical, emotional and intellectual care while the 'developmental' refers to the opportunity to maximise the resources available during childhood. The 'autonomy' interests refer to 'the freedom to choose his own lifestyle and to enter social relations according to his own inclinations uncontrolled by the authority of the adult world, whether parents or institutions'

(Eekelaar, 1986: pp. 170–1). The provisions within the Children Act which seem to offer the possibility for such autonomy follow primarily from the decision in *Gillick v West Norfolk and Wisbech Area Health Authority* [1986]. While the Gillick case was specifically concerned with whether or not a doctor could offer contraception to a girl under 16 without her parents' consent, the implications of the case were much wider. The Lords decided that a child who is sufficiently mature to understand the implications of a decision should be deemed legally capable of taking a valid decision on that issue even if the parents disagree. While there has been some debate about the intentions of the ruling (Eekelaar, 1986; Bainham, 1988) there seems little doubt that the result is to undermine fundamentally the traditional notion of parental rights to govern children. The parent's power is seen as a dwindling one which the courts would hesitate to enforce against the wishes of the child, particularly as s/he grows older. Parental power begins as the power of control but ends as little more than advice. When the child is deemed competent to make the decision, when s/he has sufficient age and understanding, the parent's power 'yields to the child's right to make his/her own decisions' (per Lord Scarman p. 189).

The Children Act has explicitly drawn upon the notion of 'Gillick competency' in deciding: whether or not children can be given leave to start or join in family proceedings (Section 10(8)); whether the child should be represented independently of the guardian ad litem (Section 41(4)) and whether the appointment of a guardian should be terminated (Section 6(7)(b)); for discharge of a care order (Section 39(1)) and for discharge or variation of a supervision order (Section 39(2)). Also, independent claims of the child are reflected in the new contact order which allows the child to visit or stay with the person named in the order rather than the other way round (Section 8(1)); in the new family assistance order which may be made in favour of the child (Section 16(2)(c)); and in the enhanced ability of an adopted child to establish contact with natural relatives by the adoption contact register (Adoption Act 1976 Section 51A as substituted by Section 88 of the Children Act 1989 and Sched. 10, para. 20(2)).

Perhaps most crucially however, a child can refuse to submit to medical or psychiatric examinations as directed by the court under a child assessment order (Section 43(8)), emergency protection order (Section 44(7)), interim care order (Section 38(6)), or a supervision order (Sched. 3, para. 4(4)) where the child is of sufficient understanding to make an informed decision. Again while the intentions of the legislation regarding such refusal seem unequivocal, the criteria and processes for deciding what constitutes 'sufficient understanding' is not clarified, and, as will be seen, that refusal can in practice be deemed as indicative of immaturity or lack of sufficient understanding.

Finally, the Children Act contains a number of provisions which have the effect of differentiating in law between young people aged 16 to 17 and younger children. The general principle seems to be that older teenagers should have a greater legal autonomy. In relation to Section 8 orders, generally no such order should have effect after the child is 16 (Section 91(10)) and no order should be made after that age. Similarly, with the new restrictions on wardship, there is in effect no longer any mechanism for a compulsory care order in relation to a 17-year-old. It is now also possible for 16-year-olds to pursue a self-referral into local authority accommodation with the authority having a duty to provide accommodation when the young person is 'in need' and when their welfare would otherwise be likely to be 'seriously prejudiced' (Section 20(3)). The legislation goes further than previously in requiring local authorities to advise, assist and befriend young people leaving their care or who are no longer accommodated by them. In certain circumstances, this requirement applies until the young people have obtained the age of 21 (Section 24). The central issue in the Gillick case, concerning the legal relationship between the legal autonomy of adolescents to be responsible for their own actions and parental responsibility for their upbringing, is left vague and obscure.

POLICY CONTEXTS AND POLITICAL BALANCES

From the outset the Government made it clear that the Act needed to be read as a whole. Consequently those Sections primarily concerned with children's rights need to be analysed in the context of the whole Act – its underlying principles, overall structures, inherent logics and, most crucially, the various constituencies and interests, which it was attempting to address.

The Act is wide ranging and comprehensive and, at one level, is concerned with attempting to modernise and rationalise the law in relation to children and families (Hoggett, 1989). Clearly however, the legislation is far more than a technical tidying up exercise. Crucially, it is concerned with trying to construct a new consensus or set of balances related to the respective roles and responsibilities of the state and the family, primarily parents, in the upbringing of children. Defining these balances lies at the heart of the Act (Parton, 1991). What it addresses is a problem which has been a major tension for the liberal state since the late nineteenth century, namely: how can we devise a *legal* basis for the power to intervene into the family which does not convert *all* families, and hence *all* children, into clients of the state? Such a problem is posed by the contradictory demands of trying, on the one hand to ensure that the family is experienced by members as autonomous and the primary sphere for raising children, while on the other, recognising that there is a need for intervention in *some* families where they are seen as failing in this primary task, and in a context where such laws are supposed to act as the general norms applicable to all. The Children Act 1989 is thus best understood as the most recent attempt by the liberal state to govern the family 'at a distance' (Rose and Miller, 1992) but taking into account the new problems posed for the family especially in a changing political and economic context (Parton, 1991; Parton, 1994).

While there is no doubt, that in the light of the Beckford, Carlile and Henry enquiries, the Act is crucially concerned with ensuring children can be protected, it is likewise clear that the primary context and agenda for reform was set by the issues demonstrated by Cleveland concerning the heavy-handed and over-interventionist state (Franklin and Parton, 1991; Parton, 1991).

There were general and increasing concerns from the mid-1970s onwards about the apparent poor and even deteriorating quality of childcare practice in the newly created generic social services departments following the Seebohm reforms (Seebohm Committee, 1968). The poor quality of skills in this area, and the failure to capitalise on the emphasis on prevention in the 1960s were highlighted by the National Children's Bureau working party (Parker, 1980) and were similarly to prove central to various Department of Health and Social Security (DHSS) and Economic and Social Research Council (ESRC) research studies (DHSS, 1985) and the Parliamentary Select Committee (Social Services Committee, 1984). Not only did it seem that there was an increase in the use of compulsory and somewhat unaccountable powers, particularly Parental Rights Resolution and the Place of Safety Order, but there was a failure to work in partnership with parents and pursue notions of family support, shared care, respite care and maintaining the links between the child in care and significant adults – particularly parents. Day-to-day practice appeared over-paternalistic and insufficiently accountable and failed to work in a planned way with parents, children and young people.

Such concerns were emerging in a period of important social and political change and ran in parallel with the growth of a number of vocal and well-organised pressure and interest groups. From the 1960s onwards, with the growth of the women's movement and the recognition of violence in the family, there was a feeling that not only may the family not be the haven it was assumed to be, but that its more powerless members, women and children, were suffering a range of abuses at the hands of men. Much of the early critical analysis and action was directed at improving the position of women, and it was only in more recent years, with the growing concerns about sexual abuse that much of the energy was directed to the position of children (Parton, C., 1990; Parton, N., 1990).

Running in parallel with this development was the growth from the late 1960s onwards of a more obviously civil liberties critique, which concentrated upon the extent and nature of intervention in people's lives that was allowed, apparently unchallenged, in the name of welfare. Initially, this was directed at the issues of mental illness and delinquency (see Taylor et al., 1980; Unsworth, 1987) but increasingly became concerned with child care issues and particularly with protecting the rights of parents over the 'natural' sphere of the private family from state interference (Morris et al., 1980; Geach and Szwed, 1983). Very much related were the critiques of liberal, due process lawyers, who drew attention to the way the administration of justice was unfairly and often unjustly applied in various areas of childcare. It was argued that the priorities of practitioners, together with the processes of decision-making failed to give due weight and consideration to the different and perhaps competing interests of family members as opposed to the concerns of the professionals themselves and their agencies which may be overly influenced by, amongst other things, protecting themselves from outside criticism.

These developments found their most explicit expression with the establishment of a number of pressure groups such as the National Association for One Parent Families, Justice for Children, the Children's Legal Centre and the Family Rights Group, which helped construct new priorities for childcare. The latter two were particularly active in lobbying during the passage of the Children Act through Parliament.

During the mid-1980s the parents' lobby also gained its most coherent voice with the establishment of Parents Against INjustice (PAIN). While its direct influence and lobbying upon the Children Act was marginal, there is little doubt that it was important in helping to organise and frame some of the central issues at play during the Cleveland affair and subsequent enquiries, particularly in the way these were presented in the media. As a consequence, the right of children to be left at home, free of state welfare intervention and removal was placed on the political and professional agenda.

While somewhat different in terms of their social location and focus of critique, we can see a growing set of constituencies developing from the late 1970s onwards which emphasised the need for a greater reliance on individual rights firmly located in a reformed statutory framework where there was a greater emphasis on legalism. Concerns around children's rights constituted just one element and were subjected to a range of interpretations and articulations.

Within an emphasis on legalism, the rule of law as judged by the court takes priority at the expense of other considerations, including that which may be deemed by the professionals concerned, as optimally therapeutic or 'in the best interests of the child'. It involves the superimposition of legal duties, rights and accountabilities upon the interventive, therapeutic and preventive responsibilities.

The conditions of possibility which emphasised the need for greater legalism also proved crucial in framing the central criteria for making decisions in the Children Act. The assessment of 'dangerousness' or 'high risk' has become central (Parton and Parton, 1989a, 1989b; Parton, 1991). In theory, the identification of the actually or potentially dangerous individual or family provides the mechanism both for ensuring that children are protected, while also avoiding unwarrantable intervention. It provides the social and professional rationale for satisfying the demands of both the child rescue lobby and the parental rights lobby. It offers the promise of identifying, isolating and removing children permanently who are in high risk, but also ensures that the innocent and low risk are left alone. Such an approach is central to the Children Act – where the threshold criteria for state intervention is 'that the child concerned is suffering, or is likely to suffer significant harm' (Section 31(2)(9)).

This emphasis on legalism characterises the Act, and while it has a variety of somewhat contradictory dimensions, it is consistent with recent changes in the wider political economy and in particular the increasing pervasiveness of the

New Right during the period. During the 1980s Government policy was based on the twin pillars of the 'free economy and the strong state' (Gamble, 1985). It stressed the importance of individual responsibility, choice and freedom; supporting the disciplines of the market against the interference of the state urging reductions in taxation and political expenditure; and while stressing the need for a reduced state, required a strong state to establish certain modes of family life and social discipline. The family was considered to be an essentially private domain from which the state should be excluded but which should also be encouraged to taken on its 'natural' caring responsibilities. The role of the state should be reduced to: a) ensuring that the family fulfils these responsibilities; b) ensuring that no-one suffers at the hands of the violent and strong. Freedom, while central, is constructed in negative terms as freedom from unnecessary interferences. The law becomes crucial in defining and operationalising both 'natural' rights and 'natural' responsibilities.

In trying to redistribute resources away from the more universal welfare provisions towards law and order, and in trying to free and reinforce the market and the family as the best way of allocating resources and insuring individual freedom, the role of the law becomes primary. Law must provide the framework for underwriting responsibilities and contracts between individuals and between individuals and the state. The emphasis also aims to make the rationale for state interventions into the family more explicit and their actions more accountable. Individual freedoms are to be defended under the purview of the law, but when the state does intervene, it does so with the full weight of the law, in the guise of the court, behind it.

Thus while the autonomy and wishes of children and young people and their rights are taken much more seriously in the Children Act than previously, this is in an overall context where the essential balances and procedures are much more legalistically framed and where the role of the court and legal thinking is central.

JUDICIAL INTERPRETATIONS OF THE CHILDREN ACT 1989

The tensions between yielding greater autonomy to most families, deemed by the parental responsibility provisions of the Act to be able to cope with the stresses and strains of family living – and in a large number of cases with family breakdown, whilst at the same time retaining grounds for intervention in those families which cannot cope, was revealed early on in judicial attitudes towards the changes brought about by the Children Act. The judges have indeed struggled judicially to come to terms with the seemingly conflicting messages purveyed by the provisions of the Act. It is proposed at this stage to consider a number of the areas of the Act already highlighted as directing attention towards children's rights and to assess the extent to which judges have been able to escape from a persistently paternalistic attitude in their dealings with children's cases. In some areas this aspect of judicial welfarism may be seen to be benevolently paternalistic, but in others it is suggested that children themselves might view the judges as deliberately taking away rights that they appear to have been given under the provisions of the Act.

An example of the benevolent paternalistic attitude displayed by many of the judges can be seen in their concerns over the changes brought about in relation to arrangements for children involved in parental relationship breakdown. In an effort to encourage greater responsibility on the part of parents and to reduce the trauma experienced by children whose parents became embattled over their custody, the Law Commission had recommended that children involved in their parents' divorces should no longer automatically be made the subject of court orders. This was achieved by amendments to Section 41 of the Matrimonial Causes Act 1973, effected by the Children Act 1989, which meant that following implementation of the Act, there would no longer be a judicial hearing with regard to arrangements being made for children following divorce. As with non-marital children, the message of the Act was clearly that parents should try to settle post-breakdown arrangements for children amicably, without resort to court orders. For children involved in their parents' divorce therefore, the arrangements made for them following their parents' divorce were simply to be set out on paper, considered on paper by the judge and approved, unless there was anything which might alert the judge to any problems requiring the court's involvement. Further discouragement to parents to bring their possible concerns about post-divorce arrangements to the court's attention, was to be found in Section 1(5) of the Act, which directs that:

> where a court is considering whether or not to make an order under the Act with respect to a child it should not make the order unless it considers that doing so would be better for the child than making no order at all.

This provision was interpreted by many as a directive against court intervention unless it could be shown to be better than making no order at all, and became widely known as the principle of judicial non-intervention. This was of course a complete misnomer since the provision directs attention to whether the order might confer a positive advantage on the child rather than declaring that there should be no intervention by means of any order at all. Nevertheless, it was felt that the message being given was that it was better for everyone if parents were allowed to sort matters out privately. Another reason for encouraging this interpretation of the provision was inevitably government concern about rising costs in divorce cases and the abolition of satisfaction hearings was calculated to produce a considerable saving both in terms of judicial time and also in relation to the Legal Aid budget.

Many judges were, however, extremely worried by this retreat by the authorities from the principle of satisfaction hearings. It was seen principally as not having been done in order to reduce conflict but as having been motivated by cost. From a children's rights perspective moreover, it could have been argued that an encouragement to parents to settle arrangements out of court with no additional direction that they should have regard to their children's wishes and feelings, nor necessarily that they should consider their children's welfare as paramount, was a very negative move. Children were denied the opportunity of discussing the arrangements made for them with a judge, formerly available through the satisfaction hearings, but given the new 'right' to seek leave to make an application for a Section 8 order (Section 10(8)) provided the child is of sufficient understanding. The child was thus denied a forum in which such issues could have been raised and the relevant information provided. The Department of Health has produced a guide for children involved in divorce and care proceedings entitled *The Children Act and The Court – A Guide for Children and Young People* (1983) but this is not made available through the court service to children who are named as the subject of arrangements considered on paper by the courts. Information is power, but many children in England and Wales have not been given the necessary information to enable them to realise that they could make applications themselves for orders under Section 8. Children and young people may wish to live with someone else or to have the opportunity of maintaining contact with some person e.g. a grandparent, aunt or friend, whom the parent caring for them has decided they should not see. Yet how do children find out about their rights to use Section 8 orders?

Those children who do manage to obtain information about their 'rights' are then faced with innumerable other obstacles. They must first seek out a solicitor, which is not easy for a child or young person, and they must then give instructions to that solicitor. In addition, fearing a flood of applications from children, the High Court Family Division issued a Practice Direction in early 1993 following the first reported case of a girl aged 14 seeking to use the provisions of Section 8 of the Act to obtain a residence order so that she could live with her boyfriend's parents (*Re AD* [1993]). This Practice Direction now provides that applications by children raise issues which are more appropriate for determination in the High Court, and states that they should therefore be transferred there for hearing rather than being heard in the lower courts, such as the county or magistrates courts. Such an approach instantly gives children, when they are informed of the position, the feeling that they are to be treated very differently from other people who might seek to make applications for Section 8 orders under the Act. In the light of case law, it would appear that even where the child succeeds in establishing that s/he has the necessary understanding to go forward with an application the High Court judges have taken an extremely paternalistic attitude on the issue of the child's right to be represented by a solicitor of their own choice rather than by the court appointing the Official Solicitor to represent the child.

While there has been considerable comment about the attitude of the judiciary in particular cases (see for example Murphy, 1993), the import of the cases reflects a very strongly-held belief on the part of many of the judiciary, that children cannot possess sufficient understanding to appreciate all the complexities of the issues arising from a consideration of an application for a Section 8 order. This is manifestly apparent from the cases of *Re CT* [1993], *Re S* [1993], *Re SC* [1993] and *Re H* [1993]. *Re CT* has been described as a case which resiles further from the principle of 'adolescent autonomy' by means of a paternalistic interpretation of subsidiary legislation under the Children Act 1989 and thereby reining in the extent to which adolescents are granted the facility for litigious independence.

(Murphy, 1993: 186)

In *Re CT* it was proposed by Mr Justice Waite that it was the court which had the final decision concerning whether a child was competent to instruct a solicitor. This view is submitted to be at odds with the actual provisions of both the primary and secondary legislation with which it was dealing and is clearly based on paternalistic concerns which, as Murphy argues, are thinly disguised and – presented as 'welfarism' – given precedence over the child's interest in self-determination. This point is made even more clearly in the decision of the Master of the Rolls in *Re S*, the second case cited above. In determining that a boy of 11 did not have the necessary understanding to seek leave to make an application for a Section 8 order, the Master of the Rolls stated that:

The 1989 Act enables and requires a judicious balance to be struck between two considerations. First is the principle, to be honoured and respected, that children are human beings in their own right with individual minds and wills, views and emotions, which should command serious attention. A child's wishes are not to be discounted or dismissed simply because he is a child. He should be free to express them and decision-makers should listen. Second is the fact that a child is, after all, a child. The reason why the law is particularly solicitous in protecting the interests of children is because they are liable to be vulnerable and impressionable, lacking the maturity to weigh the longer term against the shorter, lacking the insight to know how they will react and the imagination to know how others will react in certain situations, lacking the experience to measure the probable against the possible. Everything of course depends on the individual child in his actual situation. For the purposes of the Act, a babe in arms and a sturdy teenager on the verge of adulthood are both children, but their positions are quite different, for one the second consideration would be dominant, for the other the first principle will come into its own. The process of growing up is, as Lord Scarman pointed out in *Gillick* [cited above] a continuous one. The judge has to do his best, on the evidence before him, to assess the understanding of the individual child in the context of the proceedings in which he seeks to participate.

It can be argued in the context of such statements that too much hangs on the attitude of individual judges and the course which the proceedings may have taken. By contrast in the case of *Re H* the child aged 15¾ had been so closely involved with the conduct of the whole proceedings, that Mrs Justice Booth took the attitude that the boy had sufficient understanding to participate as a party and should be permitted to do so. Interestingly she stated that it was not for the court, in applying the test of whether the child had sufficient understanding, to take into account what the court may or may not consider to be in the best interests of the child. The boy in this case was therefore able to keep his own solicitor and legal representative, but the court took the view that the Official Solicitor should still be involved to perform the role of amicus curiae; i.e. to act as a special adviser to the court and to bring before the court any evidence which might otherwise not be put before it. Analogous to care proceedings therefore, where a child might divert from the view held by the guardian ad litem as to the course which proceedings might take and is allowed to pursue the case through his/her legal representative, the Official Solicitor, like the guardian ad litem in care pro-ceedings will remain involved in the case in order to present the court with a view as to what is in the child's best interests, even though this may conflict with what the child wants.

Further disturbing evidence of judicial reluctance to acknowledge the right of children to be in court, where from a children's rights perspective it could be argued that they should be there, is to be found in the case of *Re C* [1993]. In that case a 13-year-old girl had been present throughout care proceedings in the family proceedings court and was further present on a subsequent appeal to the High Court. The guardian ad litem had followed the provisions in the court rules which directed that careful consideration should be given to whether a child should be present during care proceedings, but the girl had indicated a clear desire to be present. The guardian ad litem felt this to be in her best interests and the magistrates had exercised their discretion under Section 95(1) of the Act to allow the child to be present in court at the hearing. None of the other parties had raised any objection at that stage, nor on the appeal. Notwithstanding this, Mr Justice Waite ruled that 'young children should be discouraged from attending High Court appeals from the justices in family proceedings'. He went on to state that it would be a pity if the presence of children were to be allowed to develop unquestioningly into a settled practice, for listening to lawyers debating one's future was not an experience that should in normal circumstances be wished upon any young child (it must be remembered that the child in this case was over 13 years of age). Therefore, he stated, where guardians ad litem were proposing to arrange for a young child to be present, he stated, they should give the question very careful thought beforehand and be prepared, if necessary, to explain their reasons to the judge. It can be seen from the facts of the case that the guardian ad litem had carefully followed these principles and the child had very much wanted to be present in court.

Further evidence of judicial reluctance to accede to a child's wish to be present in court can be found in the case of *North Yorkshire County Council* v *G* [1993]. Mr Justice Douglas Brown stated that a child of 16 could not be allowed to join in proceedings where the whole purpose of him being joined as a party was to enable the child to carry out a supportive role which he had been carrying throughout in relation to his mother, arguing against a care order being made in respect of a younger child. It was argued by the judge that there were positive disadvantages in allowing the boy to be a party since he would then have sight of all the documentation in the case which included psychiatric evidence concerning his mother. No consideration appeared to have been given to the issue of whether certain elements of the evidence could simply be produced for the child's solicitor and not actually given to the child himself.

Many other examples could be cited from case law to support the contention that the Master of the Rolls' formulation in *Re S* holds sway and that judicial considerations of what is in the best interests of the child will always override the claims of the child to any very considerable degree of autonomy. Eekelaar's claim (cited above), reflective of Lord Scarman's speech in *Gillick* to the effect that the child must as he gets older be allowed to learn from his own mistakes, does not seem to have found favour with the judiciary. It has already been noted that Section 1(3) directs the court to have regard to the ascertainable wishes and feelings of the child concerned (considered in the light of his age and understanding). Where the children's views are considered by the judges to be the 'right' ones, then the judges are happy to go along with those views. This can be seen the in case *Re F* [1993], where boys aged 12 and 9 were refusing to see their transexual father despite the recommendations of all the professionals and the views of their mother, and where the court refused to make coercive orders on the boys. It was seen also in the case of *Re S* where the Court of Appeal refused to make a contact order where the children objected to contact on the basis that their father was constantly subjecting them to religious haranguing. In that case the court of appeal stated that children of 13 and 11 were entitled to be treated with respect. Lord Justice Butler-Sloss stated that 'they were not packages to be moved around. Nobody should dictate to children of those ages as one was dealing with their emotions and their lives'. By contrast however in the case of *Re C* the wishes of the 13-year-old girl in local authority care to return to live with her 64-year-old, ill and divorced father were overruled by the judge. Mr Justice Waite said that the girl was too young to carry the burden of decisions about her own future and too young to have to bear the weight of responsibility for a parent who lacked authority and played on her feelings. The judge decided to ignore the very strong claim put forward by the girl that she wished to live with her father.

Finally, the role of judicial paternalism in overruling the rights which have been given by the Children Act, was pointed up most strongly in the case of *South Glamorgan County Council* v *W and B* [1992]. Many commentators had of course been quaking in their shoes following the decisions in *Re R* [1992], *Re W* [1993] and *Re K, W and H* [1993]. It was apparent from the decision in this last case that so-called *Gillick* provisions in the Children Act would not long survive an attack made under the guise of the exercise of the inherent jurisdiction of the High Court, and it hit us with full force in the decision of Mr Justice Douglas Brown in the *South Glamorgan* case. Here a 15-year-old girl, in a severely depressed state had refused to abide by a court order direction in an interim care order that she be removed from home to a psychiatric unit for assessment and treatment. Under the provisions of Section 38(6) of the Act, if the court makes a direction as to medical psychiatric examination or other assessment of the child, the child may, if of sufficient understanding to make an informed decision, refuse to submit to the examination or assessment. The girl had clearly and with full understanding refused assessment, but the local authority sought the assistance of the High Court and invited it to intervene through the exercise of the inherent jurisdiction on the basis of what was in the best interests of the girl, to override that refusal and order her to be removed from home and appropriately assessed. Mr Justice Douglas Brown made the order, arguing that in an appropriate case, where other remedies provided within the Children Act had been exhausted and found not to bring about the desired result, there was jurisdiction to resort to other remedies, and the particular remedy sought here was that of providing authority for doctors to treat the child, and authority, if it was needed, for the local authority social services to take all necessary steps to bring the child to the doctors so that she could be assessed and treated properly.

Thus, it has to be said, that many of the so-called *Gillick* provisions of the Children Act 1989 conferring rights upon children are in reality merely conferring strong claims for the child's voice to be heard. Those of us who have talked to children about their rights to refuse medical treatment and other forms of assessment under the Act must now retreat from such guidance and indicate more clearly to them that their refusal must be seen more in the nature of a claim to be allowed to put forward a refusal which may be overridden by a court which deems their refusal not to be in their own best interests. Many of the provisions which might have been described as children's rights under the Act should now be described more correctly as claims or interests. The judiciary, through its attitudes and actions has determined that it should ultimately be the arbiter of whether a child should be allowed to make and learn from her/his mistakes.

CONCLUSIONS

While various provisions and elements of the Children Act do appear to take children's rights more seriously and provide new opportunities for advancing the wishes, autonomy and independent actions of children and young people, this is very qualified. Not only is the Act much more legalistic in the way it is framed and the way the mechanisms for addressing the central balances are operationalised, but developments and legal cases since its inception in October 1991 provide clear evidence concerning how this is played out in practice. The articulation of children's rights, rather than constituting children and young persons as subjects, has provided a new set of strategies and mechanisms for using the voices of children as elements in the newly constituted government of families. Rather than subjects in their own right, children have become reconstituted as legal – as opposed to welfare – objects for the purpose of governing families at a distance.

CASES CITED

Gillick v *West Norfolk and Wisbech Health Authority* [1986] AC 112
North Yorkshire County Council v *G* [1993] 2FLR 732
Re AD [1993] Fam. Law 43
Re C [1993] 1 FLR 832
Re CT [1993] 2 FLR 278
Re F [1993] 1 FCR 945
Re H [1993] 2 FLR 552
Re K, W and H [1993] 1 FLR 854
Re R [1992] 1 FLR 190
Re S [1993] 2 FLR 437
Re SC [1993] Fam. Law 553
RE W [1993] 1 FLR 1
South Glamorgan County Council v *W and B* [1992] 1 FLR 574

REFERENCES

Bainham, A. (1988) *Children, Parents and the State* London: Sweet & Maxwell.
—— (1990) 'The Children Act 1989: Adolescence and Children's Rights' *Family Law* August, pp. 311–14.
Bell, V. (1993) 'Governing Childhood: Neo Liberalism and the Law' *Economy and Society* Vol. 22 (3) pp. 390–405.
DHSS (1985) *Social Work Decisions in Child Care: Recent Research Findings and their Implications* London: HMSO.
Edwards, S. and Halpern, A. (1992) 'Parental Responsibility: An Instrument of Social Policy' *Family Law* March, pp. 113–18.
Eekelaar, J. (1986) 'The Emergence of Children's Rights' *Oxford Journal of Legal Studies* Vol. 6 (2).
—— (1991) 'Parental Responsibility: State of Nature or Nature of the State?' *Journal of Social Welfare and Family Law* Vol. 1, pp. 37–50.
Franklin, B. and Parton, N. (eds) (1991) *Social Work and the Media* London: Routledge.
Gamble, A. (1985) *The Free Economy and the Strong State: The Politics of Thatcherism* London: Macmillan.
Geach, H. and Szwed, E. (eds) (1983) *Providing Civil Justice for Children* London: Arnold.
Hoggett, B. (1989) 'Family Law into the 1990s' *Family Law* Vol. 19, May, pp. 177–80.
Morris, A., Giller, H., Szwed, E. and Geach, H. (1980) *Justice for Children* London: Macmillan.
Murphy, J. (1993) 'Re CT: Litigious Mature Minors and Wardship in the 1990s' *Journal of Child Law* Vol. 5, p. 186–91.
Parker, R. (ed.) (1980) *Caring for Separated Children: Plans, Procedures and Priorities. A Report by a Working Party Established by the National Children's Bureau* London: Macmillan.
Parton, C. (1990) 'Women, Gender Oppression and Child Abuse' in The Violence Against Children Study Group *Taking Child Abuse Seriously: Contemporary Issues in Child Protection Theory and Practice* London, Unwin Hyman.
Parton, C. and Parton, N. (1989a) 'Child Protection, the Law and Dangerousness' in O. Stephenson, (ed.) *Child Abuse: Public Policy and Professional Practice* London: Harvester Wheatsheaf.
—— (1989b) 'Women, the Family and Child Protection' *Critical Social Policy* No. 24, pp. 38–49.

Parton, N. (1990) 'Taking Child Abuse Seriously' in The Violence Against Children Study Group *Taking Child Abuse Seriously: Contemporary Issues in Child Protection Theory and Practice* London: Unwin Hyman.

—— (1991) *Governing the Family: Child Care, Child Protection and the State* London: Macmillan.

—— (1994) 'Problematics of Government, (Post) Modernity and Social Work' *British Journal of Social Work* Vol. 24, pp. 9–32.

Rose, N. and Miller, P. (1992) 'Political Power Beyond the State: Problematics of Government' *British Journal of Sociology* 43 (2) pp. 173–205.

Secretary of State for Social Services (1988) *Report of the Inquiry into Child Abuse in Cleveland*, Cmnd 412, London: HMSO.

Seebohm Committee (1968) *Report of the Committee on Local Authority and Allied Personal Social Services* Cm. 3703, London: HMSO.

Social Services Committee (HC 360) (1984) *Children in Care* March, London: HMSO.

Taylor, L., Lacey, R. and Bracken, D. (1980) *In Whose Best Interests?* London: Conden Trust/Mind.

Unsworth, C. (1987) *The Politics of Mental Health Legislation* Oxford: Oxford University Press.

Chapter 4

The Criminal Justice Acts

'Justice' by geography

Barry Anderson

INTRODUCTION

The position of children and young people within the criminal justice systems of the UK is complicated by three factors. First, there are three distinctive legal systems in operation. The discussion here focuses on the criminal justice system in England and Wales; the youth justice processes in Northern Ireland and in Scotland differ significantly.

Second, the sheer volume of legislation enacted is considerable. The juvenile court was created by the Children Act of 1908, and the Children and Young Persons Act of 1933 is still highly important, more than 60 years later. But the pace of legislative change has quickened in recent years, and the Criminal Justice Acts of 1982, 1988, 1991 and 1993 were recently joined by the Criminal Justice and Public Order Act of 1994. Each of these Acts has contained major provisions concerning young offenders, and the cumulative effect can be daunting even for lawyers and specialist youth justice workers.

It is however the third complicating factor which is arguably the most significant from a children's rights perspective, since it goes to the heart of the debate about the place of children in our society. In addition to the great weight of criminal justice legislation affecting children, there is also a highly important body of childcare law, of which the most recent and probably the most important, is the Children Act 1989 (see chapter 3). Even in the 'unified' legal system of England and Wales, criminal justice policy is the responsibility of the Home Office, while child welfare is the remit of the Department of Health and the Welsh Office respectively. It is necessary only to contrast the approaches of the Children Act 1989 and the Criminal Justice Act 1991 – to the question of parental responsibility for children's behaviour for example – to appreciate what many commentators believe is an unacceptable level of inconsistency between child welfare and young offender legislation. Indeed, it is possible to argue that children in the criminal justice system suffer the 'worst of both worlds'. They are denied many of the rights and considerations extended to children in civil law, but lack the full rights of an adult in the criminal justice system. In short, there is no clear answer to the crucial question, 'Is a child who commits a criminal offence primarily to be regarded as a child or as an offender?', and therein lies the major difficulty for anyone seeking to understand the legal rights of a child who is accused or convicted of a criminal offence.

The task of implementing these somewhat ambiguous national policies falls almost entirely to local agencies. What is described as a youth justice 'system' is, in fact, a series of complicated interactions between groups of agencies and professions, in which the rights and concerns of children and their parents can easily become marginalised. The main groups involved are the police, the Crown Prosecution Service, the local authority social services department, the probation service, magistrates, justices' clerks and solicitors. Less centrally involved, but often important 'players' locally, are schools and/or education welfare officers, the youth service and voluntary organisations who run young offender projects.

Each group or agency clearly has a different role and differing objectives for their participation in the youth justice system and the way in which young people are dealt with is, to some extent, determined by the way in which these differences are resolved. It is important to recognise, however, that these significant differences can be found, not only between different agencies, but also between similar agencies in different areas of the country. Neighbouring police forces, for example, may vary considerably in their approaches to cautioning children, while their local authority counterparts may provide markedly different services to support young people on bail or to work with convicted children subject to a court order. It cannot be denied that the treatment children receive from the criminal justice system is significantly affected by such factors as where they live and where they offend. Indeed, probably the best known epigram among youth justice workers is 'justice by geography' – an ironic phrase since justice should be independent of such contingent factors. 'Justice' which is reliant on such factors is arguably not justice at all.

This chapter is in seven broad sections which analyse and examine: (1) the uncertainties and debates prompted by the diverse age-based entitlements to rights which operate within the criminal justice system; (2) the regulations governing interviews with children and young people at the police station; (3) the complexities of the decision-making procedure which establishes whether a young person under 16, suspected of an offence, should receive a caution or have their case referred for prosecution; (4) the conditions for bail, and extremely severe circumstances of remand which young people may be obliged to confront; (5) the hearing system and the possible range of sentences available; (6) the undesirable changes to Section 53 orders contained in the Criminal Justice and Public Order Act 1994; (7) a consideration of children's rights within the system.

AGE DISTINCTIONS

In England and Wales, the 'age of criminal responsibility' (i.e. the minimum age at which a child can be prosecuted for a criminal offence) is 10 years. By Western, and indeed international standards, this is low. It is not, however, the lowest in the UK: in Scotland, criminal responsibility begins at just 8 years of age.

The Scottish 'children's hearing' system, however, deals with both criminal and civil matters, operating in a relatively informal setting, and using an inquisitorial approach as opposed to the traditional adversarial system of criminal justice employed for both children and adults throughout the rest of Britain. Many today call for the adoption of the Scottish system in England and Wales, arguing that a unified system for all children at risk or in trouble is less stigmatising. An informal, inquisitorial approach, moreover, allegedly places greater emphasis on responding effectively to the young person (and so reducing the likelihood of further offending), and less on the need to secure a conviction and punish the offender. Such claims are frequently countered, however, by concerns that this apparently more liberal and progressive approach to dealing with young alleged offenders, though according them greater protection, offers them far fewer legal rights. It should, perhaps, be noted that the use of custody for young offenders in Scotland is proportionately higher than in England and Wales. In most Western countries, the age of criminal responsibility is 14 or 16; in some it is as high as 18 years of age. This does not, of course, mean that offences by younger people are ignored. Rather, they are dealt with in a way which is not dissimilar to the Scottish system, under a civil system which exists to handle all matters related to children and families.

Again, many in England and Wales argue strongly for the adoption of an approach which locates crime by young people within the context of the family and of 'normal' adolescent misbehaviour. They are particularly worried by the consequences of a provision of the Children Act 1989 which excludes criminal proceedings against children from the remit of the new Family Proceedings Court, leaving the juvenile (now youth) court, which had previously dealt with both civil and criminal matters, with solely criminal jurisdiction. It is widely perceived among those working with young people in the criminal justice system, that 'their' clients have effectively been excluded from many of the more positive provisions of the Children Act, because they are seen as offenders first and children second, and the provisions of criminal justice legislation take precedence over laws such as the Children Act.

There is undeniably a case to answer here, but again it is important to look at the outcomes of other systems as well as their underlying philosophies. Some countries with a high age of criminal responsibility also have high rates of admission to secure 'childcare' facilities. In England and Wales, the youth court now deals with young people under 18. The age of majority is therefore the same for both criminal and civil purposes. The former juvenile court heard only cases involving those under 17; the change in age-range and name, under the provisions of the Criminal Justice Act (CJA) 1991, was implemented in October 1992 but was accompanied by the introduction of new 'adult-style' sentencing arrangements for both 16- and 17-year-olds, and it might be argued that the youth court is not so much a positive development for 17-year-olds (an acknowledgement of their status and rights as minors) as an incursion on the rights of 16-year-olds. However, as will be seen in a number of the sections below, the greatest difficulty about the 1991 Act's inclusion of 17-year-olds in the youth court, is that it specifically and deliberately failed to include them in pre-court arrangements. Young people aged 17 are therefore uniquely disadvantaged, lacking not only many of the protections afforded to those aged 16 and under, but also the legal rights of those aged 18 plus (such as the right to elect for jury trial).

AT THE POLICE STATION

The overwhelming majority of police interviews with children, as with all sus- pected offenders, are conducted at police stations. Although this may seem an obvious point to make, it is important and has far-reaching implications; it also marks a comparatively recent development. Until the early 1980s it was widely considered to be good police practice to interview young people in the presence of a parent, in their own homes. The Police and Criminal Evidence Act of 1984 (PACE), however, laid down rules for the questioning of suspects which made it practically necessary for this task to be conducted in police stations. These rules cover such matters as permitted periods of detention, the manner and duration of questioning, the recording of interviews and the right to legal advice. To these general regulations are added others which are specific to juveniles (i.e. those aged 16 and under) and other groups considered to be in need of additional protection, such as people with learning difficulties or people who are suffering from some form of mental disorder. By agreement with other agencies, some police forces have extended the 'juvenile' provisions of PACE to 17-year-olds; others have not.

The most significant regulations for juveniles relate to the presence of an 'appropriate adult' during questioning and to the arrangements which must be made for children who for some reason cannot subsequently be returned home on police bail to await a possible court hearing. Part C, paragraph 3.7 of the PACE Codes of Practice provides that when juveniles are detained at a police station, their parents must be informed and requested to attend. If a parent cannot be contacted, or is unable or unwilling to go to the police station, the police must arrange for a social worker or some other 'appropriate adult' to attend. Question- ing of the juvenile can take place only in the presence of the parent or an appropriate adult, who can, if necessary, be any adult not employed by a police force. (There was, in the early days of the new regulations, a famous instance of a local police station using its cleaners for this purpose, having recently con- tracted out its cleaning services!). In practice, most social services departments now provide a 'round the clock' appropriate adult service, using specialist youth justice and emergency duty staff. This is a major undertaking by local authorities where there are high rates of youth crime, especially since they have no statutory duty to provide this or many of the other youth justice services which are generally considered to be necessary to the effective operation of the youth justice system. Social work and probation staff tend to be effective as 'appropriate adults'; they can be trained for the role and quickly become proficient through regular and frequent requests for the service. By contrast, parents are often poorly-informed and ill-prepared for the task and are less likely to be objective observers in an interview, though there are clearly other benefits to be drawn from their involvement. There is concern that the police, finding it more convenient to deal with social workers who are better briefed and less emotionally involved, sometimes fail to make adequate efforts to contact and persuade parents before calling the social services department. Whether or not this is the case, it is important to note that the young person concerned has no right of choice. At 16 years old, children in police custody may not choose to be unaccompanied, or who should accompany them; and especially where children have left home, this raises 'Gillick-style' questions about a possible conflict between the rights of children and those of their parents.

Children also have a right to be questioned in the presence of a solicitor, and 'appropriate adults' often insist on a solicitor's presence, on the child's behalf, especially where there is any disagreement concerning what has taken place. A solicitor who is present at the station in a professional capacity may not act as an appropriate adult. While the role of appropriate adults does not include giving legal advice, it can be summarised as 'seeing that everything is done according to the rules'. They should have access to a copy of the rules and an opportunity to talk to the child alone prior to the commencement of questioning.

Once questioning is completed and statements have been taken and signed, children should be allowed to return home; if necessary, on police bail. Where this is not possible, except in very rare circumstances, the police have a duty to hand the child over to the keeping of the local authority to be accommodated by them as they see fit. Even if the alleged offence is a serious one, and the police wish to bring the child before a court the following day, the child cannot normally be detained overnight by the police (PACE, Section 38(6), as amended by the CJA 1991, s.59).

Perhaps the most striking feature of the PACE provisions for juveniles is the way in which they seek to protect children without giving them any rights as individuals to determine the decisions made about them. This contrast between protection and rights is, as will become evident, a recurring feature of the youth justice system. As a child, one is afforded protections, but as an alleged or convicted offender, one loses certain rights which a child might otherwise possess.

WARNINGS, CAUTIONS AND PROSECUTIONS

If the police believe there is evidence that any person has committed an offence, they have to decide whether to take no action, take informal action, issue a formal caution, or refer the case for prosecution. Official policy in recent years has particularly emphasised the benefits of diverting young people from the formal court system by means of warnings and cautions. The Home Office Circular on

Cautioning issued for Chief Constables in 1985 and 1990, together with the Code for Crown Prosecutors produced by the Lord Chancellor's Department in 1987, firmly endorsed the view that juveniles should only be prosecuted when that is clearly in the public interest. New guidance was issued during 1994, which seeks to modify this view and limit the cautioning of young people (Home Office 1985, 1990, 1994).

Currently, a number of considerations are involved in decisions about whether or not to prosecute a young person aged 16 and under. The position for 17-year-olds varies from area to area; some police forces now include them in their 'juvenile liaison' arrangements; others do not. Perhaps the most important considerations are the seriousness of the offence and whether or not it is admitted by the accused young person. If the offence is a very serious one, the young person is likely to be charged immediately, and the case referred for prosecution, whether or not the accused person admits the offence. At the other end of the scale, police officers 'on the street' dealing with relatively minor youthful transgressions, often issue what are referred to as 'informal warnings' or 'instant cautions', which amount to a telling-off and have no formal consequences.

Where offences fall somewhere between the two extremes of seriousness, a decision is made after interview. If the young person denies the offence, the police must either take no action, or refer the matter to the Crown Prosecution Service (CPS) for possible prosecution. If the offence is admitted, the police may still choose to take no action, but they also have the option to issue a formal caution rather than to refer the case to the CPS.

It is especially important that cautions are administered only where an offence is freely admitted. It can be tempting for young people to admit an offence of which they are innocent where this will result in a prompt cessation of an interview, early release from the police station and the avoidance of a subsequent court hearing. There is an obvious danger that such considerations could be used by police officers as inducements to secure admissions and it is by no means unknown for well-meaning parents and 'appropriate adults' to urge such a course as being in the young person's 'best interests'. A caution, however, is a formally recorded finding of guilt, which will be cited in court should the young person be prosecuted and convicted of some future offence. Where a young person protests their innocence, the proper course is therefore, either for no action to be taken or for the matter of guilt to be determined by the courts.

Often, when a young person admits an offence, the police will decide to caution, without reference to anyone else, except perhaps the victims of the offence and the offender's parents. Other cases may present greater difficulties for police decision-makers, and these cases are normally referred for consideration by an interdisciplinary group of professionals, known variously as a juvenile liaison meeting, panel or bureau. Some are simply regular meetings attended by representatives of the police, social services department and probation service, often with additional personnel from the youth service, education welfare service or education department. Such meetings allow the agencies to share knowledge about young people and their circumstances, as well as about the alleged offending, in reaching a joint decision about whether to recommend a caution or prosecution. The purpose of the meetings is to ensure that difficult decisions are made on the basis of the fullest available information, and to ensure that personal or family problems which may have contributed to a child's offending are not overlooked.

There are obvious concerns, however, from a children's rights perspective, about professional gatherings to which child and parents have no access and at which information held by agencies with different roles and responsibilities is so freely shared. Again, there is a stark difference between the way in which society treats a child accused (but not convicted) of a criminal offence, and a child who is the subject of some form of childcare case conference.

Inevitably, the situation frequently arises where the appropriate response to an offence is a caution, but where the provision of some additional services or help to child or family is also indicated. This is currently a complicated 'grey' area and there have been many calls in recent years for official guidance to clarify the situation. The concern is that an offer of a caution must not be seen by young people as conditional upon their acceptance of any form of 'cautioning plus' or 'post-cautioning' support service which may also be offered. If the acceptance of such a service were, in any sense, obligatory, it would become, in effect, a sentence; but a sentence determined and carried out by a group of professionals without the authority of sentencers and without a prior court hearing.

One further outcome is possible in addition to those already discussed. The CPS may conclude either that a prosecution is not in the public interest or that there is insufficient evidence to secure a conviction. In either event, they will 'discontinue' a case – which may be the end of the matter – though a caution remains a possibility where there is an admission and the decision to discontinue is taken on public interest grounds.

The decision about whether to warn, caution or prosecute a young offender is just one stage of a lengthy process, yet it is a fairly complicated business in its own right. Perhaps its most striking feature once again, however, is the extent to which it offers young people protection rather than rights.

THE BAIL AND REMAND PROCESS

Everyone facing prosecution for an offence has a presumed right to unconditional bail; that is, to be allowed to live a normal life in the community until the case is heard. Where courts find that specific grounds are not met, however, they may withhold bail, or grant it subject to conditions. The grounds apply both to adults and minors, and relate to the need to protect the public, the likelihood that the accused will interfere with witnesses if allowed to remain at liberty, or that s/he will fail to attend court when the case is ready to be heard. The conditions which may be attached to bail include requirements to reside at a particular address, to refrain from visiting certain people or places, and to report regularly to a police station or other reporting facility. This broad framework of rules applies equally to adults and minors, but the position of people under 18 is, again, both complicated and subject to imminent change.

Some probation services and social services departments provide facilities for young people on bail; those aged 16 and over can, in theory, be accommodated in probation service bail hostels, though in practice their use for minors is considered inappropriate and a matter of 'last resort'. Many social service departments now provide bail support schemes, which offer assistance to young people aged up to 16 or 17 on bail and awaiting trial. This may include practical assistance, such as helping a homeless young person find accommodation, in order to provide the court with a 'bail address'. Local authorities have no statutory duty to provide bail support. They do, however, have a range of responsibilities to assist 'vulnerable young people' under the Children Act 1989, though there is no clear interpretation of their duty to 'assist' such young people. Again, there is a widespread feeling among social workers working with young people in trouble that young people in the criminal justice system are 'second class citizens' so far as the Children Act 1989 is concerned.

The remand process then, is not so much a complicated system as a fragmented one. Once again, it is a powerful reminder of how few rights children in the criminal justice system possess. Though the system varies in a number of respects from that which applies to adults (with the position of 17-year-olds being a continuing anomaly), young people in the remand process appear rather as passive objects caught up in a series of transactions between the agencies of justice and social welfare.

If an adult, aged 21 or over, is denied bail, they are detained in a prison or remand centre (a remand centre being a prison service establishment specifically for remand prisoners). Young adults, which for remand purposes include 17-year-olds, where possible are held in young offender institutions (prison establishments for offenders under 21) or remand centres, though they continue to be placed in the remand wings of adult prisons also, on occasions.

If young people aged 16 or under are denied bail, they must normally be remanded in local authority accommodation; it is for the local authority to decide where a young person should live, if so remanded. If a local authority believes it to be necessary, and certain grounds are established (e.g. the young person has allegedly committed a grave offence and has a history of absconding from local authority accommodation whilst on remand) the authority may ask the court at the first, or at any subsequent hearing (a remand hearing must be held every seven days), to grant a secure accommodation order enabling the authority to hold the young person in a secure unit. Places in secure units are limited in number and young people subject to secure accommodation orders are sometimes held hundreds of miles from their home area.

Boys aged 15 and 16 may still be remanded to prison establishments, subject to the same provisions as apply to those aged between 17 and 21. The CJA 1991 abolished those custodial remands for 15- and 16-year-old boys, but the government will not implement the change until there is sufficient extra secure accommodation to accommodate the extra demand which may thereby be created. They are to review the situation in 1995/6. The government's refusal to implement these provisions of the 1991 Act in October 1992 disappointed many commentators who had eagerly welcomed the initial decision to abolish prison remands for juveniles. Recent years have witnessed a series of suicides by young people remanded in custody, while incidents of self-harm and attempted suicide are now common occurrences. Young people remanded in custody while still unconvicted of any offence, are often immature and vulnerable and may be away from home for the first time in their lives. They can easily fall prey to bullying and intimidation, and may find their period on remand more harrowing than any sentence a court can hand down upon conviction.

Section 60(4) of the CJA 1991, when implemented, replaces prison remands for 15- and 16-year-old boys with a new power enabling magistrates to order the detention of any young person (i.e. female or male) aged 15 and 16, in secure accommodation, if the necessary grounds are met. Local authorities will be required to provide or purchase a place in a secure unit, but will not have any power to challenge the decision.

The Criminal Justice and Public Order Act 1994 lowers the age at which a 'secure remand' can be ordered to 12. The detention of such young children, often at a considerable distance from their homes, and when they are unconvicted of any offence, is clearly a matter of concern, though it is important to recognise that where local authorities apply to courts for secure accommodation orders, such outcomes are already possible. There is, however, widespread concern at this extension of the use of custodial remands to much younger children.

THE HEARING

Cases against young people aged between 10 and 18 should be heard in the youth court – a specialist magistrates' court. There are exceptions to this rule. If a 'youth' is jointly accused with an adult, proceedings will be initiated in an adult court and may be completed there. Adult courts should, wherever possible however, remit a case against a minor back to the youth court either for hearing or, if that is not feasible, for sentence.

Young people appearing in an adult magistrates court may subsequently find themselves appearing in the intimidating surroundings of a Crown Court (usually after a lengthy delay) as a result of their co-defendant's decision to elect for jury trial; a right which young people do not possess. Where alleged offences are serious enough, young people can be committed by a youth court to the Crown Court for trial or, upon conviction, for sentence.

Until recently, all courts, when hearing cases against children and young people, had a duty to establish that the defendant understood both the nature of the offence of which he/she stood accused, and that the alleged behaviour was 'seriously wrong'. If not satisfied on both counts, the case could not proceed. At the time of writing (November 1994) however, this legal principle known as *doli incapax* is being contested in the House of Lords. Like adults, young people have a right to be legally represented, and are entitled to legal aid for the purpose.

Before sentencing a convicted young person under 18, courts may request that a pre-sentence report (PSR) be prepared by the local social services department or probation service. Arrangements vary from area to area; often the social services department is responsible for young people up to the age of 15 and the probation service for 16- and 17-year-olds. Other common arrangements are for the social services department to have sole responsibility for the youth court, or for the two agencies jointly to staff a team of specialist youth court staff.

Pre-sentence reports should contain information on the offender which is considered relevant to the offence. It will, therefore, describe family circumstances and home background, school attendance and progress where appropriate, and previous offending history. PSRs discuss possible sentencing options open to the court and offer sentencing 'proposals' for consideration by the court.

The sentences available to the court can be divided into three groups: discharges and fines; community sentences; and custodial sentences.

Discharges and financial penalties

- An *absolute discharge* is a conviction which carries no additional punishment.
- A *conditional discharge* can best be described as an absolute discharge which can be revoked if the offender is re-convicted within a given period (usually twelve months), in which case, he/she can be 're-sentenced' for the initial offence.
- A *fine* against a young person will be assessed on their parent's income, and parents may be required to pay. Courts have a duty to consider making parents pay if the offender is 15 or under, and have the right to do so if they are 16 or 17.
- A *compensation order* is subject to the same considerations but is paid to the victim.

Community sentences

- *Attendance centre orders* require attendance at a two-hour session once every two weeks. The maximum sentence is 24 hours for young people under 16, and 36 hours for those aged 16 and under 21. Attendance centres are usually run by police officers and their 'programmes' combine such elements as drill, physical training, practical work (e.g. bicycle repair) and arts and crafts. There are junior and senior centres (with a division usually at 16) and separate centres for female and male offenders. Many areas, however, lack a female centre and a few have no centres at all.
- *Supervision orders* are available for any offender under 18. The offender is supervised for a given period (up to three years is possible, though orders for six–twelve months are the most common) by a social worker or probation

officer whose task is to 'advise, assist and befriend' the offender. Courts may include conditions in supervision orders, the most commonly-used being what are known as 'intermediate treatment' and 'specified activities' conditions. Both involve the young person's participation in additional activity, which may involve normal youth activities, an organised programme of group work or an individually tailored programme of offending behaviour work, to give three common examples.

- *Probation orders* are available for offenders aged 16 and over. They are similar to supervision orders in that the offender is required to comply with directions given by a probation officer, whose task, again, is to 'advise, assist and befriend' the person concerned. The court may insert 'adult-style' requirements in probation orders which relate to participation in probation programmes, attendance at a day centre or residence in a hostel.
- *Community service orders* are available for offenders aged 16 and over, and involve the offender in undertaking useful work in the community as a form of reparation for their offences. The work is supervised by the probation service and the maximum sentence is 240 hours.
- *Combination orders* are also available for offenders aged 16 and over, and combine a probation order with up to 100 hours community service.

Custodial sentences

There are currently two forms of custodial sentence for young people although a third is provided for by the Criminal Justice Act 1994.

- *Detention in a young offender institution* is the 'main' form of custodial sentence. It is available for both young men and young women aged 15 and over. The minimum sentence is two months and the maximum is six months for one offence and twelve months aggregate, except in the Crown Court, which may sentence to twelve months for a single offence. Prisoners usually serve half the sentence in custody and half in the community; part of the community-based period is subject to supervision.
- A *'Section 53 order'* is available only when young offenders are tried and convicted of serious offences (those which, in the case of an adult, carry maximum sentences of at least 14 years imprisonment) by the Crown Court. The name of the order refers to Section 53 of the Children and Young Persons Act 1933. Section 53(1) deals with offences of murder and manslaughter, by any offender aged 10 and under 18; Section 53(2) with other qualifying offences committed by young people aged 14 and under 18. In both cases, courts may sentence up to the adult maximum, including detention at Her Majesty's Pleasure (equivalent to life imprisonment) for murder or manslaughter.

Serious offences by children and young persons are rare, but over 200 Section 53 sentences a year have been the recent norm. Often, a young person committing a very serious offence has no previous record, but has lost self control. S/he may be disturbed and it is frequently the case that specialist help is needed. For this reason, many young people (especially those under 16) sentenced under Section 53 serve at least part of their sentence not in a young offender institution but in a secure unit.

When implemented, the Criminal Justice and Public Order Act will make significant changes to these arrangements, reducing the qualifying age for a Section 53(2) sentence to 10 and doubling all maximum sentence categories for detention in a young offender institution. Perhaps the most significant change introduced by the Act, however, is the introduction of the secure training centre for children aged 12 and under 15 who have committed three or more imprisonable offences. Since many common offences (e.g. theft) are imprisonable, it is feared that large numbers of children as young as 12 will be placed in the new centres, which are likely to be run by private contractors on five sites, catering for 40 to 50 young people each. Sentences will be up to two years.

Other outcomes which are not, strictly speaking, sentences, may also result from a court hearing. Young people may agree to be 'bound over' (in which case they are not classed as convicted). Parents may also be bound over (with a recognisance of up to £1,000) against the likelihood of further offending by the child concerned, while the Criminal Justice and Public Order Act also allows parents to be fined if their children fail to comply with the terms of a court order, such as a supervision order.

Finally, it is important to note that while custodial sentences cannot be suspended (either wholly or in part), courts may defer sentence altogether where there is a prospect of a material change of circumstances (e.g. where a child is being received into local authority accommodation or is waiting for a place in a special school). A deferment of up to six months allows courts to take such changes into account in determining their sentence.

DISCRIMINATION AND CHILDREN'S RIGHTS

Some form of discrimination in the wider sense is inevitable in any process which allows so much discretion at so many key stages. In the criminal justice system, there is strong evidence of discrimination both against black people and against women.

Though girls and young women are under-represented in the system and are initially more likely to be cautioned and less likely to be prosecuted than their male counterparts, they are also likely to receive more severe punishment if prosecuted and convicted. Moreover, girls who offend are sometimes diverted altogether from the justice system to the care system (e.g. on grounds of 'moral danger'). In its dealings with that young person, the care system can often exceed any powers a criminal court might have had if the offender had been prosecuted.

Black young people are over-represented at every stage of the youth justice process and especially in custodial institutions where they may account for a third of all prisoners. There is no evidence that black people offend more frequently or more seriously than white people however.

Section 95 of the CJA 1991 sought to discourage discrimination 'on the grounds of race, gender or any other improper ground' but it is hard to see how, in an individualised legal system which does not permit 'class action', a particular young person could show that a specific decision to prosecute, to deny bail or to sentence to custody, was discriminatory. Perhaps the only area in which young people who feel they are being discriminated against have a realistic chance of redress, is in relation to the services provided by local authorities. Local authority complaints procedures at least include offenders and alleged offenders, so that, for example, racist material in a report or behaviour by project staff can be addressed. These are, however, social welfare exceptions to the criminal justice rule.

It will be apparent from the detailed material above that the youth justice system is complicated, fragmented and essentially local in character, making for a great deal of inconsistency. Indeed, it seems appropriate to ask whether such a set of procedures can properly be described either as 'justice' or as a 'system'. Ironically, many of the complicating factors are due to the protections afforded to young people and built onto a simpler, adult-oriented structure, while some of the inconsistency arises from idiosyncratic, but often excellent, local initiatives.

The approach to protecting children in the criminal justice system is, however, at best dated and paternalistic. The passage of the Children Act 1989, with its comparatively rights-based approach, served to emphasise this fact, and to create an unhelpful dissonance between child care and criminal justice legislation.

During the 1980s, diversionary policies and practice led to a reduction of two-thirds in the number of juveniles prosecuted, and three-quarters in custodial sentencing levels, while 'criminal' care orders were abolished. The Home Office reported a reduction of 37 per cent in the number of known juvenile offenders between 1985 and 1991. In such a climate of progress and optimism, with further gains such as the abolition of custodial remands 'in the pipeline', the issue of childrens' rights was perhaps less to the fore than it should have been. With the significantly increased role for custody envisaged by the Criminal Justice and Public Order Act, there is an urgent need for closer attention to be paid to the issue of the rights of young people throughout the criminal justice system and particularly in custodial institutions. What is required is an approach to childrens' rights which does not exclude children in trouble but which sees young offenders as young people first, and offenders second.

One suggestion put forward recently has been for a charter along the lines of the recent Victims Charter, dealing with the rights of all children who enter the criminal justice system; we must never forget that children appear as victims and as witnesses also. Even this suggestion, however, would perpetuate the 'sheep and goats' distinction between deserving and undeserving young people. What price, then, a childrens' charter?

REFERENCES

National Association for the Care and Resettlement of Offenders (1993) *Juvenile Crime: Some Current Issues*, January, NACRO.
—— (NACRO) (1993) *Awaiting Trial*, June, NACRO.
—— (1993) *Seriously Persistent Juvenile Offenders*, June, NACRO.
—— (1993) *Monitoring the Juvenile Justice System in the new Youth Court*, October, NACRO.
—— (1993) *Community Provision for Young People in the Youth Justice System*, November, NACRO.

Chapter 5

Children's rights in a land of rites

Michael Freeman

Childhood in England tends to be associated with boarding schools, nannies, 'six of the best' and expressions like 'children should be seen and not heard'. When Lloyd de Mause referred to childhood as a 'nightmare' (1976: 1) he wrote in general terms, but many would confirm that childhood as experienced by English children comes close to this description. Of course, things have changed since the graphic portrayals in *Jane Eyre*, *David Copperfield* or *The Way of All Flesh*, but these changes in child-rearing and in attitudes have been recent – school-beatings were the norm a generation ago – and, perhaps not all that profound.

This must be borne in mind by anyone approaching the question of children's rights in England. True, there are references to the importance of children's rights in English case law (see for example *M* v *M* [1973]), and the UK has ratified the UN Convention (see Walsh, 1991). But its support for this was half-hearted, a number of reservations were entered[1] and an aura of complacency greeted its ratification – the government Minister in charge, Virginia Bottomley, saying publicly on any number of occasions that 'of course' English law went further than the Convention. She was referring principally to the Children Act of 1989 (on which see Freeman, 1992) hailed as each Children Act has been as a 'children's charter.[2] As we shall see, there are features of the Act which highlight a child's autonomy, but other values dominate the Act and, it may be thought, trump children's rights (see Fox Harding, 1991). The judiciary, as it has since the early 1970s, has continued to assert, as one of its number Lord Justice Butler-Sloss did in the *Cleveland* report (HMSO, 1988), that children are persons and not objects of concern (see for example *Re B* [1992]). This principle has not been upheld consistently though – even by judges like Butler-Sloss who proclaim it most vociferously.

This paper looks at some of the key provisions in the Convention and measures English law against them. In doing this it is not intended to endorse the Convention as the final word on children's rights. Indeed, there are many provisions in it, often reflections of international compromise (see Johnson, 1992), which could be re-drafted to show distinct improvements. But that is not the goal of this chapter. The goal is rather to show ways in which English law can be improved in the light of, what is currently, world consensus on the status of children. The chapter does not purport to be exhaustive of the issues raised. Each

Article of the Convention could occupy a paper itself. All that can be done here is to highlight, to point to shortcomings and to suggest improvements and modifications in English law and practice.

THE BEST INTERESTS OF THE CHILD

Article 3 of the Convention is, together with Article 12, arguably the most important provision in the Convention. It provides in sub-paragraph 1:

In all actions concerning children, whether undertaken by public or private social welfare institutions, courts of law, administrative authorities or legislative bodies, the best interests of the child shall be a primary consideration.

It will be observed that the Convention says that the children's best interests are 'a primary consideration', not *the* primary consideration or *the paramount* consideration. It is regrettable that the Convention does not set a *standard* as high as that found in English law (see the Children Act 1989, Section 1(1)). Where the child's interests are paramount, they 'determine' the course to be followed (*J* v *C* [1970] per Lord MacDermott). But on the other hand, the *scope* of the provision far exceeds the range of decisions within the remit of English law (see the Children Act 1989, Section 1). English law applies the paramountcy principle only to courts and not even to all court decisions. In adoption, the child's welfare is only the 'first consideration' (Adoption Act 1976, Section 6) (this is in line with the UN standard). In divorce, the child's welfare is not considered at all, though it is the 'first consideration' (again congruent with the UN standard) when matters of money and property are considered (Matrimonial Causes Act 1973, Section 25(1)). This is so at least in theory, for the Child Support Act of 1991 has clearly prioritised the rights of taxpayers over the interests of children.[3] In situations where one parent is trying to oust the other from the family home, because of violence or other molestation, the child's welfare is merely one consideration (Matrimonial Homes Act 1967, Section 193). The Court of Appeal was quick to point out that the Children Act had not changed the law on this (*Gibson* v *Austin* [1992]). Even in wardship, where the 'golden thread' is that the child's welfare comes 'first, last and all the time', the courts have found questions relating to children which are not governed by the paramountcy rule.

Outside 'courts of law', as narrowly construed, there are a vast range of tribunals dealing with matters affecting children which in no way are bound by the 'best interests' principle. The *Bulger* case (on which see Sireny 1994) has reminded us that criminal courts are not so constrained: in what sense can the trial processes and, indeed, the ultimate sentence in that case be said to be impressed by the best interests of the two boys involved? It tends to be forgotten that in many European countries Thompson and Venables could not have stood trial: indeed, even in England had they had the foresight to commit their frightful murder six months earlier they would have been presumed conclusively to lack the capacity for criminal activity.[4]

As far as tribunals are concerned, the list is endless, and only a few will be picked out for comment. Tribunals hearing nationality and immigration appeals are not bound by any best interests principle. Tribunals in the education system, hearing appeals on such matters as school choice, school exclusions and special educational needs are not so bound. Nor are social security tribunals, though these may hear appeals from young people of 16 and 17 denied benefits.

Outside the courts, the absence of the 'best interests' principle in any number of areas calls out for examination. Perhaps most glaring of all is the way successive Education Acts have shamefacedly refused to acknowledge children's rights in the area of education. The message conveyed by recent education legislation is very clear: the consumers of education are the parents, not the children. Similarly, housing legislation contains no 'best interests' principle: the placement of a child in 'bed and breakfast' accommodation can thus not be challenged by reference to any principle such as that in the Children Act (or UN Convention). This leaves unanswered the question as to whether a judicial review examining such a decision would be governed by the paramountcy principle, but though an interesting argument, it is difficult to see that it would succeed.

Even social services departments' obligations do not necessarily extend to giving first consideration to children's interests. Section 17 of the Children Act requires them to 'safeguard and promote the welfare of children within their area who are in need'. But 'in need' can be, and in practice is, interpreted restrictively (see Barber, 1990; Clements, 1994). There is a thin line between setting priorities and reinterpreting the legislation. The latter is unlawful, but a successful challenge to it would be difficult to mount.

The Children Act requirements have gone a long way towards ensuring that institutions dealing with children act in the best interests of those children. There are duties on community homes, voluntary homes, private children's homes, independent boarding schools (see Sections 61, 64, 67, 86, 87) though the duties as regards these have already been diluted. But these duties – to safeguard and promote the child's welfare – do not apply to maintained schools or to non-maintained special schools. There is no best interests principle either in the health service or in the penal system.

THE CHILD'S RIGHTS OF PARTICIPATION

Article 12 of the Convention requires States Parties to:

> *assure to the child who is capable of forming his or her own views the right to express those views freely in all matters affecting the child, the views of the child being given due weight in accordance with the age and maturity of the child.*

For this purpose, the child is to be given 'the opportunity to be heard in any judicial and administrative proceedings affecting the child.'

In formulating this right the Convention goes well beyond earlier international documents. It is the first to state explicitly that children have a right to have a say in processes affecting their lives. Marta Pais has argued that this converts the child into a 'principal' in the Convention, an act of enormous symbolic importance (Pais, 1992). Article 12 can be seen as a development from the child liberation philosophy of the 1970s, (see Farson, 1978; Holt, 1975) and is in line with the *Gillick* decision of the House of Lords in 1985. In Lord Scarman's words in that case 'parental right yields to the child's right to make his own decisions when he reaches a sufficient understanding and intelligence to be capable of making up his own mind on the matter requiring decision' (*ibid.*: 189).

The initial impression is thus that English law complies with Article 12. There is a lot in the Children Act to reinforce this impression. Thus, for example, courts making decisions about a child's upbringing, albeit in a limited range of circumstances, are required to have regard to the 'ascertainable wishes and feelings of the child concerned' in the light of that child's age and understanding (Section 1(3)(a)). As a second example, before making any decision in respect of a child whom they are looking after or are proposing to look after, local authorities are to ascertain the wishes and feelings of the child, so far as this is reasonably practicable (Section 22(4)). A third positive example is the range of provisions in the Children Act allowing a child of sufficient understanding to make an informed decision, the rights to refuse to submit to a medical or psychiatric examination or other assessment in the context of a child assessment order, emergency protection or other similar protective measure (Sections 43(8), 44(7), 38(6), Schedule 3, para. 4).

And yet as soon as this third example is given, and it is itself a logical progression from the *Gillick* ruling, we come up against the recent interpretational backlash, as represented by a series of cases, most notably *Re R* [1991] and *Re W* [1992]. As a result of these decisions it would seem that the *Gillick* principle does not confer upon a competent child a power of veto over treatment, but merely allows him or her to give valid consent to such treatment. A girl of 14, if *Gillick*-competent, can thus consent to an abortion, but should she refuse to consent her pregnancy can nevertheless be terminated. The *consent* of a *Gillick*-competent child cannot be overridden by those with parental responsibility, except the court, but *refusal* to accept treatment by such a child can be overridden by someone who has parental responsibility. The Master of the Rolls, Lord Donaldson, did, however, concede that 'such a refusal is a very important consideration in making clinical judgements and for the parents and the court in deciding whether themselves to give consent (*ibid.*: 639–40). Lowe and Juss have said that 'in this way . . . the court fuses the principle of child autonomy with the practice of intervention (1993). Perhaps so. But what is left to child autonomy? It is hardly surprising that in *South Glamorgan County Council* v *W and B* [1993] a first instance judge should hold that despite the statutory right of veto in Section 38(6) of the Children Act (and, presumably, also that conferred by Sections 43(8) (referred to above), 44(7) and Schedule 3, paragraph 4), the court could exercise its inherent jurisdiction to override the child's refusal. These cases show a judiciary unable to grasp the implications of the Children Act – and, it should be added, the UN Convention.

The Children Act is quite positive on Article 12, but not consistently so. It offers considerable scope for the representation of a child's wishes and feelings in the public welfare area (see Section 41). But when it comes to divorce, it is difficult to see where, if at all, the wishes and feelings of the child will get a look-in. The child is not independently represented: the emphasis on the guardian ad litem in public law is quietly overlooked in private law disputes (see Roche, 1991). It seems to be forgotten that the child may need independent representation as much when his or her parents are at war as when there is some conflict between them and the local authority, for example when abuse or neglect is alleged. It seems that there is no voice for the child in divorce.[5] In relation to divorce, the Children Act is parent-centred, not child-centred, legislation.

But then it might be asked why children should be able to express their views at the juncture of a divorce when the law provides no mechanism for them to have a say at home. In English law, as in virtually every other legal system, parents do not have to ascertain or have regard to their children's wishes before making decisions, even major ones, which affect the child. I remember as a ten-year-old being moved from one school to another and not even being told that this was going to happen until the evening before. My parents thought I'd be happier at the new school or at least so they rationalised. In Finland the Child Custody and Right of Access Act of 1983 states that before a parent who has custody

> makes a decision on a matter relating to the person of the child, he or she shall, where possible, discuss the matter with the child taking into account the child's age and maturity and the nature of the matter. In making the decision the custodian shall give due consideration to the child's feelings, opinions and wishes.

The Scottish Law Commission is also attracted to this idea. It thought there might be value in such a provision 'even if it was vague and unenforceable' for it could have an influence upon behaviour. There is considerable force in this argument. If parents were expected to take their children's opinions and wishes seriously, it is likely that they would demand similar attention to be given to the rights of children to participate by public authorities. And this, despite the Children Act, certainly does not happen at present.

A clear example of this failing is the field of education. There is a certain irony in this, for one of the aims of education is to enhance the capacity for decision-making and yet in crucial areas participation in major decisions is removed from those most affected by those decisions. Article 12(2) provides that children should be given an opportunity to be heard in judicial and administrative proceedings affecting them, but such provision is egregiously absent from school exclusion procedures, in the procedures for choosing a school and in school choice appeals and in all the discussion over such matters as the school curriculum. English education law bears little resemblance to the participatory model spelled out in Article 12.

ABUSE AND NEGLECT

Article 19 requires States Parties to:

take all appropriate legislative, administrative, social and educational meas-
ures to protect the child from all forms of physical or mental violence, injury
or abuse, neglect or negligent treatment, maltreatment or exploitation in-
cluding sexual abuse.

English law clearly targets abuse and neglect (Children Act 1989, Section 31(2)).
Parents who abuse or neglect children may be prosecuted (under the Children and
Young Persons Act 1933) and protective measures using emergency protection
(Children Act 1989, Section 44) and care and supervision orders are available
(*ibid.*, Sections 33, 35). The linchpin of the protective system is 'significant
harm' (see Freeman, 1990). A care order (or a supervision order) may be made if
a child is suffering significant harm or is likely to suffer significant harm if no
order is made, and this is attributable to the quality of parental care not being what
a reasonable parent could give. The Children Act extended the ambit of care to
include suspicion that a child is at risk (see *Essex CC* v *TLR* [1978]. Other
statutory changes recently have made it easier for children's accounts of sexual
abuse in particular to be brought before a criminal court (Criminal Justice Acts
1988, 1991). American research findings (see Gray, 1993) indicate that the
introduction of these innovatory techniques to assist the abused child to give
evidence are not working successfully – prosecutors for example being reluctant
to use them for fear that juries will believe they have a weak case. There is no
replicating evidence in England, but a suspicion that similar patterns of under-use
would be found here too. The lesson is clear: changing laws (in this case
procedures) changes nothing unless you also convert those who are to operate the
new laws or administer the processes to their value.

But laws also achieve little without the injection of resources. And one of the
lessons of the English struggle to conquer child abuse is the failure to address the
resources question. Social services departments are consistently reporting that
they have children on child protection registers with no social worker allocated to
them. Reports of inquiries into child deaths have constantly reiterated the need for
greater resources to target families at risk.

Article 19, though, goes beyond abuse in its narrow and accepted sense. It
pledges States to protect children from 'all forms of physical . . . violence'.
English law, however, permits parents to use 'reasonable chastisement' (see
Newell, 1994). The provision in the Children and Young Persons Act 1933 which
makes cruelty an offence (Section 1) specifically excludes physical punishment
(Section 1(2)). The Newson studies point to its prevalence in England and to the fact
that the use of an implement or its threat remains common (see for example
Newson and Newson, 1968). Five European countries have prohibited all
physical punishment of children (Sweden in 1979; Finland in 1984; Denmark in
1986; Norway in 1987 and Austria in 1989).[6] A recommendation of the Council

of Europe Committee of Ministers in 1985 urged Member States (the UK is one) to 'review their legislation on the power to punish children in order to limit or indeed prohibit corporal punishment, even if violation of such a prohibition does not entail a criminal penalty'.

The Children Act, while it continued the progress to outlaw corporal punishment outside the home, did not take up the issue of physical chastisement by parents. And yet nothing is a clearer statement of the position that children occupy in society, a clearer badge of childhood, than the fact that children alone, of all people in society, can be hit with impunity. There is probably no more significant step that could be taken to advance both the status and protection of children than to outlaw the practice of physical punishment. Much child abuse is, we know, punishment which as gone awfully wrong. Sweden goes even further: their Parenthood and Guardianship Code outlaws 'other humiliating treatment' as well. Is it too much to hope that England will follow the lead of Sweden and the other European countries that have declared the hitting of children to be unacceptable? For how much longer will this rite against children continue?

FREEDOM OF EXPRESSION

The Convention says the child shall have the right to *'freedom of expression'* (Article 13). This right is to include

> *freedom to seek, receive and impart information and ideas of all kinds . . . either orally, in writing or in print, in the form of art, or through any other media of the child's choice.*

The only restrictions (Article 13(2)) are to protect the rights and reputations of others (the law of defamation, for example) and to protect national security and public order as well as public health and morals. The Convention states that the child's right to freedom of expression *includes* the forms of expression listed, but it is therefore not exhaustive of them. The *'freedom to hold opinions'* in the European Convention on Human Rights is thus arguably also embraced within Article 13.

There are a number of ways in which English law fails to sustain this freedom. Governmental intrusions on school curricula, limiting teaching about homosexuality, forbidding 'the pursuit of partisan political activities by pupils' and the 'promotion of partisan political views in the teaching of any subject in the school', (how one conjectures is modern history to be taught?), restricting sex education, are all potentially breaches of Article 13.

The insistence by schools on the wearing of school uniforms is a further potential breach of Article 13. English courts have upheld headteachers' insistence on the wearing of uniforms, in one case agreeing with a head who sent home a girl who wore trousers (she had had rheumatic fever, but no doctor's letter was offered in support of her mother's decision to send her to school so dressed)

(*Spiers* v *Warrington Corporation* [1954]). The European Commission in the *Stevens* case in 1986 rejected a mother's application alleging that the rules on school uniform breached her and her son's rights under the European Convention. But it admitted that 'the right to freedom of expression may include the right of a person to express his ideas through the way he dresses'. The Commission did not think it had been established on the facts that the child had been prevented from expressing a particular 'opinion or idea by means of . . . clothing'. What then of a child refused permission to wear a CND badge, an ear-ring signifying homosexuality or a kippah proclaiming a commitment to Judaism or Zionism? The American Supreme Court upheld school students' rights to wear black arm bands to protest the Vietnam war. 'It can hardly be argued,' it pronounced, 'that either students or teachers lose their constitutional rights to freedom of speech or expression at the schoolhouse gate' (*Tinker* v *Des Moines School District* [1969]). English schools regularly breach both the letter and spirit of this right and hitherto have got away with it. But there is a strong arguable case that the Convention would find many of their practices unacceptable. It is difficult to see how they could be defended either in terms of Article 13(2).

FREEDOM OF THOUGHT, CONSCIENCE AND RELIGION

Article 14 of the Convention requires States Parties to respect the right of the child to freedom of thought, conscience and religion. Freedom to manifest religion may be subjected only to such limitations as are 'necessary to protect public safety, order, health or morals or the protection of the rights and freedoms of others'. The European Convention on Human Rights lays down a similar right, though it does so in stronger terms, emphasising the right to change religion and to 'manifest' religion in worship, teaching, practice and observance.

Nowhere does English law articulate similar norms. To conform with the UN Convention there ought to be statutory confirmation of the rights set out in the Convention. Schools which deny Muslim children the opportunity to pray on Fridays or insist upon Jewish children attending schools on Saturday clearly breach the UN Convention. English education law which gives parents a right to withdraw their children from religious worship and instruction in schools and even allows them to request special lessons in a particular religion also breaches the Convention because it does not give children similar rights. The continuing reluctance of British governments to approve funding for voluntary-aided Muslim schools – while allowing this for Church of England, Catholic and Jewish schools – is a breach of both the 'religion' Article and of Article 2 (prohibiting discrimination). Arguments by some – allegedly in the cause of children's rights – to ban circumcision of male babies, also clearly fly in the face of the freedom of religion Article. The British government has resisted the weak arguments proferred to outlaw the practice – as indeed has every other government today. The Nazis banned it of course: need one say more.

Children in care may not be brought up 'in any religious persuasion other than that in which [they] would have been brought up if the order had not been made (Children Act 1989, Section 33(6)(a)). On one level this is right, but what of the child who does not wish to be brought up in care in the religion of his (or her) family, perhaps associating it with the abuse to which s/he has been subjected? Or the child who does not wish to be brought up in any religion? In theory, the *Gillick* case should cater for such children, provided, of course, they are deemed to have sufficient understanding of the issues and sufficient maturity and intelligence to have thought rationally about them. And certainly, regulations under the Children Act (see Children's Homes Regulations, 1991) should satisfy this requirement, but in practice the Christian ethos of many childcare organisations may not make this particularly easy.

It may be noted also that wards of the court are, at least in theory, also denied freedom of religion, since the court may direct this.[7] In practice, it is doubtful whether the problem exists. Nevertheless, it ought to be made clear by statute that the powers of the wardship court, in effect the inherent jurisdiction of the High Court, cannot be used in derogation from the principle set out in the UN Convention on the Rights of the Child.

FREEDOM OF ASSOCIATION

Article 15 of the Convention recognises the right of the child to freedom of association and to freedom of peaceful assembly, subject only to restrictions that are necessary in a

democratic society in the interests of national security or public safety, public order, the protection of public health or morals or the protection of the rights and freedoms of others.

(Article 15(2))

The refusal of schools to allow union activity or, for example, CND meetings or anti-apartheid meetings or meetings to celebrate a particular national day of an ethnic group within a school breaches this Article. We have had an Education Act almost annually in recent years. Is it too much to hope that the next one will encode some basic rights for school children? Similar problems arise in the context of local authority care: it is known that the National Association of Young People In Care (NAYPIC) has had difficulty organising in some areas. Again it has to be stressed that local authorities which obstruct such activity are in breach of the UN Convention.

It is doubtful whether British public order legislation, in particular the restrictive Public Order Act of 1986, satisfies the Convention. The new offence of 'disorderly conduct' is wider than the exceptions allowed in this Article. Certainly, the police could interpret it, and have done, to restrict gatherings by young people.

THE PROTECTION OF PRIVACY

Article 16 of the Convention states:

No child shall be subjected to arbitrary or unlawful interference with his or her privacy, family, home or correspondence, nor to unlawful attacks on his or her honour and reputation.

To a large extent a child's privacy is controlled by parents or other caretakers and to a large extent also the privacy that parents can offer is related to their income and other resources. The poor have never had much privacy: their lives have always been more public than that of more affluent people. The privacy provision cannot, therefore, be entirely disentangled from another Article in the Convention which proclaims the right of every child to an adequate standard of living (Article 27). Children condemned to live in bed and breakfast accommodation, perhaps because local authority housing is sold to potential Tory voters,[8] have neither an adequate standard of living, nor any degree of privacy. It may be added that they are hardly likely to have the opportunities for play and recreational activities set out in the Convention (Article 31) or, indeed, to find the right to education (Articles 28, 29), guaranteed by the Convention, of much import.

A child's privacy is interfered with in a number of ways. Within the home this may be difficult to provide for, but in institutions, where there is widespread abuse of privacy, English law has done far too little to protect the freedom guaranteed by Article 16. Even where attempts have been made, for example, by Regulation under the Children Act, there is growing evidence that these attempts are frustrated in practice. The right to private correspondence is not protected in all institutions which house children and young persons. In some residential institutions children cannot even use toilets in complete privacy. There may be communal bathing facilities only. There are institutions in which the periods of young women are monitored by staff. In some children's homes, notably but not exclusively secure accommodation, closed circuit video cameras and two-way mirrors are used to observe children. This may be done without their knowledge, let alone their consent.

There are many other ways in which a child's privacy is invaded and to which all too little attention has been given. For example, the growing practice of advertising children for adoption with exposure of biographical details and the use of a photograph is a clear breach of this Article of the Convention. Whether it should be stopped is another matter. If adoption or another form of permanent placement is in the best interests of the child concerned, it may be thought unduly legalistic to insist upon this 'lesser' right and therefore sacrifice a 'greater' one. The Convention does after all, in Article 21, mandate those countries which permit adoption to '*ensure that the best interests of the child shall be the paramount consideration*' (a provision which, as we shall see, English law does not currently comply with). At the very least I would hope that the current 'advertising' practice would be subjected to sustained scrutiny and reasoned debate.

ADOPTION

As already indicated, English law falls short of its Convention obligations in relation to Article 21, the adoption Article.

First, the 'best interests' of the child are only the 'first consideration' in adoption proceedings in England (Adoption Act 1976, Section 6). The Convention requires them to be the 'paramount' consideration. 'First' suggests, as is indeed the case, that there are other considerations, such as the rights of biological parents: 'paramount' suggests, by contrast, that the best interests of the child should be determinative. If the report of the later Departmental Review on Adoption is implemented, English law will be brought into line with the Convention (Department of Health, 1992), but there are no immediate plans to do so.

Second, the Convention requires that the *'persons concerned [should] have given their informed consent to the adoption on the basis of such counselling as may be necessary'* (Article 21(a)). In England, counselling is not always available and, where given, often is offered after the adoption has taken place. Furthermore, English law (unlike that in Scotland) has never required the consent of the person most concerned, namely the child. Again, the recent Adoption Review will, if and when implemented, remedy this defect, at least to some extent. But it proposes the age of 12 as the appropriate one (*ibid.*, note 72, para. 95). This is unduly cautious: a child can clearly express a desire for or against a particular adoption at a much earlier age than this. I would advocate fixing the age no higher than 7. A transplant to a new family is too important a step to contemplate against the wishes of a child able to express wishes and feelings about its desirability.

Third, there is the issue of inter-country adoption. This was one of the more controversial areas covered by the Convention, with some countries, notably Venezuela, being understandably unhappy with the whole concept. (For a different perspective see Bartholet, 1993.) It needs to be said that if other provisions in the Convention were universally fulfilled (adequate standard of living (Article 27), adequate health care for mothers and children (Article 24(2)) being the most obvious examples), there would be little need for inter-country adoption. But in the foreseeable future and particularly in the light of the upheavals in Eastern Europe in the late 1980s and 1990s, there will be a felt necessity to rescue children from orphanages and bring them to more prosperous and stable countries like the UK. In the light of this it may be said that English law is insufficient to assist the process of inter-country adoption. But where intercountry adoption is allowed, it is clear that English law and practice falls short of the Convention obligation to ensure that the safeguards and standards are 'equivalent' to those existing in the case of national adoption. With the im- plementation of the Hague Convention on inter-country adoption this should change. But we must wait and see.

HEALTH AND HEALTH SERVICES

Article 24(1) of the Convention states that:

States Parties recognize the right of the child to the enjoyment of the highest attainable standard of health and to facilities for the treatment of illness and rehabilitation of health.

States are to '*strive to ensure that no child is deprived of his or her right of access to such health care services*'. The UK sets no standards as such for children's health services. There is no sense that the allocation of resources within the National Health Service reflects the needs of children. There are known to be wide regional variations in provision too. Further, poverty is strongly associated with increased risk to child health (see Department of Health and Social Security, 1980; Davey Smith *et al.*, 1990), so that full implementation of this Article requires sustained measures to eradicate child poverty. But this has increased steeply in the last fifteen years of Tory misrule (see Woodroffe and Glickman, 1993). But part of the problem is that the health of children, indeed, the population generally, is the responsibility of unelected health authorities. Their power to purchase services is now shared with fund-holding general practitioners. As the number of such GPs and the type of health care they may purchase increases, the balance of purchasing power is shifting away from the health authority. But there is no way of knowing whether GPs have the same values regarding health as health authorities or whether either of them shares the values of 'the public'. A recent study by Bowling (1992) however, indicated that doctors gave much greater priority to reducing mental illness than was given by the public. Do they target child health as the public would wish them to? We have no way of knowing.

In particular Article 24 requires a number of measures. It requires measures to be taken to diminish infant and child mortality (Article 24(2)). This has declined, but the decline has slowed, is slower than many comparable countries and is high in comparison with, for example, France, Italy and Sweden (World Health Organisation, 1992). The UK has the highest post-neonatal mortality rate of seven European countries, as reported in a 1990 study (see Woodroffe and Glickman, 1993). It also requires an emphasis on primary health care. There is concern that recent changes in the delivery of health services may work to the detriment of this, particularly as regards children.

The Article further requires measures to tackle the '*dangers and risks of environmental pollution*' (Article 24(2)(c)). There is evidence of an association between respiratory illnesses in children and the amounts of pollution in the areas where they live. Much more could be done to tackle smoking now that the evidence of the effects of passive smoking is incontestable. Smoking could be banned in public places. Cigarette advertising could be stopped, including sponsorship of sporting and other events. Taxation on tobacco products could be vastly increased. More could be done to discourage smoking by children. The right to a smoke-free environment must 'trump'[9] the so-called freedom of smokers to destroy themselves and others. Questions must also be raised about nuclear installations in the growing light of clear association between them and childhood leukaemia. An EEC Directive of 1980 was supposed to be implemented by 1982: Britain was not fully in compliance with this in the early 1990s – there were promises of full compliance by 1993 – but it is doubtful whether in the north of England in particular the air is still satisfactory.

The Article also requires appropriate pre- and post-natal health care of mothers. There are regional variations here as well as class differences and little doubt that more could be done. Health education is also inadequate. It is not, however, in the National Curriculum.

Article 24 also contains one of the most controversial provisions in the Convention. In paragraph 3, States Parties are required to take '*all effective and appropriate measures with a view to abolishing traditional practices prejudicial to the health of children*. There is legislation prohibiting female genital mutila-tion, which was the main target of the provision (Prohibition of Female Circumcision Act 1985. But see also Eaton, 1994). It cannot, however, be said that the legislation is working very effectively. France takes a more heavy-handed approach to the problem and parents have been imprisoned there for performing such acts on their daughters. Education may be thought to be a better approach, but there is little evidence of any such campaign among the communities concerned in England. There is no evidence that male circumcision, properly carried out, is prejudicial to the health of male babies. To associate this with female genital mutilation is frankly crass, though a number of children's rights advocates continue to do so. Other traditional practices have been targeted at various times: for example, the Yoruba practice of making excisions in the faces of male children was the subject of a well-publicised prosecution in 1974, *R* v *Adesanya* [1974]) though there can be little doubt that the practice continues. Ear and nose piercing arguably also falls within the purview of this Article but, in a world where children are victimised in so many more harmful ways, it hardly warrants attention.

A CONCLUDING COMMENT

This survey has shown that complacency about children's rights in England is totally misplaced. It has directed attention to some of the areas where legislative change is required, where practice needs to be better monitored, where greater thought has to be given to protecting the interests and furthering the rights of children. Progress towards these ends needs a structure. The development of this is beyond the scope of this chapter, but the following tentative suggestions will be made.

First, the UN Convention should be incorporated into English law:[10] breach of a provision of the Convention should be an infringement of English law with all the implications that this would have. Second, the concept of a child impact statement should be introduced. All legislation, including subsidiary and local, should be accompanied by an assessment of its effect on children. This should apply also to health plans, education innovations (the National Curriculum for example) and other policy changes. Third, we should follow the example of Norway (on which see Flekkøy, Chapter 13) and the other countries which have introduced the concept of an ombudsman for children.[11] The details of this are again beyond the scope of this article, but essentially the office would, I believe, be information-gathering, complaint-receiving and litigation-initiating. The structure sketched here would give some teeth to the Convention in England. The Convention has to be seen as a beginning, but the lives of children will not change for the better until the obligations it lays down are taken seriously by legislatures, governments and all others concerned with the daily lives of children

ACKNOWLEDGEMENTS

This article was written while a Visiting Professor at the University of Wisconsin, Madison and could not have been produced without library and secretarial assistance, in particular Michael Morgalla and Finessa Ferrell-Smith to whom I am exceedingly grateful.

NOTES

1 Notably on immigration and citizenship.
2 This was particularly the case in respect of the Children Act 1975.
3 Though based on a report called *Children Come First* (HMSO, 1990).
4 Ten being the age of criminal responsibility.
5 Perhaps even less of *Looking to the Future* (HMSO, 1993).
6 Germany is committed to this reform too, and it is possible that Switzerland, Poland and Canada will follow the Nordic lead.
7 It can take a decision on any matter of significance relating to the child.
8 As in the City of Westminster (so revealed in January 1994).
9 The expression is Ronald Dworkin's (1978).
10 Spain and Sri Lanka have done this.
11 Costa Rica, New Zealand and Sweden.

CASES CITED

Essex County Council v *TLR* [1978] 9 Fam Law 15
Gibson v *Austin* [1992] 2 FLR 349
Gillick v *West Norfolk and Wisbech Health Authority* [1986] AC 112
J v *C* [1970] AC 668
M v *M* [1973] 2 All ER 81
Re Adesanya [1974] *The Times* 16, 17 July
Re B [1992] 2 FLR 1
Re R [1991] 4 All ER 177

Re W [1992] 4 All ER 627
South Glamorgan County Council v *W and B* [1993] 1 FLR 574
Spiers v *Warrington Corporation* [1954] 1 QB 61
Tinker v *Des Moines Community School District* [1969] US 503

REFERENCES

Barber, S. (1990) 'Heading Off Trouble', *Community Care* 840: 23.
Bartholet, E. (1993) *Family Bonds*, Houghton Mifflin: Boston.
Bowling, A. (1992) *Local Voices in Purchasing Health Care. An Exploratory Exercise in Public Consultation in Priority Setting*, St Bartholomew's Hospital Medical College: London.
Clements, L. (1994) 'House Hunting' *Community Care* 28 July – 3 August: 20.
Davey Smith, G., Bartley, M. and Blane, D. (1990) 'The Black Report on Socioeconomic Inequalities in Health 10 Years On', *British Medical Journal* 301, 373.
Department of Health (1992) *Review of Adoption Law: Report to Ministers of Interdepartmental Working Group*: para. 7 (1).
Department of Health and Social Security (1980) *Inequalities in Health* (The Black Report) HMSO: London.
de Mause, L. (1976) *The History of Childhood*, Souvenir Press: London.
Dworkin, R. (1978) *Taking Rights Seriously*, Duckworth: London.
Eaton, L. (1994) 'A Fine Line', *Community Care* 21–27 July: 16.
Farson, R. (1978) *Birthrights*, Penguin: Harmondsworth.
Flekkøy, M. (1991) *A Voice for Children*, Jessica Kingsley: London.
Fox Harding, L. (1991) 'The Children Act 1989 in Context: Four Perspectives on Child Care Law and Policy', *Journal of Social Welfare and Family Law* 179, 285.
Freeman, M. (1990) 'Care After 1991' in D. Freestone (ed.) *Children and the Law*, Hull University Press, Hull.
—— (1992) *Children, Their Families and The Law*, Macmillan: Basingstoke.
Gray, E. (1993) *Unequal Justice*, Free Press: New York.
Holt, J. (1975) *Escape from Childhood*, Penguin: Harmondsworth.
HMSO (1988) *Report of Inquiry into Child Abuse in Cleveland* (Cm. 412), HMSO.
—— (1990) *Children Come First* (Cm. 1264), HMSO.
—— (1991) *Children's Homes Regulations*, S.1. No. 1506. Para. 11, HMSO.
—— (1991) *Children Act Guideline*, Residential Care, Vol. 4, Part I, HMSO.
—— (1993) *Looking to the Future: Mediation and the Grounds for Divorce* (Cm. 2434), Lord Chancellor's Department, London: HMSO.
Johnson, D. (1992) 'Cultural and Regional Pluralism in the Drafting of the UN Convention on the Rights of the Child' in M. Freeman and P. Veerman (eds) *The Ideologies of Children's Rights*, Martinus Nijhoff: Dordrecht.
Lowe, N. and Juss, S. (1993) 'Medical Treatment – Pragmatism and the Search for Principle', *Modern Law Review* 56: 865, 870.
Newell, P. (1994) 'Beyond Child Abuse: A Child's Right to Physical Integrity' in A. Levy (ed.) *Refocus on Child Abuse*, Hawksmere: London.
Newson, J. and Newson, E. (1968) *Four Years Old in an Urban Community*, Allen & Unwin: London.
Pais, M. (1992) 'The United Nations Convention on The Rights of the Child': *Bulletin on Human Rights* 91/2: 75, 76.
Roche, J. (1991) 'Once a Parent Always a Parent', *Journal of Social Welfare and Family Law*: 345.
Savolainen, M. (1986) 'More Rights for Children', *Journal of Family Law* 25: 113, 117.
Sireny, G. (1994) 'The James Bulger Case' *The Independent on Sunday*, 14, 21 February.

Walsh, B (1991) 'The United Nations Convention on the Rights of the Child: A British View', *International Journal of Law and the Family*, 5: 170.
Woodroffe, C. and Glickman, M. (1993) 'Trends in Child Health', *Children and Society* 7(1): 49.
World Health Organisation (1992) *Health for All Indicators* Eurostat/PC: Copenhagen.

Part III

Children's rights: Policy prescription and implementation in the British setting

Chapter 6

Children's Rights Officers
Righting wrongs and promoting rights

Shane Ellis and Annie Franklin

The appointment of Children's Rights Officers (CROs) reflects both the positive belief that children should have an advocate or champion to promote their rights, and a response to a succession of scandals in which the rights of particular groups of children were blatantly violated. The Children's Congress in 1984 – where the idea for a CRO was allegedly first mooted – as much as scandals like 'pindown', the Beck case in Leicestershire and Ty Mawr provided the trigger for the development of these posts. In practice, the goal of promoting and protecting the rights of individual or particular groups of children (an ombudswork function) has proved easier to achieve than the promotion and advancement of the rights of children as a whole.

The protection of individual children's rights is, of course, important and desirable. Bad enough that some children are denied the right to a 'normal' family upbringing; even worse that they might have been abused by that family, which may be why they find themselves in care; but far worse – although regrettably not that uncommon – is that they might be abused further by the very people intended to care for them. Such evident need explains the dramatic growth in the number of CROs between 1987 and 1993 from one to fifteen. It may also explain why all CROs work in the social services field and address the needs of children and young people in the care of a local authority.

Two additional factors explain this recent burgeoning of CROs. First, the initial appointment by Leicestershire social services in 1987 created considerable interest with professional journals publishing a number of articles examining the objectives and day-to-day work of the post. Mike Lindsay, the postholder, became a regular speaker at conferences and wrote a good deal about the work, exploring and elaborating the possibilities which the post offered (Lindsay, 1988, 1989). Second, the Children Act 1989 provided further impetus. The Act's emphasis on children's right to be heard in matters which affect them (subject to their competence to make decisions); its requirement for complaints procedures; and the departmental reorganisation needed for its implementation have each prompted further growth in CRO posts.

THE LEEDS CHILDREN'S RIGHTS SERVICE

The Leeds service was planned and negotiated before the Children Act was drafted. It reflected Save the Children Fund's broad commitment to the promotion of children's rights, but more specifically, the organisation's belief that a CRO employed by an independent voluntary agency would be more effective than a similar post located in a social services department. The establishment of the service in Leeds also reflected the outspoken commitment to children's rights of the then Director of Social Services, Norman Tutt.[1] It was a combination of ideology, moral commitment and policy intention which generated the children's rights service in Leeds.

The Partnership Agreement between Leeds Social Services and Save the Children sets out the following six aims for the work:

1   To ensure that children in receipt of services from the department are informed of their rights, as embodied in the Children Act 1989 and the UN Convention on the Rights of the Child.
2   To examine particular cases in respect of social services provision with a view to influencing future procedure/services especially with regard to residential care.
3   To monitor city council policy and practice, as it affects children's rights, and advise senior management where change is required.
4   To raise awareness in the city council, and outside, about children's rights issues and how they are affected by local government policies and practice.
5   To increase consumer participation/consultation in respect of social services provision. (A range of methods and forums may be used to achieve this aim.)
6   To make available to Leeds City Council the experience gained elsewhere in enhancing children's rights and to promote Leeds' experience more widely to influence other councils' policies and practice.

The agreement was negotiated between officers of the two agencies although the aims and the funding for the post were agreed by Leeds' Social Services' Child Care Sub Committee and by Save the Children's UK Advisory Committee. Social services contribute 66 per cent of the costs of the project, with Save the Children meeting the rest. The salary of the CRO post amounts to approximately two thirds of the project's budget with the remainder allocated to secretarial support, publicity and travel expenses including those of the young people who are involved in the project.

Leeds Children's Rights Officer – Shane Ellis – is employed and managed by Save the Children which provides him with a work base, telephone and address, establishing his independence from the social services department. This independence brings a number of obvious advantages. First, it guarantees the CRO's integrity as a children's advocate. Second, young people can see that the officer is not 'part of the system'. Third, the officer has the support of colleagues who work on rights issues in other Save the Children projects and a line manager, who shares responsibility for the work and offers support in specific conflicts with the department. Fourth, the officer manages an independent budget and enjoys a greater degree of administrative and secretarial support than would be available in social services. Fifth, he has regular 'face-to-face' meetings with the Chief Officer as part of the agreement between the two agencies, which enables him to short-circuit the hierarchy of the department when necessary. Finally, the CRO cannot be forced to undertake work which is not considered to be properly within his remit. This last point is crucial. It would be easy for a CRO to be diverted into a number of roles within the department, for instance as a Complaints Officer, especially in times of scarce resources.

But there are a number of potential disadvantages which may derive from being employed by an independent agency. An officer positioned outside the department could more easily be marginalised. CROs are dependent for information on departmental managers and their effectiveness could be undermined very easily if departments withdrew their goodwill. CROs who work for a local authority will have a line manager, possibly even an assistant director, who is responsible for the work and wishes to defend it.

The Partnership Agreement also sets out the management arrangements for the service and specifies a number of groups with differing functions.

The main management body is the Partnership Review Group which is responsible for planning and resourcing the work and resolving any problems or conflict. Members of the group include the CRO and the Assistant Divisional Director (Save the Children Fund – Yorkshire) who is his line manager and the Assistant Director (Residential and Daycare) and the Residential and Daycare Manager (for Children from Social Services).

There are two advisory mechanisms. The first is provided by a 'board' of coopted adults drawn from a variety of backgrounds whom the CRO can consult individually or as a group over specific issues. There is also the Young People's Forum, composed of young people in care, which meets regularly to discuss their proposals for change in the department's provision of services and to offer feedback to the CRO on request. The purpose of both advisory groups is to act as a sounding board or 'think tank'. It is important to consider carefully when a response from the CRO is necessary and what form that response should assume. On both counts, the Advisory Board supplements the line manager to help formulate decisions.

Finally, the agreement outlines an annual reviewing mechanism, under the title of a Consultation and Review Body, which reviews the previous year's work and suggests priorities for the future. The proposals which arise from the Consultation and Review Body are submitted to the Partnership Review Group for approval. The composition of the Consultation and Review Body is intended to include a majority of young people – for three reasons: to enable staff and other adults to hear young people's views of the service; to ensure that proposals for future work are consistent with the aims of a children's rights service (there are, unsurprisingly, instances when young people's views are at odds with those of adults, especially departmental staff, although these may not arise as often as expected); to guarantee that the service's own commitment to children's and young people's right to participate in decisions which affect them is implemented within its own structures.

CASE WORK AND RIGHTS ISSUES IN LEEDS

The Partnership Agreement establishes the role of the Leeds Children's Rights Officer as informing children and young people of their rights; acting as an advocate for them when necessary; listening to their concerns and sometimes to those of their carers and supporting them if they have complaints to make; ensuring that their views are taken into account in the development of new policies and practice within the department; promoting their rights more generally.

This section discusses examples of individual case work, as well as broader aspects of the work which the Children's Rights Service has been involved with during the first two years of its operation. Illustrative examples have been chosen to suggest the diverse issues which the service seeks to resolve, their widely differing causes and the range of recommended solutions.

Bulk buying

'It's great here, the staff are brilliant and the food is good, but I hate the toothpaste', one young person commented during a visit by the CRO to a community home in the city. It soon became apparent that this particular boy wasn't the only person concerned about young people's lack of choice about such a basic requirement.

Children and young people being looked after by a local authority are supposed to receive quality care which resembles an ordinary home life as much as possible. But in community homes in Leeds, bulk buying of food, cleaning materials and toiletries including sanitary protection, from a central purchasing unit denies young people choice and fails to reflect the way in which young people in families would shop for these commodities. Toothpaste and other basic requirements are ordered on official forms and delivered weekly instead of being bought at the corner shop or supermarket where young people living in families would buy these products. Despite widespread criticism by the Social Services Inspectorate and other children's charities the bulk buying system has persisted in Leeds far longer than in many other authorities.

The CRO raised this issue in the regular meeting with the Director of Social Services. Proposals were presented to the department within two months of the start of the service, suggesting a change in policy. There was resistance from some homes and from finance personnel within the department, who offered arguments about economies of scale, but a pilot scheme was established. At the time of writing (January 1994) six homes are now purchasing from local supermarkets although some of them still fail to involve young people in shopping.

Ending bulk buying in all children's homes is still a priority for the service. The new Director of Social Services, Keith Murray, has given assurances that bulk buying will end in the near future.

Children's consent

An 11-year-old boy wrote to the Director of Social Services complaining that an advertisement, accompanied by his photograph, had been published in the *Guardian* without his prior knowledge and consent. The advertisement, which was seeking foster carers, was undoubtedly well-intended, but the boy did not want anyone outside of the care system to know he was being looked after. More importantly, he felt his social worker should have consulted him beforehand.

During a visit from the CRO the boy made it clear that he did not want the social worker concerned to be sacked or disciplined, nor was he seeking compensation for the upset and distress which the placing of the advertisement had understandably caused him. He simply wanted an apology from his social worker and an assurance that this would not happen to him or anyone else in the future.

The CRO wrote to the social worker on the boy's behalf, expressing his views on the matter and requesting that she visit the boy and apologise to him; the social worker agreed. A further letter was sent to the department suggesting that in future all children and young people should be involved in preparing advertisements and that written consent should be obtained from anyone aged 10 and over. This has now been agreed.

Basic information rights

Leeds Social Services Child Care Policy, drawn up by officers and members in 1989, sets out the rights which young people can claim while in the department's care. They include the right of a young person to read their file; to attend reviews; to receive good health care; to have their ethnic and cultural background respected and to be free from racial abuse or harassment wherever they live. The list continues to embrace other rights including education, finances, privacy and leaving care. The document was written for staff in the department but it was never distributed to children and young people.

In December 1991, the service established a working group, which met over six months, to produce a guide for all children and young people aged 12 years and over, incorporating the Child Care Policy. The working group consisted of young people who were currently living in care, ex-care users, residential and field social workers, foster carers and representatives from the Jewish Welfare Board and local leaving care projects. The role of the CRO was to chair the working group and produce a booklet targeted at young people, which covered issues and topics of interest to them, but which at the same time was acceptable to members and officers of the council.

Many people commented on the drafts and offered large numbers of amendments; during such a protracted process, it was often hard to sustain the interest and enthusiasm of the young people in the group. In June 1992, however, the council approved the draft which was published as an A5 booklet entitled *You and Your Rights* (Leeds Social Services, 1992). The booklet is intended for all young people whether in residential or foster care. The 109 different topics, which range from 'abuse' to 'volunteering' and include discussions of 'bullying', 'disability', 'juvenile justice', 'religion' and 'special needs' are listed alphabetically and include discussion of the rights embodied in the Child Care Policy document. A list of useful addresses and telephone numbers for agencies such as The National Association of Young People in Care (NAYPIC), the Children's Legal Centre (CLC) and the Citizen's Advice Bureau (CAB) is appended. *You And Your Rights* also contains a freepost envelope addressed to the Director of Social Services to be used for either comments or complaints.

The booklet aims to inform young people and their carers about their rights, to promote a better understanding of the care system and the mechanisms available for redress of grievance if the system is failing them in anyway.

Home closure

The decision of Leeds' Social Services Committee, in February 1992, to close one of it's children's homes was considered by the Children's Rights Service to be illegal, because it contravened the Children Act 1989 by failing to consult the young people who were resident in the home. The staff and young people at the community home, which catered for ten young people, decided to contact the Children's Rights Service for advice and support.

The service helped them to register their formal complaint about the closure under the provisions of the Children Act 1989. A meeting was arranged with the Director and Senior Management Team of the department; legal advice was sought and a solicitor was appointed to act for the young people; the residents were also helped to give their views to members of the Social Services Committee.

The Children Act 1989 and Article 12 of the UN Convention on the Rights of the Child each support the right of children to be consulted in such circumstances. The social services department must take into account the wishes and feelings of the children and young people involved in any such closure. This challenge by the young people, supported by the Children's Rights Service, was to be the first real test of the council's commitment. It resulted not only in delaying the proposed closure of the home pending a judicial review, but also in the council drafting and agreeing new procedures to avoid such action being taken again.

The young people involved gave their views to senior officers and members on several occasions with tact, diplomacy and honesty. The home finally closed in early September 1993, by which time most of the residents had left and moved to new homes as part of proper care plans.

Living conditions

The physical state of some community homes in Leeds was a major concern to the CRO, young people and the staff who worked and lived in them. In December 1992 a series of four visits to community homes was arranged by the service for the Chair and Vice-chair of the Social Services Committee, two senior officers within the social services department and the young persons adviser on the Social Services Committee.

The purpose of the visits was to ensure that politicians and managers were made fully aware of the deplorable condition in which some children were housed. The staff in the four homes visited were carrying out their role to the best of their ability, but confronted considerable difficulties in trying to work with young people in such poor physical surroundings. Much of the furniture including beds, wardrobes, seating, curtains, kitchens and carpets, was in a poor state of repair. At least one home needed re-roofing urgently.

In March 1993 following a report to the Children's Services Sub-Committee by the Children's Rights Service, a refurbishment programme commencing in the 1993/94 financial year was announced and a figure of £250,000 set aside for this purpose.

Although the visits in December 1992 and the committee report and press coverage at the time prompted action by the council, it is not yet clear what long term effects this may have for the project; politicians and senior officers are not typically enthusiastic about such negative publicity. But the action brought about much needed change for the benefit of both young people and staff.

Complaints

Many young people who contact the service do so because some thing or someone is making them unhappy. They might be being bullied by other young people, feeling powerless in decisions being taken about their future, or frustrated by rules made by staff in community homes. The CRO's role is not to investigate complaints but to provide children and young people with support, advice and advocacy should they decide to make complaints, either formally or informally.

The regulations governing complaints procedures are long and tiresome to most adults. To a young person of twelve, thirteen or less, they can be off-putting, lengthy and frustrating, especially if, in the end, the complaint is not upheld. The service tries to ensure that young people receive advice about the best way to pursue a particular concern or complaint; this may require the CRO to make a telephone call to clarify and resolve an issue for the young person. On other occasions, it may mean helping a young person to make a formal complaint to the department or on occasions referring them to a solicitor.

Some complaints made by individuals are shared by other young people and carers. A child in residential care, for example, complained that the £20 birthday allowance was inadequate. It soon became clear that many children shared this view. The sense of grievance was fuelled by the knowledge that children in foster care received up to £80 on their birthdays. There was no rational reason for this discrepancy and, following a submission by young people, the committee agreed that in future they should receive the same allowance wherever they live.

A children's rights service must try to guarantee that young people are informed of their rights and allowed to exercise them. But it must also be concerned to listen to young people and carers and ensure that sensible suggestions for improving services are put forward and, where possible, acted on.

CHILDREN'S RIGHTS OFFICERS – PROBLEMS AND ISSUES

All CROs have a difficult job. They are on the margins of the department and frequently viewed with suspicion by colleagues. Fighting for children's rights and redress for their grievances is not always guaranteed to win popularity, especially when it leads to criticism of individuals or reprioritisation of jealously guarded budgets. Although these posts have grown, at least in part, in response to scandals in residential care, the bread and butter of their work is the 'systems abuse' enacted by monolithic and financially stretched bureaucracies on children they purport to 'look after'.

The work in Leeds is unexceptional. It is certainly comforting that there is no evidence of serious abuse by residential staff and carers in the city, but, as the examples above illustrate, there are plenty of issues about the treatment of children by the department, which the department is not always happy to deal with. There are several instances where practice is at odds with agreed procedure, even at odds with the law. It is very common, for example, to find childcare reviews are being held without compliance with agreed protocols. Chairs do not necessarily check that decisions agreed at previous reviews have been carried out; they do not always conduct proceedings in a style which encourages the young person concerned, or their parents, to participate. Worse, reviews can be supplanted by an informal 'planning meeting' which enables professionals to make decisions without clients' knowledge or involvement. The complaints procedure in Leeds does not follow the requirements concerning the involvement of independent persons, which is specified in the Children Act, because the department has taken a decision that the costs are prohibitive.

The greatest difficulties, however, arise from the lack of basic support, supervision and training available to residential care staff. Leeds, like all social service departments, designates different uses for its various community homes: short-term and remand; reception into care; long-term; preparation for leaving care. It is sometimes necessary for a home to change its function, but experience suggests that to date staff have had little or no help in adjusting to the different needs of the new group of young people for whom they will be caring. One home, for example, was changed from a remand unit into a long-term establishment. Staff were given no time, training or even information to enable them to understand how to achieve this change and consequently a number of complaints were received from new residents that they were being treated as though they were on remand and were being subjected to all sorts of unnecessary regulations. When the CRO took up this issue with the officer in charge and the department, the staff were angry and felt criticised for doing what they thought the department had asked them to do (or rather never asked them to stop doing). It is much more common for problems to arise because of staff's lack of understanding than from deliberate abuse. But the department seems to be so financially and organisationally stretched that it cannot manage to establish simple supervision, team building and training to enable staff to work better. At the time of writing another reorganisation of residential homes is underway, with accompanying proposals for staff development, but it is unclear whether this will effect real improvements for young people or staff.

These problems have been acknowledged and discussed in a series of recent reports relating to residential care (Howe, 1992; Skinner, 1992; Utting, 1992; Warner, 1992) but there is insufficient impetus from either central or local government to implement the recommendations and secure improvements in the care of children being looked after by the local authority. At the Leeds Children's Rights Service Consultation and Review Day, social services staff suggested a long list of rights issues which they wanted the CRO to tackle, but none of them expressed the feeling that they could effect positive changes in the services which they actually deliver. It was clear that practitioners and first line managers in Leeds felt quite powerless to bring about improvements in the delivery of services.

THE CHILDREN'S RIGHTS OFFICERS ASSOCIATION

All CROs, regardless of their employer, express feelings of isolation in their role. The potential to be unpopular and marginalised within their departments, together with the very real dilemmas described above, led the CROs to establish their own association. The meetings offer space to discuss problems and air issues with others who work in similar circumstances. As the Association develops, it intends to become a voice for children's rights within social services. The Children's Rights Officers Association aims to set standards and advise authorities wishing to establish new posts.

The Association began as a network for mutual support, meeting quarterly in different locations. This format continues although the meetings have had to be structured to set aside time for business and to enable an increasingly large group to share information effectively. Proceedings confirm that all CROs find their work difficult and isolating, although some who are in neighbouring authorities do manage to offer mutual support in a sustained way. Members report being dependent on the personal support of individual managers in their departments and the majority feel under-resourced for their workload. Many CROs are based in inspection units, although the conflict this might present has rarely been considered; a significant number have a key role in investigating complaints within their departments, or managing the complaints procedure.

Very few CROs have their own budget and have to vie for money from general departmental budgets to produce leaflets and information for young people. Some do not even have an independent phone line to enable young people to contact them without going through a social services switchboard. In these circumstances it is hard to avoid the perception among young people that the CRO is just 'part of the system'.

The difficulties experienced by all CROs in achieving improvements in children's rights without alienating departmental support for their work begs a question about the nature of their role.

RIGHTING WRONGS OR PROMOTING RIGHTS?

The Leeds Children's Rights Service has been an important development for children and young people looked after by Leeds social services. The service has contributed to real improvements in the state of children's homes; in departmental policy and practice on a range of issues such as bulk buying, home closures and leaving care procedures; in the information available to children and young people about their rights; in young people's ability to make a complaint and get it heard.

But given the massive difficulties social services currently face in terms of public, political and media hostility to their work and client groups, which is translated into resource constraints, distrust and the low esteem of social work as a profession, especially of untrained residential workers, it is too much to expect individual CROs to transform services. Promises to consult young people before the closure of homes can take a back seat when 'nimbys'[2] and the local press join forces in bashing councillors'/officials' careful plans for an integrated care service. Homes can be closed almost overnight and policies revised as quickly, leaving good practice a poor relation to political expediency. CROs alone cannot change this.

Good care services require good management; effective selection, recruitment and induction processes; regular staff supervision and continued staff development; and all this within a common value framework and a clear shared purpose. When this is in place then CROs may be really effective in enabling children's and young people's perceptions to be voiced and to be heard. Until then they resemble the sorcerer's apprentice: bailing out an unrelenting and formidable tidal wave. In the present climate CROs should be pooling the lessons deriving from their work and using their Association to campaign for improvements at a national level, beginning with the effective implementation of changes recommended in the recent reports on residential care.

At a local level CROs must continue to redress the wrongs suffered by children who are looked after by the local authority. They must continue to act as the department's conscience, ensuring that managers and staff do not ignore children's rights, or subordinate them to the crass needs of the bureaucracy. They must continue to lift the carpets and see what has been swept underneath them.

NOTES

1 Although certain individuals were pivotal in establishing the Children's Rights Service, the Partnership Agreement was between the Save the Children Fund and Leeds Social Services and not individuals. The agreement and the Children's Rights Service remain unchanged even though Norman Tutt left the Authority in 1992.
2 'Nimbys' stands for not in my back yard – it is used as a collective noun for individuals and groups who campaign against the location of homes/hostels for disadvantaged groups in their neighbourhood.

REFERENCES

Home Office (1985) *The Cautioning of Offenders*, Cm. 14/85.
—— (1990) *The Cautioning of Offenders*, Cm. 59/90.
—— (1994) *The Cautioning of Offenders*, Cm. 18/94.
Howe, Lady (1992) *The Quality of Care* June 1992 Local Government Management Board. (A discussion of pay, conditions of service, training and qualifications of residential staff.)
Lindsay, M. (1988) 'Child's Rights Officer By Appointment' *Childright* July/August 1988 No. 49 pp. 16–19.
—— (1989) 'The Children's Advocate' *Community Care* 25 October 1989 pp. 23–4.
Skinner, A (1992) *Another Kind of Home* November 1992 HMSO. (A review of residential care in Scotland.)
Utting, Sir W. (1991) *Children in the Public Care* HMSO. (A review of residential care in England, with special reference to monitoring and control of residential care, following the 'Pindown' scandal in Staffordshire.)
Warner, N. (1992) *Choosing to Care* HMSO. (An examination of the selection and recruitment of staff to children's homes, following the prosecution of Frank Beck for abuse of children in Leicestershire.)

Chapter 7

A Minister for Children

Joan Lestor, MP

Children's rights is an emotive phrase which often causes puzzlement in industrialised societies. In our affluent corner of the world, the argument goes, we are able to care for our children: feed, clothe and nurture them. So when we think of children's rights, our thoughts fly automatically to the Third World, where poverty and underdevelopment often rob children of their childhood. We are wrong to be so complacent, for children in our own society also lack rights, recognition as individuals and respect.

The scale and nature of the deprivation is, of course, different to that experienced by children in other parts of the world. But then, so is the lifestyle of their parents and the challenges facing their governments. Unlike countries ravaged by war and famine, we have the resources and the time to build a sensitivity and responsiveness to the weakest and least vocal of our fellow citizens into our institutions and communities. We also have a duty to do so.

Our hopes and ambitions for the future are vested in our children. Few, if any, parents want less for their children than they themselves already enjoy. Most parents work hard to establish, so far as they are able, a stable and loving home environment to act as a springboard for their children's talents and abilities. But parents need help, from their extended family, from friends and from the wider community. And government, it is agreed, should give a lead and legislate in support of children, irrespective of the domestic setting into which they are born and reared.

All governments, of course, will claim they are doing this already, albeit to differing degrees. Even successive Conservative governments since 1979 have produced landmark legislation – such as the Children Act 1989 – although without supplying the resources essential to its successful implementation. But in Britain there is a tradition of non-intervention in matters of family life, which are viewed as residing predominantly in the private realm. For their part, children are still considered in the perception of too many adults to be the property of their parents, and any efforts to promote the cause of children's rights are often readily interpreted as undermining traditional 'family values' and parental authority (see chapter 14). For these reasons we still do not have a Minister for Families nor a Minister for Children in Britain despite strong pressure from voluntary agencies working with families.

Within the European Union, the debate has focused on the limited competence of Europe to legislate on family policy. It was only in 1983 that the European Community acknowledged the need to take account of the impact on family life of economic, social and cultural policies. The result has been an increased emphasis on directing help towards families and children most at risk. But few European Union countries possess coherent policies for the family, and even fewer take full account of any impact of policies on children. In Britain, the last decade has witnessed a government which has quite consciously attempted to off-load responsibility for families and children from the State back on to families themselves.

But change is coming slowly. The United Nations Convention on the Rights of the Child was a much more significant declaration than many people realised initially. It was important, of course, because it established for the first time, a universally agreed set of rights for children. But it also stimulated debate within the developed world about a meaningful interpretation and implementation of those rights. Member countries in the European Union, for example, are contributing towards a European version of the Convention, and the European Commission has recommended the appointment of a Minister for Children in each member country. Clearly, there is now a widely recognised need to respond more directly to the rights and needs of children at home as well as in other continents.

A MINISTER FOR CHILDREN: THE CASE OUTLINED

In Britain, the most significant barrier to formally acknowledging that children's rights is a major political issue is children's lack of a national political champion. Other countries have appointed people to help children assert their rights claims and have, with varying degrees of success, given children a political voice. Norway, for example, has had an Ombudsperson for more than a decade and in 1990 appointed a Minister for Children (see chapter 13). Other European countries have Ministers for Children or Youth Affairs, but with very narrow briefs; some Canadian provinces and Australian states have made similar appointments. But there has never been a central government department established and headed by a senior Minister, to oversee and coordinate policy developments affecting children from birth to voting age.

The Labour Party general election manifesto in 1992 carried such a commitment, signalling its intention, if elected, to appoint a Minister charged with listening to children and promoting their rights. The Minister would work in tandem with an independent Children's Rights Commissioner. The idea was not new, having been first proposed in Britain more than two decades ago, but it was the first time a national political party had endorsed the idea; it enjoyed widespread support from all the major children's charities.

I believe the case for a Minister for Children and for a Commissioner for Children's Rights is irrefutable. I know some will ask 'Why should we treat children differently from other identifiable sections of society?' The answer is simple. Children are the largest minority in Britain's democracy without a political voice of their own. They do not have a vote, but they constitute almost one quarter of the total population (13 million children and young people). Because they do not organise or lobby decision-makers, however, they are all too often the statistically unrecognised victims of bad policies (Jackson and Jackson, 1981).

It is easy to forget that laws passed by Parliament and directed at adults also have an impact on children's lives. So easy, that we have overlooked their needs year after year. When we gave the go-ahead for tower-block housing, for example, we condemned thousands of toddlers to an environment devoid of the opportunity to play. More recently when Parliament passed the Child Support Act, a law which saves the Exchequer money, the cost to the lone parent or the second wife or husband but also their children is very burdensome in emotional, physical and sometimes financial terms.

Children, because they continue to be viewed as property rather than as individuals in their own right, do not have their needs adequately met by the loose and largely informal partnership which exists between parents and the state. Successive governments have failed both to acknowledge and offer redress against the injustices inherent in a system based on constant renegotiation between these two adult parties, and which largely ignores the needs, interests and rights of a third; namely children.

The view that children's rights are commonly abrogated is widely held. APPROACH, ChildLine, the National Children's Bureau and the Association of Directors of Social Services (ADSS) have suggested:

> Attitudes to children, as reflected in public and political debate and in the media, are punitive and ill-informed; children are frequently scape-goated for problems created by adults. The built environment, transport and environmental policies are seldom friendly to children and children's welfare is seldom considered when these issues are under review. Concepts of ownership of children and of them being objects of concern rather than people, persist within the family, in institutional settings and in the wider society in sharp contrast to the principle of children's rights which was accepted by the Government when it ratified the UN Convention in 1991.
>
> (All Party Parliamentary Group for Children, 1993)

This consensus prompts an obvious question: Why do governments turn a blind eye to the realities of children's lives? Ministers have easy access to policy advisers both within and outside Whitehall. Voluntary agencies and campaigning organisations regularly produce quality research and well-argued proposals which would significantly improve the lives of thousands of children and young people. Indeed, as a politician seeking answers through the parliamentary system, I have frequently been referred to such research and proposals by ministers who argue that they constitute the most reliable source of statistical information on a range of issues from the numbers of young runaways to children who care for sick or disabled relatives. So the detailed information is available, some of it funded directly or indirectly by government, although it is not centrally collated, examined and interpreted. Government cannot therefore be confident of assessing with accuracy the impact of its policies on children. It can also avoid direct responsibility for the results of its actions.

It is my view that much of the information about children's lives makes uncomfortable reading; and that once government gives it official recognition, pressure will be put upon it to set targets – in child homelessness for example – and to develop policies which work directly to meet those targets and respond to the needs of those children.

The very existence of such information would be an irresistible force for policy change. In some policy areas children do not feature at all. There are no figures, for instance, showing how many children are homeless – only estimates based on average household size of how many live as members of homeless families. Given that many such families have larger than average numbers of dependent children, official figures substantially underestimate the problem. The appointment of a Minister for Children and an independent Commissioner for Children's Rights would automatically generate demands for more information.

So we need a political voice for children, a rights champion and much more information. We also need to carry out a thorough overhaul of the way Whitehall and its local government counterparts function. The current arrangement, whereby seven government departments parcel out responsibility for children with none being charged with taking an overview for the well-being of the 'whole' child, obviously fails children and young people. In particular, it fails those children who find themselves caught in the grey area of overlapping departmental responsibilities. In these cases, it is only when tragic or shameful individual experiences hit the headlines – the physically abused child or the youngster abused while in residential care, the Kings Cross Station rent boy – that the government takes action. The policy response is invariably piecemeal, short-term and, above all, cheap. It is a firefighting operation, often conducted under the glare of media publicity rather than a sustained and systematic policy response. As the Children's Society expresses it:

> Administrative restructuring and poor inter-agency cooperation has led to our failing children and young people with behaviour problems. Labelled as 'young offenders', 'beyond parental control', 'having learning difficulties' or 'mentally ill' depending on which agency they come into contact with, these young people cannot and do not neatly fit into any one system. As a consequence they are often passed from one agency to the next – dictated to as much by the laws of supply and demand as by their own needs.
>
> (All Party Parliamentary Group for Children, 1993: 7)

Within departments, structural changes to service delivery often fail to take proper account of children's needs. As the ADSS points out:

The recent reorganisation of health authorities into purchasers and trusts along with the opting out moves current in education has led to considerable fragmentation in services to children. For example the multi-agency approach to child protection – fundamental to Government policy on this issue – is put in serious danger by the disassembly of the health and education services. Strategies must be developed to ensure that child protection can be developed cooperatively.

(Ibid.)

In recent years, new laws – particularly relating to local authority responsibilities – have been introduced which failed to take full account of existing legislation, leading to diverse interpretation and confusion. The example given by the British Psychological Society and Social Information Systems refers to children with special needs:

while the Children Act consolidates childcare law it is still at odds with other legislation governing children, for example the Education Act 1981 [now 1993]. How do health, social and education services – with their separate legislations and, some would argue, their differing underlying philosophies – integrate to provide a single comprehensive service for children with special needs?

(Ibid.)

A MINISTER FOR CHILDREN: A CATALYST FOR CHANGE

So how would the Minister for Children function? Starting up a new department from scratch is a very daunting enterprise. The Whitehall machine is long-established and lacks enthusiasm for change. In the past, governments may have tinkered with the system, occasionally combining two departments only to separate them again, as in Trade and Industry for example, or grafting a junior ministerial post, such as Minister for Disabled People, onto an existing department. But typically, governments have fought shy of innovations which might unsettle the status quo. Ministers understandably become territorial and unwilling to embrace changes which might result in a diminution of their powers. For these reasons, strong and persuasive arguments have to be made, both publicly and privately, for the creation of a new Department headed by a Cabinet Minister.

The role of the new Minister and her or his department should be viewed as supportive and complementary to existing portfolios. The Minister's primary responsibility should be to argue children's case within government. The overall objective should be to help to make Britain more 'child-friendly' and to counter the fragmentation of services which currently exists in so many areas of service provision for children and young people. In practice, this would mean taking responsibility for coordinating initiatives across departments; taking the lead on overseeing implementation of key child-focused pieces of legislation; and chairing a Cabinet Committee which would call on each department to review its policies, administrative practices, existing and proposed legislation. The Minister would act as a constant reminder to colleagues of the need to include assessments of the impact of policies on children during all stages of the policy formulation process.

In consultation with colleagues, the Minister would propose 'partnership' schemes, drawing together several departments with shared and overlapping responsibilities around a specific policy area. Perhaps an example will illustrate the point.

How can Government best help 16–18-year-olds make the important transition from childhood to adulthood? If children are our future, we should be putting great efforts into encouraging them to play an active part in society, at all levels and at the earliest opportunity. Yet, as the British Youth Council argues, 'Young people are too often seen as passive recipients of established policy, rather than active citizens within society' (1993: 19).

The disaffection young people feel often leads, at best, to apathy and at worst to juvenile crime. The BYC goes on to recommend the introduction of a coherent legal framework for young people's rights as independent citizens; the introduction, at central and local government level, of a coherent and strategic policy towards young people, and legislation requiring government to consult with young people in the development of policy relating to them.

So a joint policy-making committee of Ministers looking at this issue would examine the interrelated areas of social security, housing, education and training, employment, juvenile justice and the residential care system. For the first time Ministers would be encouraged to look at the whole issue, rather than simply their small segment and to coordinate the delivery of services in the interests of young people.

Similar projects would concentrate on children in their early years (education, health, social security, housing, employment, environment); the impact of advertising on children and young people (health, education, home office, food and agriculture); juvenile offenders (education, home office, health, social security, environment); and race (education, training and employment, home office, health and social security).

Developing a political response to children and young people will demand a dramatic change of *approach* to policy development. Issues which affect both children and parents will have to be examined at the earliest stage with the benefits to children to the fore. Childcare provision, for example, should stem from an assessment of what is best for the child, not the working parent. If childcare is a good thing, then it is good for all children. The provision of nursery education and universally available, affordable, quality childcare should therefore be established as part of a wider strategy which extends the child protection network and helps develop a child's social potential. The needs of working parents would also be met but as a bonus, not as the primary purpose of the policy (see chapter 10).

Civil servants would liaise interdepartmentally and report to the junior minister on progress. In addition, individuals would be seconded from the statutory and voluntary sectors and staff would be encouraged to interchange between departments and the Minister's office. Such flexibility and exchange of experience and information is vital if the department is to make a deep and lasting impact on the Whitehall culture.

The Minister would be directly responsible for commissioning research on children's lives and would produce an annual report, after consultation with the Commissioner, the voluntary sector and local government. This statement would have to be considered by Cabinet before decisions were taken which might have an impact on children.

The role of Minister and Commissioner would be complementary. The Minister would help draw up policy, the Commissioner would be consulted on it and would monitor its impact and effectiveness. The Minister would work within government as a catalyst for change and a policy coordinator. The Commissioner would be free to criticise from the outside and would have additional responsibilities and powers, for example to conduct formal investigations on issues of significant and symbolic importance. Both the Minister and the Commissioner would actively seek the views of children and young people. They would also be charged with monitoring effective service provision at central and local government level and by other service providers to identify any groups of children whose needs are not being met. This would be a close working relationship and each would benefit from the existence of the other.

Children are potentially the most important catalyst for social change. The very process of recognising children's rights and needs; identifying the policies which could respond to those rights and needs, implementing those changes would not only dramatically improve the lives of the children themselves. Of necessity, it would also result in an improvement in the lives of their parents.

A Minister for Children is an idea whose time has come. We ignore the rights and needs of children at our peril. The appointment of a Minister would send the clearest signal that children and young people have a central place in our society as present and future citizens.

REFERENCES

All Party Parliamentary Group for Children (1993) *A Message to Parliament Concerning Children from interested Associations and Organisations* London: National Children's Bureau.
British Youth Council (1993) *Looking to the Future; Towards a Coherent Youth Policy* London: BYC.
Hantrais, L. (1993) 'Towards A Europeanisation of Family Policy' in R. Simpson and R. Walker (eds) *Europe for Richer or Poorer* London: Child Poverty Action Group.
Jackson, B. and Jackson, S. (1981) *Childminder* London: Penguin.
National Children's Home (1993) *The NCH Factfile 1993* London: NCH.
United Nations (1991) *1994 International Year of the Family* Vienna: UN.

Chapter 8

The Children's Rights Development Unit

Gerison Lansdown

When the Polish government first proposed the need for a United Nations Convention on the Rights of the Child on the eve of the International Year of the Child in 1979, the idea was largely supported by every member of the UN except for the UK. The UK government took the view that such a Convention was both unnecessary and inappropriate, although they agreed to participate in its development if other countries believed it was a suggestion worth pursuing; they did. A drafting committee was appointed which worked across the subsequent decade to produce the Convention which was adopted by the UN General Assembly in 1989. The Convention establishes a set of minimum rights for children, but it is nevertheless a radical document which brings together for the first time in an international treaty children's welfare rights and rights to protection but also acknowledges children's claims to civil and political rights. If implemented fully, it would dramatically improve the status of children in society

The UK government ratified the Convention in December 1991. By ratifying, the government made a commitment under international law to comply with its provisions. But governments may enter reservations where they feel unable or unwilling to commit themselves to certain principles in the Convention; these reservations are stated at the point of ratification. In the UK, the government entered the maximum of three reservation expressing its unwillingness to provide any special protection to 16–17-year-olds in the labour market, to amend the immigration and nationality legislation to achieve compliance with the relevant Convention Articles and eschew the practice of placing young people with adults in custody. Having ratified the Convention, governments are obliged after two years, and subsequently every five years, to report to a UN Committee on the Rights of the Child on progress towards implementation of the principles and standards it contains. The committee was established under the terms of the Convention and consists of ten international experts in the field of children's rights. The experts, who are elected by the governments of countries who have ratified, scrutinise the reports and comment on measures taken by the different governments to promote the rights of children in their respective countries. Through this process the committee will develop interpretations of each of the Articles to provide a frame of reference for individual countries against which to evaluate their own law, policy and practice. The committee aims to establish a dialogue with governments through which it will be possible to raise awareness of good practice in respect of children's rights. It has issued guidelines suggesting that governments should use the opportunity provided by the need to produce a report, to encourage wide-ranging debate and consultation and to conduct an extensive review of policies as they affect children. The UK government's first report was presented in January 1994, but they neither consulted over the production of the report nor is there any evidence of the application of the principles of the Convention to recent legislation and policy development (see especially chapter 4).

Early in 1990, a recommendation to the Gulbenkian Foundation suggested that a 'secretariat' should be set up to ensure that once the Convention had been ratified by the government, the various Articles in the Convention would be treated with due seriousness and implemented as fully as possible. After consultations with key organisations, the foundation appointed a consultant to take wider soundings. There were a number of possibilities for the organisational form which the secretariat might assume: a coalition of representatives from key children's organisations; a small specialist unit located within an existing organisation; a free-standing organisation with an explicit brief to focus exclusively on promoting the Convention. The response broadly favoured a new, independent, but short life unit. The foundation next established a steering committee to progress matters by forming a company and seeking charitable status and funding. It was proposed that the project should be called the Children's Rights Development Unit (CRDU); it should be funded for three years with a brief to promote the fullest possible implementation of the UN Convention in the UK. Funding was obtained from many of the large charitable trusts together with grants from most of the key child welfare organisations; the CRDU began its work in March 1992.

STRUCTURE OF THE CHILDREN'S RIGHTS DEVELOPMENT UNIT

The first task of the Unit was to create an organisational structure for its work which ensured the fulfilment of three central principles:

- the implementation of the Convention should apply equally to all children throughout the UK and the interests of children in England, Scotland, Wales and Northern Ireland had to be adequately represented.
- the work of the Unit should be informed as fully as possible by the views and experiences of children and young people.
- the work of the Unit would be based on the widest possible consultation and collaboration with professionals, academics and other interested individuals.

Creating a UK perspective

It was necessary to establish a dialogue in each jurisdiction within the UK to identify the most effective means of ensuring that the interests of all children would be adequately reflected in the work of the Unit. In Scotland, discussions with the Scottish Child Law Centre produced an agreement that a policy co-ordinator funded by the Unit and based in the Law Centre would provide a focus for the promotion of the work. In Northern Ireland, a Children's Rights Alliance had been formed with members representing the key child welfare organisations. It was agreed that the CRDU would fund a policy coordinator based in Belfast for whom the alliance would act as a resource and support. A close working relationship was established with Children in Wales to ensure that the perspectives of Welsh children were also appropriately reflected in the Unit's work. Four staff were to be based in a London office.

Involving young people

Article 12 of the UN Convention states that children have a right to express their views freely on all matters of concern to them and to have those views taken seriously. It was crucial that the Unit's work was rooted in this principle. One of the posts created in the London office was a Youth Development Worker whose primary function was to develop the necessary contacts and networks of children and young people to provide this input. It was also intended that a third of the membership of the Council, the Unit's management body, should be allocated to young people.

Consultation and collaboration

The Unit was established on the basis that it would provide a focus for promoting the Convention throughout the UK. It was to serve both as a catalyst for encouraging action to be taken towards implementation, and also a filter for gathering and disseminating expertise and knowledge which exists in the field of children's rights. It was essential for the pursuit of these objectives, that the Unit worked collaboratively. It was intended that this approach would both strengthen the Unit's contribution in promoting the Convention, and would also open up debate and interest to the widest possible range of organisations and individuals.

THE FOCUS OF THE UNIT'S WORK: MONITORING IMPLEMENTATION AND RAISING AWARENES OF THE CONVENTION

The work of the Unit fell into two broad areas. Raising awareness of the Convention and its potential application to law, policy and practice was of critical importance. Without widespread knowledge of its provisions, the value of the Convention as a tool for arguing in support of social change in respect of children would be lost. Consequently, a key part of the Unit's work has been to disseminate information to both adults and young people about the existence of the Convention, to provide guidance and assistance on how to translate the Articles into policy and practice, to inform the media of its provisions and to try to use media to promote them and to lobby politicians to apply its principles to new legislation and policy.

The primary task, however, has been to monitor the implementation of the Convention in the UK. In 1992, the Convention was still very new. The UN Committee had not had an opportunity to develop any detailed interpretations of any Articles or to establish indicators of rights against which it might be possible to test the extent of our compliance with them. It was necessary to construct an overall picture of the state of children's rights in the UK in order that we could begin to assess what changes might be necessary. In order to do this, we needed to tease out the meanings of many of the Articles in the context of an in-dustrialised country such as ours. How, for example, could we begin to evaluate what is meant by 'an adequate standard of living' (Article 27)? What in the UK setting represents the 'best possible health' (Article 24)? How do we assess compliance with a principle that a child's best interests must be the primary consideration when decisions that affect them are being made (Article 3)? We began work on the production of a UK Agenda for Children – a systematic analysis of the extent to which law, policy and practice in the UK complied with the principles and standards in the Convention. The UK Agenda also identified areas where a lack of information made it extremely problematic to assess the extent of UK compliance with the Convention, while at the same time offering recommendations for change which would promote greater levels of compliance with the requirements of the Convention. This report would be submitted to the UN Committee as an alternative perspective on the state of children's rights in the UK. The methodology for producing the report involved the following processes.

Creating a network of interested organisations and individuals

It was important that the report was based on the widest possible collaboration and consultation. It needed to draw on the expertise and experience of a broad range of professionals in relevant fields. Accordingly, the first task was to construct a questionnaire which was circulated to all health authorities and trusts, local authorities, key national voluntary organisations, interested academics and professional associations. The questionnaire sought to establish whether respond-ents were interested in participating in a consultative process and, if so, with which Articles of the Convention they were primarily concerned. Initially 1,000 questionnaires were distributed in England and Wales with additional copies circulated in Scotland and Northern Ireland. Several hundred completed quest-ionnaires provided the basis for an extensive network on which to draw for the production of the report.

Production of consultation papers

The Convention contains over 40 Articles relating to different rights of children.

It was decided that rather than produce papers in relation to each individual Article, it would be more constructive to identify the key policy areas addressed by the Convention and then to examine all the Articles of relevance within that policy framework. The areas identified were: education, day-to-day care of children, play, health, poverty, environment, child labour, abduction, personal freedoms, physical integrity, youth justice, armed conflict, nationality, immigration and refugees, international obligations. In all these areas, there are three underlying principles which have application – Article 2: the requirement that all the rights in the Convention apply to all children without discrimination, Article 3: the requirement that in all actions affecting them, the welfare of the child must be a primary consideration, and Article 12: the rights of the child to express a view and be taken seriously in all decisions that affect her or him. The implications of these Articles were considered in every policy paper.

Having established the central themes, initial research was undertaken to explore the relevant law, policy and practice in each area and evaluate it against the standards and principles embodied in the Convention. In some of the subject areas, an exploratory seminar was convened with interested experts invited to identify current concerns in relation to children's rights. Consultation papers were then produced which identified key areas where there was either an explicit breach of the Convention or where there would need to be changes to legislation, its implementation or levels of resourcing if the UK was to achieve full compliance. All consultation papers appended recommendations designed to ensure greater compliance with the Convention. Most of the papers were produced by the Unit itself but, in some areas, other organisations were commissioned to produce a draft. Once written, the papers were distributed for consultation to all interested organisations and individuals.

Ensuring a UK wide perspective

There are marked differences in legislation, the administration of statutory services and cultural experiences within the four jurisdictions in the UK. It was obviously essential that these differences were reflected in the UK Agenda. We identified a number of areas where the experience in Scotland and Northern Ireland was of sufficient difference to require a separate paper being produced; for example, youth justice in Scotland and armed conflict in Northern Ireland. Where the differences were more marginal or were quantitative rather than qualitative, such as in issues around poverty, it was agreed to circulate the same paper and rely on the feedback from participants to identify critical regional concerns that needed to be addressed. Separate consultations and seminars were convened for a number of the policy areas in Scotland and Northern Ireland.

Involving children and young people

The Agenda needed to be informed as fully as possible by the views of children and young people. We achieved this objective through two main strategies. First, the CRDU produced a two sided document, with each policy paper that was drafted, which set out the key rights addressed in the paper and asked a number of questions about the extent to which the particular rights under consideration were respected in practice. When the papers were distributed, every participant was invited to use the document as a basis for discussion with any groups of young people with whom they were in contact and to send any details of the discussions to the CRDU.

Second, the CRDU organised between 30–40 consultation sessions with children and young people throughout the UK. These groups ranged from ages 8–16 and sought to reflect the wide disparities in life experiences of children in different circumstances. Some discussions, for example, were based in schools or youth clubs, others were with young people looked after by local authorities, or who were leaving care, others involved young people who were caring for sick or disabled parents or who had been abused, or were homeless. The discussions were wide-ranging and produced a wealth of material which was able to inform and strengthen the analysis in the agenda.

Finalising the Agenda

Once the comments had been received, each consultation paper was redrafted and the recommendations finalised. The Scottish, Welsh and Northern Ireland perspectives were incorporated together with the views and experiences of young people. In some subject areas, a follow-up seminar was convened prior to redrafting to explore any contentious or unresolved issues. We drafted a statement of endorsement of the Agenda which we asked every participating organisation to sign. These organisations were then listed in the final draft to demonstrate the breadth of expertise and support on which the Agenda was based. The Agenda was then published in the form of 15 booklets as a comprehensive analysis of the state of children's rights in the UK as tested against the Convention.

WHAT DID WE LEARN?

The completion of such a wide-ranging and comprehensive overview of law, policy and practice relating to children, allowed the CRDU to identify some significant issues concerning children's rights. It was apparent, moreover, that the UK is failing to comply fully with every single Article in the Convention. While there is an awareness of the rights of children to be protected from abuse, exploitation, violence, armed conflict, drugs and abduction, the reality is that for many children these rights are not being safeguarded adequately. On occasion, it is the legislative framework which is at fault, while on others it is the failure to translate the legislation fully into practice; sometimes it is simply that there are inadequate resources with which to guarantee the protection of children.

Similarly, there is a broad recognition in UK society that children have social rights. Free full-time education, free access to health care, child benefit, free prescriptions and dental and optical care all testify to the acceptance of a social responsibility for the promotion of the rights of children to certain standards of care. A complex web of social security benefits exists to prevent families falling below minimum standards of living. Yet the massive rise in unemployment which characterised the late 1980s, together with changes in the structure of employment leading to greater numbers of workers in part-time and temporary jobs, has led to a considerable growth in child poverty. This poverty, compounded by government policies on housing during the 1980s, has also contributed to the serious escalation of homelessness and has meant that for many children, the very basics of an adequate diet, warmth and security are absent from their lives.

So, it is evident that in many ways there is a clear dissonance between society's professed commitments towards children, and the effective implementation of those commitments. In the sphere of children's civil rights, however, society has not yet even got as far as expressing the commitment. The rights of children to freedom of expression, of religion, of association, the right to privacy and to physical integrity are not fully respected in law and are regularly breached in practice. It is not possible in the context of this chapter to examine all the issues of concern but it is worth examining some of the most consistent and significant examples of failure to respect children's rights.

Powerlessness

Article 12 states that the government

shall assure to the child who is capable of forming his or her own views the right to express those views freely in all matters affecting the child, the views of the child being given due weight in accordance with the age and maturity of the child.

The theme which emerged from *every* group of young people without exception was that they felt that adults did not listen to them, did not respect them, did not take them seriously, did not value what they had to say. They felt this in respect of their personal relationships with parents, in school, in foster and residential care, at a wider level with regard to the media, politicians and policy-makers. There is a general feeling amongst many young people that childhood is characterised by low status, little power and almost no control over the outcomes of their lives. These views were echoed by many of the professionals working with young people.

The Children Act does introduce a requirement on the part of courts and local authorities making decisions in respect of children and young people, to 'ascertain their wishes and feelings' (Sections 1(3)(a), 22(4)), and this requirement is consistent with the duty embodied in Article 12. It is evident, however, that day-to-day practice needs to change very considerably before it begins to impact on the lives of children. Children looked after by the local authority continue to experience a sense of impotence and alienation from the system and little appears to have improved since the Act's implementation. We do not have a culture of listening to children – and changes in legislation will achieve little unless backed up by fundamental changes to procedures, training of all staff working with children, and the introduction of formal measures designed to elicit the views of young people and act on them. Compliance with Article 12 would require that all providers of services for children:

- ensure that children have adequate information appropriate to their age with which to form opinions. Children in a hospital setting, for example, need to be informed about who is responsible for telling them what is happening, what the implications of treatment are, side effects, options that are available, implications of not having the treatment, whether it will hurt, how long it will take. Information is crucial to the capacity to make informed choices.
- provide children with real opportunities to express their views and explore options open to them. A serious commitment to respecting children and their right to participate in matters of importance to them – whether they are in school, in care or in hospital – means it is imperative to make sure that children have ample opportunity to explore the issues facing them. Their doubts, anxieties and confusions must be addressed if they are going to be involved effectively. In assessing a young person's competence to be involved in decision-making, it is important to consider the young person's own views about their competences. The ability of a child to make decisions reflects not simply the child's competences but on the respect shown by others for those competences.
- listen to those views and consider them with respect and seriousness and tell children how their views will be considered. There is obviously no point in listening to a child's views if you have no intention of taking them seriously. It is necessary to be clear about what aspects of the child's care or education or health or play he or she can be involved in. In order to allow children to be involved in decisions about themselves, adults need to be prepared to listen and respect them and speak in partnership with them, not as substitutes for them.
- let them know the outcome of any decision and, if that decision is contrary to the child's wishes, make sure that the reasons underlying the decision are explained fully.
- provide children with effective, accessible and genuine avenues of complaint, supported by access to independent advocacy on any occasion when a child feels they have been mistreated or ignored or abused in any way.

It is not only in the public sphere that change is needed. Many children clearly feel that they are powerless within the family to have their views heard and taken seriously. The UK Agenda recommends that the law should be changed to impose a requirement on parents, so that in reaching any major decision relating to a child, the parents should ascertain the child's views and give due consideration to them, subject to the child's age and understanding. This provision does exist in countries such as Finland and Sweden and indeed in their Report on Family Law, the Scottish Law Commission (1992) found that there was widespread support for comparable provision here. The incorporation of such a provision in law would be an explicit recognition of the right of children to participate in decisions that affect them and represent an affirmative statement of their status within the family as individuals and not merely the property of their parents.

Discrimination

Discrimination was the second major theme which ran through almost every policy area. Article 2 states that all the rights in the Convention must apply without discrimination to all children. Yet it is clear that whether for reasons of poverty, ethnicity, disability, sexuality, or immigration status, many children are denied rights which are fundamental to the Convention. Black children are more likely to be living in families where the parents are unemployed, they are more likely to experience homelessness and they are more likely to be living in poor quality housing; their parents are more likely to be low paid. Black children are more likely to experience difficulties in accessing the health and social services that they need. The services that they do receive will often fail to address their particular cultural and religious needs. Afro-Caribbean children are more likely to be excluded from school and there is serious cause for concern about the rising numbers of racist attacks being experienced by members of minority ethnic communities. This catalogue of discrimination is powerful testimony to our failure to comply fully with Article 2 and with it the denial for many children of significant other rights.

We have no legislation rendering it unlawful to discriminate on grounds of disability. Disabled children remain substantially marginalised from most main-stream activities which able-bodied children take for granted. Article 23 stresses the right of disabled children to opportunities for the fullest possible social integration. Yet, despite the 1981 Education Act with its qualified duty on LEAs to place children with special educational needs in ordinary schools wherever possible, analysis of Department of Education and Science (DES) returns shows that there was only a 4 per cent decrease in segregation between 1982 and 1989 (Swann, 1989). Many disabled children remain excluded from mainstream schools, from mainstream play opportunities, from integrated day care, from access and many other cultural opportunities available to other children.

Poverty

Poverty and the consequent failure of many children to achieve an

> adequate standard of living for (their) physical, mental, spiritual, moral and social development

(Article 27) was a dominant theme in our consultation. Government figures published in July 1993 (HMSO, 1993) reveal that there has been a widening of the gap between rich and poor in the UK over the past 14 years. Using the definition of poverty as those living on less than half the average income, there are now 13.5 million people, including 3.9 million children, living in poverty. This compares with 1.4 million children in 1979 and now represents one-third of all children. Alongside the growth in numbers of children living in poverty, we have also witnessed a massive rise in the numbers of homeless families and homeless young people living on our streets. In 1991, about 420,000 adults and children were accepted as homeless by local authorities in England alone (Burrows and Walenkowicz,1992). The official figures on homelessness have tripled since 1978. Shelter estimate that almost 150,000 young people become homeless every year (Shelter, 1989). Many of these children and young people are being denied the right to the best possible health (Article 24), to opportunities for play (Article 31), the right to adequate housing (Article 18), the right to family life (Article 9), the right to education (Article 28). Perhaps even more importantly, poverty denies children the rights of citizenship; the right to respect and value as a member of society. There is a prevailing and widespread view within the UK, reinforced by many government ministers, that the poor are responsible for their poverty. The impact of these views is that the *physical exclusion* from participation enforced on poor children as a consequence of their poverty, is compounded by a *social exclusion* created by social attitudes of condemnation and blame. Such exclusion is inimical to the promotion of the child's development necessary for compliance with Article 27, runs counter to the requirement in Article 2 of the Convention to ensure all the rights it embodies to all children, and indeed breaches the spirit of the Convention as a whole.

Support for parents in promoting their children's rights

The Convention is explicit in its recognition that parents have the primary responsibility for caring for children and promoting their rights, but is equally clear that the state has a vital role to play in supporting parents in that role. Article 18 stresses that governments must

> *render appropriate assistance to parents and legal guardians in the perform-*
> *ance of their child rearing responsibilities and shall ensure the development*
> *of institutions, facilities and services for the care of children.*

In fact, much recent government policy has been significant for its attempt to withdraw from that responsibility. Publicly funded day care – a vital resource for parents – is woefully inadequate in this country. Day care for under-threes provides for 2 per cent of children in the UK, compared with 30 per cent in France and 48 per cent in Denmark (see Moss, 1990). More than 95 per cent of French and Belgian children are in nursery schools from the age of three; figures for Italian and Danish children are 85 per cent. In Britain the figure is around 25 per cent with most children attending only part-time. The Children Act with its gate keeping concept of 'in need' is far removed from a broad-based commitment to support for all parents. Minimal recognition is given in employment to parental responsibilities – 14 weeks paid maternity leave but no statutory rights whatever for fathers to have leave at the birth of a child, and similarly no statutory provision for leave to care for sick children. It is difficult to reconcile this virtual workplace denial that children exist, with the requirement in Article 3 of the Convention to promote the best interests of the child and to provide the necessary legislative and administrative measures to ensure the care and protection of children. The impact of the Child Support Act with its powers to penalise mothers for non-disclosure of details of fathers is inconsistent with the promotion of children's welfare. How does the reduction of a family's benefit, already below what is an inadequate allowance, tally with the government's professed motivation to protect children's interests? Similarly, the rigid formula for assessment of maintenance is proving problematic for many fathers who find that the weekly maintenance they are now required to pay denies them sufficient income with which to sustain the costs of continued contact with their child. Thus, the legislation is impeding the right of the child to continuing contact with absent parents set out in Article 9 of the Convention.

CONCLUSIONS

Despite the Children Act 1989 – with its shift from a legal concept of parental rights to one of parental responsibilities – the language of parental rights is still very much with us, and with it a belief that children's rights threaten the exercise of those parental rights. The views and opinions of children and young people are as yet given scant status and there is still a prevailing perception of them as irresponsible, irrational and incapable of making informed choices. We continue to regard children as the property of their parents and not as individuals in their own right. How else can we explain the fact, for example, that children have no legal rights to express a choice of school, to be given a hearing if excluded from school, to be able to refuse consent to treatment, to protection from all forms of physical violence. But if we expect parents to be the key agents with responsibility for promoting their children's rights, they must be given the power to exercise those responsibilities. Adequate benefit levels, secure employment, access to affordable housing, high quality and affordable day care, and employment legislation which acknowledges the existence and rights of children are all central components of a society which supports parents and respects children. The impetus for change afforded by the UN Convention does offer a unique opportunity to re-examine our legislation, our policy and practice and our attitudes towards children. Failure to do so will not only represent a breach of our international obligations, but will mean the perpetuation of discriminations practised against the largest minority group in our society – the 13.2 million children living in the UK.

REFERENCES

Burrows, L. and Walenkowicz, P. (1992) *Homes Cost less than Homelessness* Shelter: London.
HMSO (1993) *Households Below Average Income 1979–1990/91* HMSO: London.
Moss, P. (1990) *Day Care in the European Community 1985–90* Commission of the European Community, Brussels.
Scottish Law Commission (1992) *The Report on Family Law* HMSO: Edinburgh.
Shelter (1989) *One Day I'll Have a Place of My Own* Shelter: London.
Swann, W. (1989) *Integration Statistics; LEAs reveal local variations* Centre for Studies in Integrated Education.

Chapter 9

The rights and wrongs of children who care

Jo Aldridge and Saul Becker

'When I think about all those years I cared for my dad, it makes me angry, not because I had to care for him – I *wanted* to care for him – but because I was left alone to cope with his illness for so long. I wasn't just doing ordinary tasks like other kids might do around the house. I was having to cook for him, beg for money and food parcels so I could feed him, take him to the toilet, clean him up when he couldn't get to the toilet – because he couldn't get up the stairs towards the end.'

'No one should have to see their parents like that, when they lose all their bodily functions. I loved my dad and I couldn't bear to see him losing his dignity – getting more ill before my eyes. But because I loved him, I wanted to be with him. I wanted to look after him. I just wish someone could have helped me and that those who interfered in our lives and made them difficult could have left us alone.'

'All I ever wanted was to talk to someone and someone who could have warned me about my dad's fits, caused by his brain tumour.'

'It's too late for me now. My dad died and I'm no longer a "young carer", but for all those other kids out there who are in the same situation I was, then something should be done to help them. Not take them away from their mum or dad, but to help them care without worrying, without being frightened.'

Jimmy, aged 16 years

From the age of 13 Jimmy nursed his dying father on his own for three years. His mother had left home, taking Jimmy's sister with her. Caring for his father was a profoundly traumatic experience for Jimmy. They were very close and Jimmy was devastated when his father died. During the years of caring Jimmy refused to attend school. They had very little money, were prosecuted for trying to defraud the Department of Social Security and taken to court for non-school-attendance (his father was fined, Jimmy was put on probation). Jimmy had to beg for food parcels and was having to undertake domestic and very intimate personal tasks for his father, including toileting him. He also had to take him back and forth to hospital, and cope with his violent fits, which were a consequence of a brain tumour. Throughout the caring period no paid professional ever offered any constructive support to Jimmy who was afraid that either he or his father would be 'taken away' and put into an institution. When his father died, Jimmy was offered the choice of going to live with his mother or being put into care.

DEFINITION AND SCOPE

Jimmy, like tens of thousands of other children, is a child carer. The Carers National Association (CNA) has referred to young carers as:

> children and young people, who, in the absence of appropriate practical support from outside agencies, take responsibilities in the care of a relative at home. This might be a parent, grandparent, brother or sister with a disability or in emotional distress. They may be alone undertaking basic household tasks or full nursing care. Or in many families, children provide a great deal of emotional stability whilst the adults are under stress. The effects on children of a parent's long-term illness or disability go largely unrecognised.
>
> (Carers National Association, 1992: 1)

The CNA refers to 'young' carers – a group which includes children and young adults. However, our concern in this chapter is with 'children' who care – people under the age of 18 with the legal status of children. We believe that the issues confronting children as carers, in particular their needs and rights, are distinct from those confronting young adult carers.

The story of children who care is an account of choice and responsibility turned upside down: of children having to perform the most basic, personal and intimate tasks, becoming their parents' parent. The contribution of child carers, however, is very much hidden; it is rarely acknowledged or recognised in the literature on community care, informal care or children's rights, and has largely been ignored by policy makers at national and local levels.

And yet, the discussion of child carers poses fundamental challenges to conventional wisdom and understanding of the nature of caring, childhood, dependency, citizenship and children's rights. Child carers face real and fundamental tensions arising from their experiences as carers and as children, and from cultural, social, economic and legislative pressures that attempt to define and construct their roles, rights and responsibilities.

DISCOVERY AND CONSTRUCTION

Child caring is not a recent social phenomenon. Images of children who care can be traced through creative writing with the novels of Dickens and Hardy offering obvious examples. In Dickens' *Little Dorrit* (1857), the character takes on the role of 'little mother' and takes responsibility for her family at a very early age. By the time little Dorrit is 13 she is housekeeper and 'mother' to her brothers and sisters.

Images of the child carer can be traced back even further. In her work on children in history, for example, McLaughlin (1974) reports that at the beginning of the eleventh century there is evidence that, due to the death of one or both parents, young children were cared and provided for by their older brothers or sisters. By the thirteenth century – when life expectancy was around 30 years of age – children who survived infancy were themselves more likely to be orphaned at an early age and forced into caring for other members of their family. Through the fourteenth to sixteenth centuries many orphaned children, from the age of seven, were often apprenticed or hired out as servants – to provide care in *other* families.

More recently, the writings of children's author Jamila Gavin have included stories of child carers, such as little Effie, who

'every day had to support the huge body of her invalid mother and help her from bed to wheelchair to bathroom to wheelchair, and finally, at the end of the day, back to bed again. Even the nights weren't her own . . . but Effie also had to see to her brother, Jackson and sister, Seraphina . . .'. Little Effie was, indeed, 'God's own child'.

(Gavin, 1991: 7)

This commitment, often against all the odds, has also been portrayed by the media as 'courageous'. As a reward for their bravery and selflessness, some child carers can expect to receive a golden heart from Esther Rantzen, or shake the hand of Princess Diana at the annual Red Cross Care in Crisis Awards. The media has helped to construct the image of the child carer as a child of courage – God's own child.

While novels, and media images, tell us something about the changing nature and experience of child carers, surprisingly little knowledge has been gained from academic research or official statistics. Consequently, there is a considerable research literature which focuses on the lives and needs of informal (unpaid) carers in the community, but most of this fails to examine in any depth the particular experiences and needs of *children* who care (Fallon, 1990). The 1990 General Household Survey of Carers indicates that there are about 6.8 million people in Great Britain who are looking after a sick, disabled, or elderly person (Office of Population Censuses and Surveys (OPCS), 1992). It is impossible, however, to derive from these data, or, for that matter, from any other official data sets, the numbers and characteristics of child carers. In effect, children who care have been excluded from official data collection procedures and analyses, and correspondingly, from the wider policy debates on community care and children's rights. So, for example, nowhere in the guidance to the National Health Service and Community Care Act (finally implemented on 1 April 1993) are child carers specifically mentioned, despite the principle of the Act which is based upon listening to carers and providing for their needs. Indeed, to a large extent the effectiveness of recent community care changes relies heavily on the contribution of informal carers. In many thousands of households this contribution will be provided by children.

It is only more recently – from the late 1980s – that child carers have become more recognised, and their experiences and roles have become more documented. As a consequence of a few small-scale pieces of work (see for example Page, 1988; O'Neill, 1988; Bilsborrow, 1992), and through the work of the Carers National Association Young Carers Project (CNAYCP) (see for example, Meredith, 1991, 1992), there is now more open discussion and awareness of the needs of children who care. Child carers are themselves being given a voice, especially through the CNAYCP. A number of conferences organised by the CNA have given young carers a platform to talk about their experiences, needs and rights. Apparently, child carers are *not* asking for opportunities to receive golden hearts or shake hands with royalty, but would prefer instead to be given recognition and support in their caring roles. This is not a message that some policy makers will want to hear: it is far simpler to give child carers tokens or awards, rather than finding the resources or commitment to address their needs. It is far easier to talk about, and construct children who care as 'children of courage' or 'God's own children', rather than child carers with needs and rights.

THE EFFECTS OF CARING ON CHILDREN

Our research (Aldridge and Becker, 1993a, 1994) has found that child carers are often deprived of their childhood; they are fearful, isolated and excluded. They receive no payments for their 'labour of love', and they are denied access to social security benefits as they are classified as children. Many experience difficulties with school attendance and in forming and maintaining social relationships. Many live in families experiencing poverty and exclusion.

The effects of caring on a child can be manifold and complex. This is certainly the case where the nature and extent of caring responsibilities are intense – in those circumstances where the child carer is the sole provider of care; where there are no other adults in the home aside from the care receiver, and where the care receiver's condition is such that it requires constant attention.

Caring can severely restrict children's lives. It can have implications for their physical and psychosocial development as well as their educational prospects. Many child carers are forced to lift and carry their parents up stairs and from one room to another. This can often cause injury to the child (or indeed the parent) or exacerbate existing injuries. Friendships and social activities are also severely impaired when children undertake primary caring responsibilities. They often have to forgo socialising, and friendship networks can suffer as a result. Caring can also place a 'silent curfew' on children so that when they do go out, they often have to return early to carry out their duties, or the care receiver can put pressure on children to return early to the family home.

Many child carers are persistently late or absent from school. Their educational performance can be severely restricted. Their aspirations for the future are often very narrowly defined, if defined at all (Aldridge and Becker, 1993b).

PUNISHING CHILDREN FOR CARING

Although many key medical, health, social services and education professionals may be involved in families where there is a long-term illness or disability, they are not necessarily identifying primary carers where these carers are children. Indeed, where identification generally has taken place, subsequent interventions have very often been punitive in nature (Aldridge and Becker, 1993c). Social workers and education welfare officers have threatened to pursue care proceedings for non-school-attendance or because the child is considered to be at risk; community care assistance (home help) has been withdrawn from families because a young child is considered to be 'old enough' to cope; general practitioners have ignored child carers when considering the medical care and treatment of their patients; other professionals, while in contact with the 'care receiver' have failed to engage with the needs of child carers, assuming that what is good for the parent is also good for the child who cares.

To be punished for caring is hard to comprehend when you are a child. The messages that this gives children during a critical stage in their psychosocial development may influence the way they perceive, and value, caring and family responsibility in adult life.

CHALLENGING RECEIVED WISDOMS

As we have noted above, the discussion of child carers poses fundamental challenges to many conventional wisdoms. Some of these challenges are examined below.

The first challenge is to the traditional values placed upon caring in childhood. It has been suggested, by feminist writers and others, that the caring role can provide women with part of their feminine identity (it is more than another species of work: see Lewis and Meredith, 1988), and that caring is an important part of childhood, family and social development. Intensive caring by *children*, however, is likely to distort child identity and childhood development because of the 'adult' and intense nature of the caring process and experience. Indeed, recent research (Bilsborrow, 1992; Aldridge and Becker, 1993a) indicates that caring not only damages the physical and mental health of some children, but that, in effect, it also denies child carers the experience of childhood.

The second challenge is to traditional values placed on work and employment. Caring is often considered a 'labour of love'. Child caring is essentially unpaid work which, because of its intensity, has profound implications for children's development and opportunities. Society does not, generally, expect young children to be in full-time or even part-time work situations to the extent that their education, physical; intellectual and social development are compromised. When children are caring, however, this is exactly what is happening. Furthermore, child carers experience multiple and interrelated deprivations – their childhood is undermined, and they forgo incomes that many other children are able to receive through part-time paid employment. Child caring has many of the negative associations of full-time work with few, if any, of the benefits or rewards.

The financial circumstances of child carers is at the centre of a third challenge – a challenge to traditional notions of dependency. The social security system does not financially accommodate child carers (Aldridge and Becker, 1993d). As they are not adults they cannot receive income support in their own right, except in severe circumstances; consequently they are not eligible for the carer's premium, nor can they apply for social fund payments. They are similarly excluded from receiving other 'passported' benefits. Very occasionally a child carer over 16 may receive invalid care allowance, where eligibility has been proven.

Children who care may receive no income maintenance from the state, and no wages for their labour. And yet, the cared-for person(s) will receive child benefit and/or child additions in respect of the children who care for them. The social security arrangements, and safety net provision of income support and the social fund, work against the financial independence, security and stability of child carers, and reinforce traditional notions of dependency that construct the child as dependent on the adult. These institutionalised assumptions have very powerful effects on self image and lifestyles, and are reinforced through the day-to-day arrangements that govern the interchange between adults and children, between parent and child. In the case of child carers, it is the parent who is dependent for support – indeed, dependent for the very basics of life, including such intimate tasks as toileting, washing and dressing. The Children's Legal Centre manifesto states that:

> The social security system should provide children and young people with adequate living standards and promote independence rather than perpetuating financial dependence on parents.
>
> (Children's Legal Centre, 1992: 12)

This is particularly so for children who care.

The fourth challenge is to the received wisdom on social citizenship. In particular, child carers may experience some of the harshest, yet most invisible forms of poverty and exclusion. With no independent income of their own, with contradictory tensions from legislation on community care, children's rights and social security, with pushes and pulls from cultural, racial, gender-role expectations and systems of discrimination, child carers may be denied the opportunity to participate fully as children in society. Similarly, they are denied the rights of social citizenship that pertain to adulthood. They cannot vote, they have restricted legal rights and they experience the social exclusion and restricted opportunities that correspond with limited income and severe poverty. They are denied the (adult) rights of social citizenship because of their legal status as children, and yet they take (adult) responsibility, and (adult) accountability, for the primary care of others, often with no help or support from professionals paid to care.

RECONSTRUCTION: FROM GOD'S OWN CHILDREN TO CHILDREN WHO CARE

The problematic position of child carers also arises from contradictory pressures contained within current legislation and philosophy concerned with children's rights and community care. The Children Act 1989 defines and clarifies the rights of children – and implies a notion of childhood that is safe and protected: Section 17 of Part III of the Children Act states:

It shall be the duty of every local authority (a) to safeguard and promote the welfare of children within their area who are in need; and (b) so far as is consistent with that duty, to promote the upbringing of such children by their families, by providing a range and level of services appropriate to those children's needs. For the purposes of Part III a child shall be taken to be in need if (a) he is unlikely to achieve or maintain, or have the opportunity of achieving or maintaining, a reasonable standard of health or development without the provision for him of services by a local authority, or (b) his health or development is likely to be significantly impaired, or further impaired, without the provision for him of such services.

(Section 17 (10))

Child caring imposes real strains on this view of childhood – on the rights and needs as children – because where children are carers, they are essentially providing care and security *for* their dependant, often at the expense of their own childhood, welfare and needs.

The community care legislation (DoH, 1989, 1990) promotes a different tension. By encouraging people to stay in the community for as long as possible, and by enabling and facilitating the development of networks for community care, there is a key role envisaged for informal care (indeed the White Paper acknowledges that informal carers will continue to be the main providers of care). So one strand of legislation is establishing a framework for community care and support of carers, while another strand attempts to protect children and establish their rights. There is a tension between the two when children are carers.

The critical question to be addressed here is: should child carers be viewed and treated as children of courage – 'God's own children' – children in need or children who care? The neglect of child carers by professionals, and the absence of a clearly-defined policy agenda for child carers, partly arise from the difficulties inherent in answering this question, and from the problems of 'classifying' child carers' experiences and needs. For the media the answer is far simpler: the child carer is God's own child, a child of courage to be applauded and rewarded with some symbol or token. The media has generally failed to penetrate and engage with the contradictions of the child-caring experience. But at the policy level, especially given the growing evidence about lifestyles and need, the 'God's own children' approach is hard to sustain. Local social services/social work departments, charged with statutory responsibility for community care and child care, have been unsure as to whether child carers fall into the policy and practice domain of child care committees or community care committees. This is despite, or even because of, the Children Act and community care legislation. This 'boundary' dispute has led to the needs of children who care going largely unidentified in the local resource allocation and planning process. At national level too, despite the advances made by the CNA Young Carers Project and the publication of recent research findings, child carers are rarely, if ever, mentioned in DoH discourse on community and informal care, discourse on children in need, or for that matter, in the literature of the children's rights movement more generally. To a large extent, therefore, child carers remain obscured from the various policy making arenas. When they are recognised they are constructed as brave and courageous. This is undeniably true – children who care *are* brave and committed to their tasks – no matter how painful these might be to their loved ones and to themselves. But child carers are now asking for more than golden heart awards.

Recent qualitative research has attempted to give a voice to children who care: it has tried to provide child carers with the opportunity to construct their own image, and to define their own needs (see Aldridge and Becker, 1993a). This is in part both the method, and epistemology of qualitative research: to embrace the insider view – to report from the perspective of those studied, to be concerned with process rather than merely social structure (Bryman, 1988). When given that opportunity to speak, to be reported and to be heard, child carers see themselves as key providers of care as well as children with special needs. Many child carers want to be listened to as children *and* as carers. The development of services for child carers, and a policy agenda, will need to take account of this essential duality in their function, experience and needs.

It will also have to take account of the need to protect child carers, and their loved ones, from themselves and from each other. The impact areas of caring on children have much in common with the impact of other forms of child abuse and neglect: low personal esteem, lost childhood, growing up before time, insecurity and instability within family life, impaired psycho-social development, poor educational achievement, silence and secrets, few friendships, few opportunities. Further research also reveals that child carers very often experience tight parental control from the person they care for. Additionally, the parents of child carers often fail to recognise that their child – their carer – has specific needs as a child, as well as a carer (Aldridge and Becker, 1994).

A RIGHTS BASED APPROACH

A World Health Organisation (WHO) study (1982) identified four categories of need in relation to children's development: the need for love and security; the need for new experience; praise and recognition; and the need gradually to extend their responsibilities in the family environment. The research reported above reveals that most, if not all of these needs are often undermined by the caring experience.

The *gradual* extension of responsibilities among children bears little relation to the actual experience of most children who care. The WHO study suggested that such responsibilities should start with very simple personal routines. Child carers' routines on the other hand were often of a very demanding and intimate nature. Their introduction to adulthood (whilst still a young child), and to caring, was often unexpected and sometimes violent. Most child carers appear to have little choice in taking on their caring tasks. They are often 'elected' into caring responsibilities and then socialised into the role (Aldridge and Becker, 1993a).

The challenge ahead is to 'ensure the opportunity for optimal flowering of each individual's autonomy' (Doyal and Gough, 1991: 207). Young carers need to be given the recognition, opportunity and support to flower as individuals, children *and* carers. Guidelines or approaches for action, therefore, need to be based upon child carers' own statements of need, upon their own construction of child caring. It is important that adults, and paid professionals in particular, do not impose their own ideals concerning child carers' best interests. A starting point when considering the way forward is to acknowledge the unique situation of each child carer, so that any assessment of their needs is made on an individual basis. What is right for one child carer might not be right for another.

Furthermore, any guidelines for service delivery must inevitably be based on philosophical and pragmatic principles. These include the recognition and observation of children's rights, practical policy recommendations based upon these rights, and pragmatic considerations in relation to professional intervention and service arrangements. Alderson (1992: 156) has suggested that 're-thinking childhood in terms of rights opens the way for children to be consulted more fully in defining their interests'.

In the remainder of this chapter we outline some of the general principles that might serve to guide the development of specific responses and services to children who care. The framework we suggest is based upon the understanding that children who care are both children and carers, and have rights as such. We wholly accept, indeed much of this chapter has highlighted, the tensions inherent in being a child and in being a carer at the same time. Nonetheless, the child carers in our studies wanted to hold on to both of these worlds. What they wanted from others, including paid professionals, was for their contribution to be acknowledged, recognised and valued, and for some help in the performance of daily routine chores and intimate personal tasks. No child carer was asking to be 'taken away' from the caring role, nor were they asking for their loved one to be taken away. What they were asking for was someone to talk to (who would listen and understand) and for a little help now and then.

It is difficult to frame a set of guidelines or recommendations that rest comfortably between the contradictions and tensions inherent in being a child *and* a carer. A starting point, however, is to identify a set of rights that can form the bedrock from which more detailed and specific guidelines, recommendations or approaches can be developed. These rights are tantamount to a statement of principle. We believe that child carers, as children and as carers, have:

- the right to self-determination and choice (to be children, carers or both)
- the right to be recognised and treated separately from the care receiver
- the right to be heard, listened to and believed
- the right to privacy and respect
- the right to play, recreation and leisure
- the right to education
- the right to health and social care services specific to their needs
- the right to practical help and support, including respite care
- the right to protection from physical and psychological harm (including the right to protection from injury caused by lifting etc.)
- the right to be consulted and be fully involved in discussions about decisions which affect their lives and the lives of their families
- the right to information and advice on matters that concern them and their families (including benefits and services, medical information etc.)
- the right to access to trained individuals and agencies who can deliver information and advice with appropriate expertise, in confidence
- the right to independent and confidential representation and advocacy, including befriending or 'buddying'
- the right to a full assessment of their needs, strengths and weaknesses, including full recognition of racial, cultural and religious needs
- the right to appeal and complaints procedures that work
- the right to stop caring.

NEEDS AND SERVICES

Moving beyond this statement of rights, to consider more specific service provision and professional interventions, requires us to consider a number of other factors and issues. However, a general 'test' for any service development or provision will be the extent to which it measures up against – indeed promotes – the set of rights identified above.

Child carers' lives, both as carers and as children, are fraught with anxiety, stress and uncertainty. As a consequence of the time they have to give to caring, their living conditions are often painful and distressing and their futures bleak. Child carers need to be given the recognition, opportunity and support to develop as individuals and as children, but they must also be able to make their own decisions about caring – whether to continue caring, whether to accept services and outside support when appropriately offered, or whether to stop physically caring for their parent.

Clearly such issues are embedded in the notion of children's rights and are tied up with the boundaries demarcating acceptable familial responsibility and accountability. Any guidelines or approaches for action should be based on the clear expression of those rights and child carers' own constructions of need. These needs – especially for services – are modest. All the child carers in our studies said that what they needed most was 'someone to talk to', someone who would befriend them, understand their circumstances, empathise and represent them without further threat of a 'cascade of intervention' or separation from their families. The fear must be removed from provision and support – the fear of isolation, uncertainty and punishment.

Child carers also said they needed information and advice. At present, many are not receiving the information which is crucial to their day-to-day quality of life, and which could give them the opportunity to better express their own needs in terms of services. The provision of information need not be a severe burden on resources and finances. The development of 'resource and information packs' for young carers and their families could provide much of the information – on advice and counselling agencies, benefits, medical information or 'helplines' etc. – that is needed.

The development of such resources, and other new services or arrangements, will need to take full account of the racial, cultural and religious needs of child carers and their families, as our statement of rights reminds us. But they will also have to take account of educational ability and literacy. Some child carers cannot read or write. They will need access to information that is not in written form.

The development of befriending and information services may indeed provide for some of the child carers' most pressing needs. But unless the wider issues concerned with the position of child carers in society are addressed, children will continue to be punished and abused for caring. Some of these issues are fundamental. For example, at what age should it be acceptable for a person (child) to take *responsibility* for the care of their parent, for toileting them, for showering them or for dispensing medications? At what age should a child be *accountable* for this care? Will the age for responsibility and accountability depend on the sex of the child and the sex of the parent, or the 'ability' or 'maturity' of the child or – like the legal age for marriage, sexual relations, the vote – will it be fixed for all? These questions need answers, then actions.

At a practical level child carers' needs must be included in future community care plans. With the implementation of the National Health Service and Community Care Act, social services now play the lead role in assessing the needs of carers and users. It is therefore imperative that effective training and assessment procedures are established to ensure child carers are both identified and assessed. Where children are the primary carers, this should automatically trigger a full assessment of their needs. These assessments ought to be conducted jointly by professionals concerned with community care and children's needs. This way, the needs of child carers both as children, and as carers, can be taken into account. It will be the responsibility of the professionals concerned to work towards reconciling the contradictions between the roles, and the service needs, of children who care.

Service planners and providers will have to be made more aware, to be trained, sensitive and pro-active – rather than just responding to crises as they arise. It will also require far better inter-agency and inter-professional communication. Young carers have often fallen into the gaps between social services and education, and between health and social care. Agencies need to work together for children who care, rather than against them. The critical question for professionals must be: how can child carers be enabled to care, and be protected in their child and caring roles, without their family life being torn apart by heavy-handed child protection procedures? The answer is to be found by listening to the stories of children who care, and respecting their right to be both children and carers.

REFERENCES

Alderson, P. (1992) 'Rights of children and young people', in A. Coote (ed.) *The Welfare of Citizens: Developing New Social Rights*, London: Rivers Oram Press.
Aldridge, J. and Becker, S. (1993a) *Children Who Care: Inside the World of Young Carers*, Department of Social Sciences: Loughborough University.
—— (1993b) 'Children as carers', *Archives of Disease in Childhood*, 69: 459–62.
—— (1993c) 'Punishing children for caring', *Children and Society*, 7(4): 277–88.
—— (1993d) 'Excluding children who care', *Benefits*, 7: 22–4.
—— (1994) *My Child, My Carer: The Parents' Perspective*, Department of Social Sciences: Loughborough University.
Bilsborrow, S. (1992) *'You Grow Up Fast as Well . . .' Young Carers on Merseyside*, London: Barnardos.
Bryman, A. (1988) *Quantity and Quality in Social Research*, London: Unwin Hyman.
Carers National Association (1992) *Young Carers Link*, March.
Children's Legal Centre (1992) 'A children's manifesto', *Childright*, March.
Department of Health (1989) *Caring for People: Community Care in the Next Decade and Beyond*, London: HMSO.
—— (1990) *Caring for People: Policy Guidance*, London: HMSO.
—— (1991) *The Children Act 1989 Guidance and Regulations*, London: HMSO.
Dickens, C. (1857) *Little Dorrit*, reprinted 1985, Harmondsworth: Penguin.
Doyal, L. and Gough, I. (1991) *A Theory of Human Need*, London: Macmillan.
Fallon, K. (1990) 'An involuntary workforce', *Community Care*, 4 January.
Gavin, J. (1991) *I Want to be an Angel*, London: Mamouth.
Lewis, J. and Meredith, B. (1988) *Daughters who Care*, London: Routledge.
McLaughlin, M. M. (1974) 'Survivors and surrogates', in L. de Mause (ed.) *The History of Childhood*, London: Souvenir Press.
Meredith, H. (1991) 'Young carers: The unacceptable face of community care', *Social Work and Social Sciences Review*, 3: 47–51.
—— (1992) 'Supporting the young carer', *Community Outlook*, May: 15–17.
O'Neill, A. (1988) *Young Carers: The Tameside Research*, Tameside Metropolitan Borough Council.
Office of Population Censuses and Surveys (OPCS) (1992) *General Household Survey of Carers*, London: HMSO.
Page, R. (1988) *Report on the Initial Survey Investigating the Number of Young Carers in Sandwell Secondary Schools*, Sandwell Metropolitan Borough Council.
World Health Organisation (1982) *Manuals on Child Mental Health and Psychosocial Development*, Geneva: WHO.

Chapter 10

Children's rights in their early years
From plaiting fog to knitting treacle

Gillian Alexander

British public authorities have traditionally viewed young children in negative terms and labelled them variously as 'under 5s' or 'under 8s'; both phrases covertly signal, 'not yet old enough'. Young children in the UK have proved an awkward group for policy makers: difficult to categorise, difficult to provide services for, and difficult to listen to. They have been the subject of much debate, but there has been little consensus about what constitutes the 'best interests' of such children. The idea that young children might claim the right to be involved in decision-making has largely been rejected. The concept of children under 8 being rights-holders constitutes a fundamental challenge to a value system which, at root, believes that children should be seen and not heard. Government, locally and centrally, has chosen the easy option. Publicly-provided services for children in their early years are scanty, stigmatised and tokenistic. They are under-resourced, low-status and discretionary. Constantly vulnerable to funding cuts, early years services in the UK are a shocking reflection of the status and value placed upon young children and those who work with them.

During the late 1980s and early 1990s, however, approximately 20 local authorities have established early years services to unify and coordinate services for children in their early years. The Children Act 1989 gave local authorities increased responsibilities for regulating services for children under 8 and provided a legislative framework for increasing the quality and quantity of services more attuned to the needs of children, parents and the wider community.

This chapter is written from the perspective of an operational manager with overall responsibility for establishing an early years service within the Metropolitan Council of Kirklees in West Yorkshire. My argument is that the fragmented and marginalised state of early years services reflects the failure to organise them around the needs and rights of the whole child. Early years services have, instead, been developed to service broader economic needs and a range of segregated professional interests. Consequently, any attempt to unify early years services is likely to prove an uphill struggle. As a colleague at Kirklees commented, it is rather akin to moving from plaiting fog (an activity over which the manager has very little control) to knitting treacle – a situation where the manager has one large sticky mess in her lap. The theme of this chapter is that the development of a unified and seamless garment of early years services will only be achieved if the promotion of children's rights becomes a guiding principle. This chapter examines some of the challenges, opportunities and practical implications of developing early years services within a children's rights framework.

THROUGH GLASS DARKLY: A HISTORICAL PERSPECTIVE

The development of services for younger children has been an *ad hoc* and spasmodic affair, rarely informed by a clear view of children as people or as consumers of those services. The dominant theme in the development of services has been that children should be considered as mere objects rather than subjects: objects in the way of women's participation in the labour market; objects of professional debate about their needs and best interests.

Barriers to women's economic participation

The two major periods of expansion in services for younger children coincided with the two world wars which created a pressing need for women to enter the labour market (Cohen, 1988; Cohen and Fraser, 1991; Penn and Riley, 1992). During the First World War 108 day nurseries were built very rapidly across England and Wales, but were dismantled shortly after its conclusion. The advent of the Second World War, witnessed a policy reversal with the number of day nurseries increasing from 14 in 1940 to 1345 in 1943. More recently the so-called 'demographic time-bomb' and the longer-term shift in the workforce from manufacturing to service industries, has again prompted the need for women's participation in the labour market, with the consequent need for childcare services. The Government White Paper 'Employment into the 1990s', argued the case in these terms:

> Employers cannot expect to recruit as many young people, especially well qualified young people as they have in the past. They will have to tap new services for their recruits . . . employers must recognise that women can no longer be treated as second class workers. They will need women employees, and must recognise both their career ambitions and domestic responsibilities.
>
> (HMSO, 1990: 94)

Current government policy allocates the costs of childcare to employees and parents. Unlike the wartime expansion, recent growth in childcare services has benefitted only a small minority of working women and has excluded the mass of women working in low paid, unskilled, part-time jobs (see Penn and Riley, 1992). An important development during the 1980s and 1990s has been the development of an equal opportunities for women lobby which has linked the need for childcare provision to the argument for women's rights to participate in the labour market on equal terms with men (Cohen, 1988).

The best interest of the child

Children have been the subject of heated professional debate about their needs and best interests throughout the history of early years services; the manifest content of the debate has often reflected economic circumstances. During periods of 'boom', when women's participation in the labour market has been a necessity, arguments in favour of day nurseries as being educationally, physically and socially good for children have enjoyed prominence. During periods of 'slump', however, the dominant view has been that home is the best place for the pre-school child except where parental inadequacy (usually maternal) required special services. This latter view, legitimised by the psychoanalytical theories of maternal deprivation propounded by Bowlby, asserted that mothers of young children should not go out to work; Tizzard suggests persuasively that the theory is not supported by research evidence and simply represents a response to market pressures. But these views legitimated the policy that publicly-funded full-time daycare services for children should be developed only on the grounds of welfare, and prompted a perception of public sector daycare as a stigmatised, ghettoised welfare service for children in need.

The other major characteristic of early years services in the UK has been a division between those services which have been developed in response to the care needs of children, and those which have been developed for educational purposes. In the 1970s the Plowden report established educational provision as the main focus of early years services in the public sector. Education was seen as a way of rescuing society's helplessness and compensating for social disadvantage. Between 1966–87 the number of children receiving some form of pre-school provision provided by local authorities increased from 15 per cent to 47.6 per cent. A substantial part of this expansion however was created by converting full-time places into part-time places and by increasing the number of under 5s in reception classes (Drummond, 1989). During this same period there was also a major increase in the number of playgroups, providing community-run pre-school provision for young children. Part-time nursery education in no way caters for the care needs of the child, and the educational model of 2½ hour sessions per day creates major difficulties for parents and employees. This division between care and education has created two significant difficulties. First, a publicly-funded daycare system which provides for children on the grounds of welfare alone and a part-time nursery education system which provides for less than 50 per cent of the under 5s population, has created a number of service gaps filled on an *ad hoc* basis by expensive private-sector provision and the voluntary sector. Second, the division between care and education has led to a situation where children routed through daycare provision are missing the benefits of early years education.

THE CONTEMPORARY CONTEXT

The provision of services for children in their early years has been characterised to date by conflicting ideologies, low priority, and lack of direction and co-ordination at central government level. Perhaps unsurprisingly, this has resulted in a fragmentation of services at local level. Within local government, services are typically the speciality of three front-line service departments: education, social services and leisure. Other departments – for example economic development and personnel – may also be involved in issues about provision. Additionally public agencies, external to the local authority, may be involved in action on childcare e.g. Training and Enterprise Councils and a whole array of voluntary and community organisations are involved in developing models of work with children and plugging gaps in service delivery at local level. Each of these service departments and agencies holds different values concerning the needs of young children and their parents, which are expressed in a distinctive departmental philosophy and language. The professionals within those departments are governed by different professional boundaries and interests, career patterns, employment conditions, training structures and pay. Additionally each local authority service department is covered by its own statutory responsibilities and legislative requirements, and may well have its own separate grant aid criteria, some services overlap – particularly in the area of playschemes and out-of-school clubs.

The overall effect has been divisive. The one factor which unifies services across this diversity of departments and agencies is low status. Early years services are given a low priority by every department. Staff are likely to be women and at the bottom of the service in terms of pay and recognition. This low priority generates predictable outcomes. Early years services are generally characterised by:

Fragmentation and division: Services for young children are compartmentalised and patchy. This has led to instability and inefficient use of already inadequate resources. The rigid departmentalism of services has created divisions and debate. Nursery education makes claims for the child-centredness of their approach and the need for teaching professionals to support children's early learning. Playgroups make claims for parental participation and argue for the cost effectiveness of the early admission of children into reception class. These are, of course, services targeted at 3- and 4-year-olds and separate the needs of the child from the needs of the parent. None cater for the needs of the working parents, but it is often seriously suggested that parents may put their own needs i.e. the need to work, above the perceived needs of the child (as judged by the professionals). This division is reinforced by the training routes available to early years workers. The education lobby regard nursery teachers as indispensable to the promotion of good services, while social services and the private sector tend to regard teachers as a luxury and consider that Nursery Nurse Examining Board (NNEB) trained staff (who are cheaper to employ) are sufficient to provide for the education of children. Playgroups consider that short Pre-School Play Group Association (PPA) courses are sufficient, while childminders are least likely to have any training at all. This rigid compartmentalisation inevitably restricts the flexible development of services and reinforces professionalism at the expense of the client. It also leads to a lack of coordination and a tendency to resist change.

Low status: Recent legislation has confirmed the non-statutory status of early years services. The 1980 Education Act removed any obligation from LEAs to provide nursery education and emphasised the discretionary nature of the service. The 1993 Education Act makes no changes to this. The Children Act 1989 only requires local authorities to provide daycare services for children in need. This has largely been defined by local authorities as children in need of protective services and disabled children.

Lack of investment: Early years provision has suffered from lack of resources. Services for young children in the UK are frequently poorly accommodated, poorly staffed and poorly equipped. As a non-statutory service, early years provision is vulnerable to funding cuts and increasingly tighter resource allocation has been targeted on priority groups.

Low levels of provision: As an inevitable consequence of low status and lack of investment, the UK has some of the lowest levels of publicly-funded childcare services in Europe. We have: the lowest percentage (2 per cent) of places for under-3s in publicly-funded childcare services as a percentage of all children in that age group; the lowest proportion (with Portugal) of publicly-supported provision for children between 3 and compulsory school-age; less than 0.5 per cent of out-of-school hours care for school-age children.

Unequal access: The *ad hoc* nature of early years service development has resulted in unequal access to services. Access is largely influenced by issues of geography, levels of political support, social class and ethnic origin. Levels of nursery education provided by local authorities range from 8 per cent to 86 per cent. A survey conducted by Osborne and Millbank (1987) reported substantial social inequality in access to pre-school provision. Of the most disadvantaged in their study, 46 per cent had received no form of pre-school education, compared with 10 per cent of the least disadvantaged. Osborne and Millbank also found that 46 per cent of Indian and Pakistani children and 35 per cent of Afro Caribbean children had no pre-school experience, compared with 28 per cent of white European children. Black and ethnic minority children were much more likely to be placed in day nurseries than white children, with Moss (1988) reporting that nearly 14 per cent of all children in day nurseries were from ethnic minority groups.

PUTTING CHILDREN FIRST: A LOCAL AUTHORITY RESPONSE

The lack of coherent, well-resourced and responsive services for young children in the UK is the inevitable result of the lack of a national strategy for young children. It is also the result of a failure to develop services on the basis of the needs and rights of the *whole* child. Each competing service has developed models of provision which meet different aspects of need as perceived by professionals. As a consequence children and families have become compartmentalised and slotted into models which, it could be argued, serve the best interests of service providers rather than the interests of the child. As a consequence children in daycare do not gain access to the same degree of nursery education as their peers in a nursery class. Working parents face a dilemma when their children reach the age when they could attend a nursery class. Do they move them and make complicated care arrangements to suit the 2.5 hour session, or do they leave them in a care setting and run the risk that they miss out on a pre-school education?

Current arguments in favour of early years services have drawn upon a wide range of guidance. Arguments have been made linking the centrality of early years services to economic development, crime prevention, the prevention of teenage pregnancies and the promotion of equal opportunities. Viewed from these perspectives children are seen as a problem to be solved. It is important to remember, however, that the incoherent development of young children's services has been a direct result of the fact that the development of childcare services has been prompted by the need for women's participation in the labour market. The major impetus for childcare services during the 1980s originated from the debate about equal opportunities for women. Without marginalising the importance of this argument, it is important to emphasise the rights of children. It is important to recognise that a coordinated approach to developing young children's services must be underpinned by a commitment to children's rights in the early years and the belief that children benefit from the best that we can provide rather than the least we can tolerate. This will require a radical shift in the current organisation and delivery of children's services. It will require organising services and models of provision which focus on the needs and rights of the whole child, the responsibilities of parents (male and female) and the support needs of parents and communities in promoting the best interests and welfare of their children. The concept of young children as rights-holders has been a difficult one for adults to grasp. Fundamentally it requires an attitude shift from viewing children as objects to viewing children as consumers and citizens with rights to quality services which ensure their survival and development, rights to protection and rights to participate in decision-making.

Clearly significant change in the organisation of young children's services at a national level will be dependent upon a national childcare strategy with clearly stated goals and objectives and a targeted public investment programme which would fund improvements in quality and an expansion in the quantity of provision. Ultimately, if the UK is to provide the resources our children so richly deserve, and put us in line with our European partners, a lead government department responsible for all services for children must be established (see chapter 7). Despite the absence of a committed central government, there are measures which local authorities can take to generate change at a local level.

Unifying early years services – the theory

Ensuring that services for young children meet the needs of children and parents will require a reappraisal of existing local authority provision and the development of a new vision of services for young children. Local authorities must ensure that services are organised and delivered effectively. This means breaking down traditional departmental barriers and developing shared objectives. This requires structural change. But fundamentally, it requires a clearly articulated statement of goals and values to govern the direction of services which seek to reflect and enhance the rights of children.

Goals and values

A new direction for early years services within the UK must be underpinned by a clear statement of goals and values. Five seem central.

- *Children come first*: Every child has a right to depend upon adults to provide the conditions which enable them to reach their full potential. We all bear responsibility for all our children and it is essential that parents and carers should receive the necessary support to ensure their children achieve the best possible start in life.
- *Children have a right to be recognised as people with views and interests.* They have a right to be listened to and to participate in decision-making on issues which affect their lives.
- *Children should have the opportunity to be part of a family and community*, to experience a stable learning and caring environment which enhances their esteem as individuals, their dignity and autonomy, self-confidence and enthusiasm for learning, and respect for others and which ensures they are free from discrimination.
- *Parents, carers and communities need to be supported in promoting the interests and welfare of their children.* Children need strong adults upon whom they can depend to provide love, security and the financial resources to ensure they access an adequate standard of living. Early years services must be rooted in local community infrastructures and provide real choices for families, particularly those living on low incomes.
- *Children have a right to safe play environments* which provide a whole range of opportunities for autonomy, social development and recreational activity. Children and families also have a right to participate in the services provided by the retail, cultural and tourist sectors.

Structural and management issues

The Children Act 1989 recognises the fundamental role local authorities have to play in planning, coordinating and reviewing service provision for young children. If local authorities are to have a meaningful impact on the delivery of services at a local level however, a number of areas will need to be addressed:

- *A unified structure and strategic planning.* It is important that local authorities give political commitment to unifying early years services by establishing member committees to deal corporately with services for young children. The committee should have an influence on policy making and have delegated powers on separate budgetary provision for a unified service. This would increase local authorities' ability to act as a strategic planner of services.
- *Integration.* New models of provision need to be developed which demonstrate ways of meeting the care, education and play needs of children on an integrated basis whatever the setting – whether it be group-based provision for under 5s, out-of-school provision for 5–12-year-olds or childminder provision.
- *Affordability.* Current central government policy places the responsibility to pay for childcare on employers and parents. Local authorities, however, can consider ways of re-modelling existing provision to create access for low income families and develop strategies for local authority childcare subsidy.
- *Quality.* Local authorities have a key role in supporting quality developments both through their statutory duties to inspect and register provision and through the provision of training, advice and consultancy. It is also important for local authorities to facilitate a debate on issues concerning quality to promote a shared ownership and consensus. A strategic approach to quality assurance in the early years will involve integrating registration, inspection, training, advice and support.
- *Quantity.* Local authorities are planners and developers and should facilitate the expansion of childcare provision in response to local needs. In the current climate however, local authorities cannot be the sole funders of expanding provision. Inevitably expansion will be dependent upon the extent to which a local authority can attract further investment and external funding. It is vital, however, that local authorities should play the major role in channelling investment within a strategic framework. A recent Department of Employment initiative which targeted investment in childcare via the Training and Enterprise Councils, could be a worrying and fragmentary trend.
- *Resources.* Undoubtedly improvements in early years services can be made by the reorganisation of existing council resources. But significant action on the quality, quantity and affordability of provision will require additional resources. Clearly this is problematic in the current context of local government in the UK.
- *Partnership working.* Local authorities are not the only providers of services for young children. There is a wide and diverse range of interest groups in the early years field. The challenge is to provide a framework for working in

partnership which draws on the strengths of the wide range of agencies and enables coordination, cooperation and meaningful consultation. Additionally, it is important to recognise the important role parents play in supporting their children's early learning. Parents are the prime educators of their children. It is important to de-professionalise early years education and recognise that learning with parents at the levels of both policy and practice will be central to the effective development of early years services.

- *Access and choice for parents*. Local authorities are information holders and must provide information about service provision to enable parents to make meaningful choices concerning the needs of their children.
- *Training*. Developing integrated models of service delivery will involve the creation of an integrated approach to early years training for all early years workers. Inevitably this will require a unified and coherent qualification system which would allow greater mobility and progression within the various professional roles relating to children. In the short term however, local authorities as providers and enablers of training can promote the integration of in-service training, and coordinate the implementation of NVQ assessments in childcare, education and playwork.
- *Listening to children*. Opportunities need to be developed to ensure service providers and regulators listen to children's views about the nature and direction of services.

The Kirklees Early Years Service – theory into practice

A handful of local authorities including Southwark, Leeds, Lewisham and my own authority, Kirklees, have recently established unified early years services. These services are in the initial stages of development but it is worth considering some of the early lessons.

In keeping with many early years services the development of the Kirklees Early Years Service (KEYS) was politically initiated and actively promoted by members. The rationale for the formation of a unified service was described by a member in the following terms:

> At the moment childcare and related services are provided through the Social Services, Education, Personnel, the Rolling Programme and Leisure Services. The services tend to be only a small part of the overall service provided by the particular departments and as a consequence, they may not be a service priority. There is no effective way of co-ordinating what is provided across departments and, as a result, although individuals are working well, the services are not always provided in the most effective, positive way.
>
> (Smith, 1991)

The outcome has been the formation of a single unit of management responsible for the unification, coordination and development across the authority. A joint Social Services and Education Childcare Sub-Committee oversees the service, makes policy decisions and has delegated responsibility for a ring fenced budget. The committee has been delegated all statutory duties under the Children Act 1989 with respect to daycare facilities for children under 8, including duties to inspect and register all facilities and to carry out the Section 19 triennial review of children's services.

The service has the following key objectives: to provide a framework for coordinating and managing quality under 8s provision within Kirklees; to increase the quantity, quality and choices of affordable daycare and early years education for children under 8 years of age; to manage and coordinate developments in existing local authority provision to establish quality standards of care and education in under 8s services and make coordinated responses to need; to encourage, advise and assist providers to work within a coordinated framework to meet the council's objectives. Former LEA nursery schools and social services day nurseries have been transferred into the service. The key functions undertaken by the service are outlined in Figure 10.1: Kirklees had to choose between social services and education as the lead service department in which to locate the early years service. The eventual choice was education which is generally viewed as a universal, non-stigmatised service which has a greater resource potential.

Progress to date has been significant and shares much in common with developments in early years structures in other local authorities. Developments include:

- attracting funding from the European Regional Development Fund to establish two new age-integrated care and education centres to provide childcare for 0–12-year-olds
- developing a 'quality assurance' scheme which links inspection and registration with advice, support consultancy and training; producing a directory of child-friendly services which encourages providers in the retail, leisure, cultural and public sectors to develop inclusive child-friendly facilities
- establishing an Early Years Training Strategy which provides an integrated training programme for *all* under 8s workers and links with NVQ standards and higher education accreditation
- launching a childcare database linking into local access points which enable parents to gain easy access to childcare information
- raising the profile of childminders as key childcare professionals; channelling European Social Fund investment into a new childcare training programme in areas of disadvantage
- remodelling existing service provision within the service to expand the availability of low-cost daycare for families on low income
- piloting ways of enabling early years providers to work together at a local community level to support children's learning in whatever setting they are in e.g. childminder, at home, nursery class, day nursery, private nursery
- establishing Early Years Forums to encourage cooperation, collaboration and consultation on a Kirklees-wide basis and at a local community level

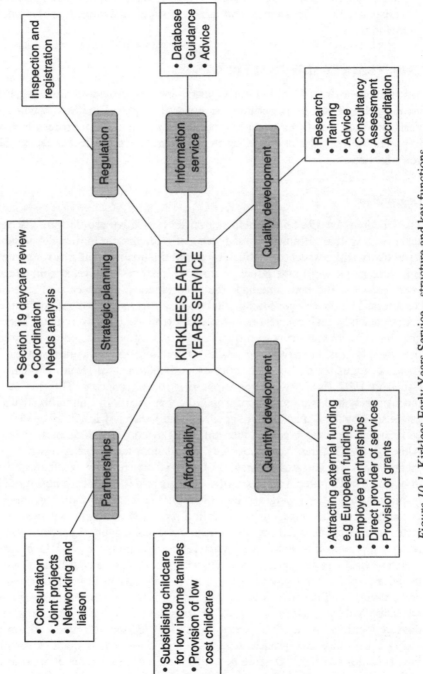

Figure 10.1 Kirklees Early Years Service – structure and key functions

- subsidising low cost childcare for low income families; developing methods of listening to children and parents as part of the annual inspection of childcare facilities.

CONSTRAINTS AND CHALLENGES

The establishment of unified early years services provide a framework for creating change and an opportunity to break through the impasse which early years provision has faced to date. But change is a long-term process and it is important to recognise at the outset the constraints and challenges facing early years services.

Legislation

The Children Act 1989 has provided a raised legislative profile for early years services as well as a framework and terms of reference for unified departments, particularly with respect to establishing minimum quality standards for services. But three major legitative issues continue to restrict the development of early years services. The first is perhaps the most obvious; the absence of sufficient resources. The provision of quality services is expensive, but the Act was not accompanied by major increases in resources from central government. There is growing concern that the cost of quality will inevitably be passed on to parents. Increasingly concerns are being raised by parents and providers about quality standards regulated by Local Authorities. A Department of Health circular was issued in 1992 (LAC (93)1) in response to these concerns. This has led to inconsistency and ambiguity concerning the framework of minimum standards established by the Act and lack of consensus about what is meant by quality.

A second difficulty concerns the conflicting outcomes of different legislation. Although the Children Act encourages local authorities to break down departmental divisions in the early years field, the legislative framework enhances those divisions. The Children Act stresses the strategic role which local authorities play in planning and developing services (Section 19), but education legislation is encouraging the 'atomisation' of education provision through grant-maintained status and local management of schools. As a non-statutory service, nursery education provision is increasingly vulnerable to funding cuts, and the extent to which an LEA can strategically plan nursery education on a coordinated basis is threatened. Additionally, separate legislation requires separate inspection procedures and criteria. The Education Reform Act 1988 governs the inspection of nursery education and the Children Act 1989 governs the inspection and registration of daycare facilities. As a consequence there is no legislative framework for enabling a coordinated approach to ratios, curriculum development or environmental health standards. Despite best efforts to ensure a universal approach to children's services, children technically have different legislative rights and entitlements with respect to the setting in which they are placed.

Third, the extent to which dominant ideology conflicts with the Children Act 1989 guidance within the judicial system was clearly evidenced in the now famous 'Sutton case'. Department of Health guidance clearly states that corporal punishment should not be used by any registered carer (the Children Act, 1989 Guidance and Regulations Volume 2, p. 36). However when the London Borough of Sutton refused to register a childminder who refused to undertake not to use corporal punishment Judge Wilson upheld the decision of Magistrates on appeal, stating that parents can delegate their responsibilities to others including smacking. This has called into question the extent to which the Act provides a framework for promoting the best interests of the child.

Changes in local government

Central government, throughout the 1980s, introduced wide-ranging legislation to restructure local government and restrain local authority expenditure. The fragmentation of local government has been the major theme of central government reform. There has been an increased sharing of responsibilities and the delivery of services with a range of other agencies and institutions. A number of government appointed quangos e.g. Training and Enterprise Councils have been established as part of this trend.

Within this environment, the early years services are under increasing pressure. There is growing concern that the recent Education Act 1993 will have a substantial impact on the resources available for nursery education. Traditionally those LEAs committed to nursery education have spent above their central government allocation through the Standard Spending Assessment for nursery education. As LEAs face increasing pressure to resist funding cuts to compulsory education however, funding for non-compulsory nursery education will face increasing pressure.

The resource constraints facing local authorities mitigate against the development of unified early years services. Consequently, the extent to which local authorities can have a major impact on the quality, quantity and affordability of early years services will be limited. It is also clear, however, that the very existence of an early years service will ensure that a coordinated response to resisting draconian budget cuts is made possible.

Professional and departmental boundaries

Breaking down professional and departmental boundaries which have developed over decades will take time, and will require more than a simple transfer of personnel into a new structure. Two issues are of relevance here. First, early years services lack 'clout'. They are often placed within large lead departments (usually education or social services) but, without sufficient 'clout', the service can be marginalised and overshadowed by the dominating concerns of the lead department.

Second, problems arise from the diversity of workers' career patterns, pay and conditions. The principal occupations involved in early years service provision are teachers, social workers, nursery nurses, nursery assistants, and playworkers. Their pay and conditions of service are split between the three main local government bodies for teachers, administrative, professional, technical and clerical, and manual workers. The training avenues have developed on an *ad hoc* basis and there is little flexibility to allow transfer and progression through related occupations. These discontinuities are major constraints in delivering a comprehensive service to young children. Staff may subscribe to a common philosophy regarding the development of a unified service, but in principle change will be resisted so long as staff feel their terms and conditions of service are under threat. This is a difficulty facing all early years services in the UK and will require a joint approach across local authorities at a national level to consider strategies for change.

Practice issues

Developing skills in listening to children and enabling them to participate in decision-making, is an area of considerable difficulty for practitioners. A major challenge for early years services is to develop the skills, mechanisms and commitment to ensure that children have a voice. There are few practice examples to draw on in the early years field. In Glasgow a project focusing on 'philosophy for the under 5s' has considered strategies for developing children's decision-making skills, and in Denmark a range of initiatives are in place which aim to encourage children's participation in decision-making, particularly in out-of-school facilities. It is clear, however, that children are key consumers of services and ought to be consulted and enabled to participate. Out-of-school provision is particularly relevant here, since traditionally children have been the major decision-makers regarding how they spend their leisure-time after school hours. Annual inspections of provision provide additional opportunities for children's voices to be heard. Developing work in this area is an important challenge if we are to enable children to move from being passive recipients of services – objects in a system – to consumers and citizens with rights.

BUILDING BLOCKS FOR THE FUTURE?

It is always difficult to raise your head above the day-to-day cut and thrust of budgetary and legislative contraints, competing ideologies and organisational bureaucracies, to catch a glimpse of what the future might look like. But there is undoubtedly a climate of change in the UK, and early years issues are once again inked clearly on the agenda. There is a growing consensus about the importance of early years education and the need for childcare services. The reasons underlying this consensus are mixed. The need for childcare services has become a priority because of the need for women to participate in the labour market.

Arguments can also be heard which emphasise the importance of early years education in the development of 'good citizens' – citizens who do not engage in criminal activities, who become productive workers, and who are unlikely to become single parents. But if history is not to repeat itself, it is important to re-define this agenda, to separate the needs of the economy from the needs and rights of children, and to promote the concept of young children as citizens with rights and entitlements. Children have a right to care and education services in their early years which ensure their parents are able to provide an adequate standard of living *and* that they benefit from educational support. Children have a right to play in a safe and caring environment. Children have a right to be listened to and to participate in decision-making on issues which affect their lives. This must include involvement in decisions concerning their education, care and play arrangements as well as rights within the judicial system. A redefinition of the early years agenda will only be possible if local authorities take the initiative. This will involve developing services which start with the interests of the child – rather than the best interests of services and professionals – and organising services in a way which will recognise the mutuality of interests between children and parents. It must involve breaking down traditional barriers between care, education and recreation and developing new integrated models which are more attuned to the needs of parents, families and communities. New united early years services are an important step forward. Constrained as they are by conflicting legislation and increasing resource constraints, they provide an opportunity to demonstrate different ways of providing early years services, and therefore can begin to raise expectations of the level of service provision children deserve in their early years. If they are not to fall by the wayside, it is vitally important that early years services resist the temptation to promote children as objects to be removed, or problems to be solved; nor must they present children as barriers to economic recovery or as the single parents and criminals of the future. The underpinning rationale for early years services must be that children are citizens and rights-holders and that their interests and rights can only be met by a seamless robe of services. It is crucial to move on from plaiting fog to knitting treacle – and much further beyond even that!

REFERENCES

Cohen, B. (1988) *Caring for Children: Services and Policies for Childcare and Equal Opportunities in the United Kingdom*, Commission of the European Communities.

Cohen, B. and Fraser, F.W. (1991) *Childcare in a Modern Welfare System, Towards a New National Policy*, Institute for Public Policy Research: London.

Drummond, M.J. (1989) 'Early Years Education: Contemporary Challenges' in C.W. Deforges (ed.) *Early Childhood Education* British Journal of Educational Psychology, Monograph Series Number 4.

Government White Paper (1990) *Employment in the 1990s* HMSO: London.

Moss, P. (1989) *Childcare and Equality of Opportunity*, Report of the European Childcare Network.

Osborne, A.F. and Millbank, J. (1987) *The Effects of Early Childhood Education*, Clarendon Press: Oxford.

Penn, H. and Riley, K. (1992) *Managing Services for the Under Fives*, Longman: London.

Pugh, G. (1988) *Services for the Under Fives, Developing a Co-ordinated Approach*, National Children's Bureau: London.

Smith, A. (1991) 'Early Years Services in Kirklees', unpublished paper presented to Kirklees Metropolitian Council.

Tizzard, B. (1986) *The Care of Young Children – Implictions of Recent Research*, Working and Occasional Papers, Thomas Coram Research Unit: London.

Chapter 11

Rights for children who are disabled

Margaret Kennedy

I want to discuss the rights of the disabled child in the context of child protection, since this is an area which I have studied for many years. In considering disabled children's protection requirements, as well as the various ways in which these have been denied, it is best to proceed from an historical perspective with a particular focus on the concepts of 'lives worth living' and 'futility'.

THE HISTORICAL AND IDEOLOGICAL CONTEXT

Many of us know of the Holocaust and the extermination of the Jewish people, but perhaps fewer people are aware of the extermination of the *untermenschen* or 'sub-humans'; the name given to those people who had an inherited or genetic disease or a physical or intellectual impairment. They were not to live. In 1939 Hitler authorised the extermination of *die vernichtung lebensunwerten leben*; 'lives not worthy of living'. Children marked with a plus sign were to die, those with a negative sign could live. All the 'pluses' were ordered to one of twenty-eight institutions including some of Germany's oldest and highly respected hospitals, rapidly equipped with extermination facilities (Morris, 1991). The Nazi euthanasia programme killed an estimated 300,000 disabled people in addition to 6,000,000 Jews (Wolfensberger, 1992).

The legitimation of 'deathmaking'

Some commentators believe this ideological legacy continues in modern times. Wolfensberger for example, has argued that society 'has made an unexplicated but nonetheless real, commitment to the legitimization of practices of all sorts of "deathmaking" of its unwanted devalued classes' (Wolfensberger, 1992: 19). He defines deathmaking as 'any action or pattern of actions which either directly or indirectly bring about or hasten the death of a person or group, thus deathmaking actions range all the way from explicit, overt, and direct killing that may take a long time to exert its effects and may be very difficult to trace, and it can include active participation as well as silent, unobjecting collusion' (Wolfensberger, 1992: 19). Wolfensberger is alarmed by the increasing legal sanction of deathmaking and suggests there may be a growing support among the general population for killing disabled people, as long as this is undertaken 'scientifically'; which usually means the involvement of physicians in medical settings. Such 'death-making' is not uncommon in the UK.

A recent well-known case of 'deathmaking' involved Anthony Bland who was left in a persistent vegetative state (PVS) following the Hillsborough disaster. His parents wished for the withdrawal of nutrition and hydration. The House of Lords declared such withdrawal to be lawful, basing their judgment on an assessment of when life has become 'futile'. The *Oxford Dictionary* defines this as 'useless, ineffectual, vain . . . lacking in purpose', concepts central to the various medical uses of the term (Gillon, 1993: 67). But obvious ethical problems arise when the term 'futile' is applied to treatments which doctors (or even the vast majority of people) may consider to be more harmful than beneficial, *but which in the patient's view might be beneficial*. There is a clash of opinions here concerning what constitutes 'benefit for the patient', but the issue is evidently less about the *meaning* of 'futility' than *whose assessment* of futility should count in a particular case (my emphasis).

For disabled children euthanasia may not be the most significant issue. Undoubtedly, the clearest evidence of societal support for 'deathmaking' derives from shifting attitudes towards abortion. In 1990 an amendment to legislation controlling human embryo research introduced a new time limit of 24 weeks for all abortions except when the foetus was 'seriously handicapped', when the mother's life was at risk, or when there was a risk of permanent injury to the mother if the pregnancy continued. Where a foetus is diagnosed as having a physical or learning disability, termination of the pregnancy is now legal – right up to the moment of birth (Morris, 1991: 67). Those in favour argued that the quality of life of such babies and children was intolerable, that the burdens imposed on their parents was insupportable and that they constituted a high economic and social cost. Lord Habgood, Archbishop of York pointed out that the legislation meant 'seriously handicapped people may be destroyed simply because they are seriously handicapped' (House of Lords official report, 18 October 1990, col. 1049).

As a disabled person, I am predictably appalled by legislation which, had it been enacted when my mother was pregnant, might have meant that I would not have been encouraged to enjoy the right to live because of pressures brought to bear on parents to terminate pregnancy in the event of disability. 'To give ourselves the right to judge someone else's life as not worth living', Morris claims, 'is to enter the same ideological framework as the German physicians in the third Reich' (Morris 1991: 54).

I do not believe I have strayed from child protection issues in the preceding discussion. Child protection rests on the value and respect which is invested in the child. When the child is judged to be of little value or is not respected, services for that child will be less. Hence it is the first prerequisite of child protection to value children; all children.

The Children Act and disabled children

It was unfortunate that the Children Act 1989 placed disabled children into a 'special' category labelled 'children in need'. An essential ingredient in child protection is to empower children to enable them to value themselves; perpetrators of child abuse tell us that it is the devalued child they target (Conte, 1989). Legislative perceptions that disabled children are less capable and require placing in a distinctive category ('children in need'), transmits negative messages to society, parents and children; even to abusers. It does not say 'these children are powerful and valuable' but suggests they are weak and incapable of independence; children automatically become 'in need' on diagnosis of impairment. Disabled children have been taught to be good victims (Senn, 1986).

There are also moves to have registers of disabled children – although no other children are registered because of an aspect of their bodily functions! We do not, for example, register children who have fair hair or brown eyes. This might seem a ludicrous comparison at first glance, but I would argue that when such differences are defined and categorised, prejudice and discrimination is allowed space and opportunity for growth. It has been argued that these efforts to discriminate positively (which I argue is negative discrimination), were intended to enhance rather than diminish service provision. But what is not always appreciated is that to suggest, on the one hand, that disabled children (and adults) are being catered for positively, while on the other hand, continually labelling them negatively and categorising them within mainstream service provisions, gives out two opposing messages. Disabled children are part of society and therefore should be included in the Children Act and yet they are not part of society and should be segregated into categories and onto registers! The latter is eroding society's capacity to value disabled children and adults. For disabled children the most significant rights must be the right to life (Article 6 of the UN Convention). This is not necessarily the starting point for the discussion of non-disabled children, but it must be for disabled children. The next most important right is to be regarded as of equal value to non-disabled children (Article 2). Disabled children must not be segregated, labelled or characterised as 'special' children; this de-humanises and isolates them.

DISABLED CHILDREN AND ABUSE

Disabled children have been perceived as so distinctly different to non-disabled children that, until recently, they have not been considered within child protection services. When they are included, workers and managers alike are completely unable to understand the nature and implications of disability in relation to child abuse.

Three very important myths have developed which allow child protection workers to deny the existence of abuse within the disabled child population. These myths originate in the perceptions discussed above, which see disabled children as different from other children. First, disabled children will not be targeted by abusers because they are not attractive or because people feel sorry for them. Second, sexual abuse of disabled children is not as harmful as for other children because they don't understand what is happening and/or because they don't feel it. Third, disabled children are more likely to make false allegations concerning abuse. How are we to assess these myths?

The first myth is simply not true. There is ample evidence to suggest that disabled children are at least equally at risk of abuse as non-disabled children. While there is no research which conclusively proves that disabled children are abused more frequently than non-disabled children, there are a considerable number of studies which argue that children who are disabled are at an increased risk of abuse (Kelly, 1992; Westcott, 1991, 1993). One study suggests a 50 per cent risk increase for sexual abuse of people who are disabled (Sobsey and Varnhagen, 1990). The second myth suggests that disability 'protects' from the harmful effects of abuse, that not understanding somehow translates into not being disturbed by the abusive events. But we know that even young non-disabled children, who may not understand the events, can nevertheless be profoundly disturbed by them. The logic that a child paralysed from the waist down may not feel penetration (sexual abuse) and therefore it would not be harmful, denies the fact that this child still has hearing, sight and intelligence to understand the secrecy and power of the abuser's manner and behaviour.

So far as the third myth is concerned, it is important to note that many disabled children use other forms of communication such as Sign Language or Blissymbolics, and find it incredibly difficult to disclose abuse. There is moreover a great likelihood that they will be disbelieved because of stereotypical perceptions of them as 'less capable'.

Although all the rights in the UN Convention apply to all children equally, whatever their race, sex, religion, language, disability, opinion or family background (Article 2), there remains a predominant belief that disabled children's rights are secondary to non-disabled children's rights. When I asked a child protection policy maker what she was including in child protection policies to cover disabled children, she pondered and then replied 'let me sort out the normal children first' (Kennedy and Kelly, 1992). Although many child protection policies do not mention the specific needs of disabled children at all, policy makers can get away with this discrepancy by arguing 'disabled children are children first therefore the same policies apply'. Again, I'm struck by the inconsistencies of the argument when the Children Act claims they are not and places disabled children within a special category of 'children in need' and onto registers.

The 'children first principle' has denied very many rights to disabled children. The most noteworthy being the right to an identity. The 'children first principle' denies disability and impairment completely. It is as if it doesn't exist. The denial is functional. If the impairment can be denied, it becomes easier to discuss the need for additional services. It becomes a simple progression to argue that child protection policies for disabled children are adequate since they are children (not disabled children). Because there is no impairment (!!) there is no additional need. Policies for non-disabled children therefore suffice. But do they?

PROTECTING DISABLED CHILDREN

Pro-active safety and prevention programmes

Whatever we may think of safety and prevention programmes, research suggests they have some value. It is important therefore that disabled children have access to the potential benefits of such programmes. But disabled children's accessibility to these programmes is hindered by three particular difficulties.

The first hurdle to confront in implementing them is the attitude of some teachers. My experience has shown that the myth that 'abuse doesn't happen to disabled children', combined with efforts to keep disabled children powerless, means that some teachers are unwilling to empower children in the way these programmes intend. It is widely believed, for example, that disabled children (and adults) should be grateful for their care and that challenging anything is an inappropriate role for the disabled child (or adult!). There is also a very deeply-rooted reluctance to encourage disabled children to learn about sex and sexuality, reflecting, at least in part, a eugenic belief that such children were not intended to reproduce. It follows that they do not require education along these lines. Consequently, very few schools for disabled children use Kidscape.

The second difficulty in implementing any such safety programmes is the question of their relevance and appropriateness for disabled children. Most safety codes require voice/English (communication), mobility/dexterity, cognitive ability, sight. Children are advised to say 'no', to get away somehow, and to tell someone about things that worry or frighten them. But it is very difficult if you are learning-disabled or use Makaton signing either to challenge an adult's abusive behaviour or to confide in a trusted adult about the experience. The adult may not be able to receive the message because they do not understand Makaton or because they do not believe the child. There is a good deal of anecdotal evidence to suggest that disabled children are less likely to be believed. Their particular impairment is often perceived to make the child less capable and prone to 'get things wrong' or to make the child 'disturbed' and likely to seek attention. It is not unusual therefore for disclosure to be discounted, particularly if the child has continual intimate daily care from a number of people. The multi-disabled child who requires washing, feeding and toileting may be disregarded on the grounds that the careworker was 'only washing your bottom' (Westcott, 1993).

Trying to escape an abusive situation may be complicated by visual impairment or mobility impairment. If the blind child is in a strange place, running away (even walking away) will be extremely problematical since blind and visually impaired children need to be familiar with their environment in order to negotiate it.

For the wheelchair user, removing oneself from a room which has heavy doors opening inwards, or steps, is well-nigh impossible. A child with muscular dystrophy, moreover may require the wheelchair to be pushed if it is not a powered one.

The third factor limiting accessibility to these programmes is the lack of accompanying literature to which the disabled child can relate. There are examples of good practice. The National Deaf Children's Society's book *You Choose* is produced in Sign Supported English (illustrations) and English. Many deaf children relate to the book very excitedly simply because they see deaf children with hearing aids in the illustrations and pictorial representations of their sign language. The deaf children *know* this book is for them. But while the book is very accessible to deaf children it may not always be available. Those deaf schools who do not allow deaf children to Sign, will not use the book. Their attempts to make children 'normal', by encouraging speech, takes precedence over safety!

The investigative interview

Increasing numbers of disabled children are reaching the stage of the investigative interview, as practitioners begin to realise that disabled children are and can be at risk of abuse. The workers entrusted with the interview tend to react in one of two ways. Some adhere strongly to the 'children first' principle and regard disabled children like other children. Consequently they employ inappropriate and inadequate methods and techniques for interviewing. Others regard disabled children as very distinctly different to non-disabled children and feel disempowered, de-skilled and unable to cope adequately with the situation.

Since most child protection policies and procedures are designed for nondisabled children (including the recent Memorandum of Good Practice (MOGP)), workers typically adopt a 'hit and miss' approach to the interviewing of disabled children.

Although the recent MOGP suggests the use of interpreters if required, it fails to offer the worker any guidance on how to use the interpreter. Recent publications describe in detail the implications of using an interpreter (British Sign Language and Sign Supported English) or a facilitator (Blissymbolics or Makaton) in the investigative process (Marchant and Page, 1993; Kennedy, 1993). The National Deaf Children's Society, Keep Deaf Children Safe Project, trains Sign Language interpreters for the role of interpreting in child protection investigative interviews, but a parallel course, training child protection workers in using Sign Language interpreters is not yet available. Many disabled children do not use speech to communicate and this one factor has major implications on a system of enquiry wholly based on voice communication. It is important to acknowledge and consider alternative forms of communication, as well as the fact that many children may not have been taught the vocabulary necessary for investigative interviews involving suspected sexual abuse.

Many augmentative communication systems censored sexual words or words describing body parts. It was felt both distasteful and unnecessary to teach such children these words! Ultimately the hurdles to the investigation can be so great, that police, crown prosecution and social services, do not consider taking disabled children through the criminal process.

The criminal process

We must remember that people who staff the various agencies of the criminal system have been subjected to society's values, prejudices and stereotypes about disabled children. Mostly these stereotypes are negative, perceiving the child as incapable and/or disturbed because of their impairment. There are particular difficulties if the child does not have speech – many courts seem reluctant to invest the disabled child's statements with any credibility. There are other difficulties. Many courts for example are not physically accessible for disabled children. The style of questioning within the court is alien and confusing to many disabled children. A recent publication, *The Child Witness Pack* contains only a single paragraph concerning disability:

> if your child has a learning or other disability: Being a witness at court is an experience no child finds easy. For children with a learning disability, it can be even more difficult, especially if the disability affects the child's speech or hearing. Remember your child may need extra encouragement and support both before and on the day of the trial.
>
> (Department of Health, 1993: 3)

This is the entire guidance for parents in the child witness pack. It fails to address many of the concerns raised by children such as: 'What if I'm about to have an epileptic fit and I'm giving evidence?'; 'What if I'm diabetic and need sugar but I'm in court and I've forgotten it?'; 'What if my hearing aid battery goes flat while giving evidence?'; 'What if my urinary catheter starts to leak?'; 'What if I cannot hear the barrister's questions?'; 'How do I know who everyone is?' (blind child). Children worry about such details. We know also that defence barristers have used the child's disability to discredit their statements. How do we help the child to cope with this?

The survival process

This title may seem puzzling. When drafting its training pack the ABCD Consortium – comprising The National Deaf Children's Society, The NSPCC, Chailey Heritage and Way Ahead Disability Consultancy – decided to abandon the medical model in discussions about the care and support of abused disabled children. Words such as 'therapeutic', 'therapy', 'diagnosis' and 'symptoms' were not used. We felt very strongly that the medical model with its emphasis on illness, treatment and recovery, produced the opposite of empowerment and served to stigmatise both the disabled child and the abused child. We did not regard disabled children as ill or in need of treatment in order to recover (become 'normal'); nor did we consider abused children to be ill. We recognised that abused children were harmed by their experience, but we did not wish to label their justifiable and understandable hurt, anger and sense of betrayal, as 'illness', but rather as a positive and healthy response to an abusive and discriminatory action by an abuser. The appropriate response therefore seemed to be to restore the child's integrity and sense of self-worth; a replacing of what has been taken away, not a cure.

The process towards survival therefore demands ways of working which do not stigmatise even further. Regrettably many workers feel de-skilled in the face of disability and refer the child to psychiatric services. Many abused children are so referred; a practice which stigmatises and may further 'medicalise' a child's experiences. When working with disabled children it is important to consider the possible impact of their impairment on ways of working. Take, for example the case of helping a child to express anger towards a perpetrator. One way might be to draw a figure, pin it on a wall and have the child throw bean bags at it. But if a child with cerebral palsy and athetoid movements of both arms, is unable to control his or her arms effectively, such a technique may not be appropriate, and another way must be found to help the child express their anger. Art, drama and play therapies are ideal for these children but require a great deal of imagination and flexibility from the worker. Finally it is important to understand that a disabled child who has been abused has been *doubly* oppressed because they are disabled and because they are children. Both aspects need to be addressed if the child is to be a stronger, more assertive child, able to believe in themselves and take control of their lives.

CHILDREN'S RIGHTS CHARTERS

The rights of disabled children have tended to be framed within a 'welfare' perspective which interprets rights claims as entitlements to a service rather than the entitlement to be an active participant in decision-making. This approach is under challenge from an increasingly militant coalition of disabled persons' groups (Jenkins, 1993). Jenkins has designed an excellent training pack on children's rights, containing 80 cards on which are written statements about various children's rights, but only four cards relate specifically to a disabled child. The pack offers six case histories to be used to explore the rights of children in the particular cases, but none focus on a child who is disabled. The marginalisation of disabled children, so evident in the *Child Witness Pack* is replicated here.

The Chailey Heritage Charter of children's rights

Children's Rights Charters do exist. The Chailey Heritage Charter involves disabled children in a unique way. The focus of this charter is not on 'welfare' entitlement to a service, but stresses the more fundamental importance of valuing the disabled child. The children at Chailey Heritage have very complex, often multiple disabilities. Many of them do not use speech to communicate. The charter is simple and comprises two sections. The child receives one section; the adults who care for the child receive the second. Both parties are advised about the ethos of the charter and children may complain if the specified rights are abrogated. The child's section of the charter is reproduced below.

Charter of Children's Rights

When I am at Chailey Heritage, wherever I am, whoever I am with, whatever I am doing, I have these fundamental rights:

being valued as an individual means:-

– being cared for and treated as unique.
– being talked to and about by my own name.
– being consistently cared for across settings.
– being encouraged to be me.
– being given enough time to take part, to do things for myself.
– to understand and be understood.

being treated with dignity and respect means:-

– being addressed with respect; never referred to or about as if I am my disability, nor as if I am one of my needs, nor as if I am a piece of equipment, nor finally as if I am hardly a child at all.
– being involved in conversations; never being talked about as if I am not there.
– having my privacy respected at all times and in all places.
– having all information about me treated carefully, kept safe and shared only with those people who need to know; never discussing me in the presence of another child.
– being given the best possible care that can be provided.
– being involved in decisions that affect me: being actively encouraged to express my views and where these cannot be taken into account, then told why.

being loved and cared for as a child first means:-

– having the same rights and choices and, as far as possible, the same kind of life as other children of my age and culture.
– consistent care from staff who really care about me and know me well.
– being actively supported as part of a family: having my parents fully involved in any planning for me and acknowledged as ultimately responsible for me.
– having access to communication equipment at all times, and being listened to and heard when I need to communicate, even if it takes a long time, and even if I am not easy to understand.

- being given information about what is happening before it happens, being given explanations of procedures before they occur.
- being given opportunities to play.

being safe means:-

- not being exposed to unnecessary risks.
- being protected from abuse:
    Physical abuse includes any physical punishment or unnecessary rough handling.
    Emotional abuse includes malicious teasing and taunting, unjustifiably ignoring me, controlling me through fear, shaming or humiliating me or deliberately misinterpreting my communication.
    Sexual abuse includes any sexual act or contact with me.
- being part of a service that is integrated; not having to hear things that may undermine my faith in the service as a whole.
- knowing that I have all of these rights, all of the time I am at Chailey Heritage, and that these rights can only be denied with good cause.

Other charters for disabled children

Other attempts have been made to produce disabled Children's Rights Charters. The National Union of the Deaf (NUD) produced the *Charter of Rights of the Deaf* in 1982 which looked closely at the United Nations Declaration of the Rights of the Child and studied the deaf child in relation to this. Many of the rights for deaf children contained in the NUD document considered the rights to Sign Language. The document describes what it calls 'the dummification process' and challenges oral/aural education for deaf children.

> THE DUMMIFICATION PROCESS – a terrifying side effect of the oral-only method of communication and instruction in the education of the deaf: meaning the turning of deaf children into dummies, who understand very little of the world about them and who 'stare blankly' when spoken to. These results of Oralism discussed in this book, affect not only language development, but emotional maturity and self-respect, and are noticed throughout deaf school leavers since 1945 who received their education in the oral-only method which they could not understand fully. After a few years of exposure to sign language and the deaf community, a lot of improvement is noted in the subsequent ten years. But the Dummification Process leaves its mark in many ways as discussed throughout the book.
>
> (NUD, 1982: 13)

The NUD were attempting to illustrate the value of Sign Language for deaf children, but also to re-establish the deaf identity as well as enhance self-esteem and respect; it also wished to restore a valuable language to deaf children. It challenged all attempts to 'force' deaf children to speak and suggested that denying Sign Language was an infringement of deaf children's rights. Such a stance portrays the deaf child not as a hearing child who happens to be deaf, but as a Deaf child.

DISABLED CHILDREN'S RIGHTS – CHILD PROTECTION

This chapter has focused predominantly on child protection and disabled children's rights in this regard. The Children Act 1989 (section 17) states: 'It shall be the duty of every local authority to safeguard and promote the welfare of children within their area who are in need'.

For the purpose of the Act, disabled children are considered (automatically) to be 'in need'. While we might disapprove of this categorisation, Section 17 establishes unequivocally that disabled children have a right to welfare.

I have argued that these rights claims must be met from conception but, since the right to life has not always been upheld in the UK, it is not surprising that in the area of child protection disabled children have a second-class service.

Disabled children are asking for certain rights which will enable them to grow and develop in an environment which is not abusive and which promotes a positive identity for them. The foundation for child protection rights must remain the right to life and the right to a positive and full identity i.e. as a disabled child.

A disabled child summarising the rights discussed in this text might ask for the following: (reference to points made in the text are bracketed).

I have the right:

- to life (deathmaking policies: p. 147)
- to be regarded as of equal value to other children – not to be stigmatised and segregated (children in need/disability registers: p. 149)
- to be included in mainstream society without labels and/or conditions (that is to become 'normal': p. 149)
- to be acknowledged as being at equal risk of abuse as non-disabled children (myths: p. 150)
- to be believed when I disclose abuse (myth: p. 150)
- to proper research being conducted concerning the risks of abuse (p. 150)
- to be considered equally in child protection policy and practice and not as a secondary consideration ('let me sort out the normal child first': p. 150)
- to have my full identity valued positively (I'm not just a child but a disabled child: p. 150)
- to information that might keep me safe (safety and prevention programme: p. 151)
- to have full access to that information (presented in appropriate and useful ways, in my form of communication if necessary: p. 151)
- to be included (pictures of me) in mainstream child protection materials (p. 152)
- to have access to sex education and the vocabulary which is necessary to disclose abuse should it happen (body parts, sexual vocabulary: p. 152)

- to a language in which to disclose (Sign Language, Deaf children, Makaton, Bliss, Rebus etc.: p. 152)
- to appropriate investigative interviews conducted by skilled workers who understand my additional requirements because of impairment (p. 152)
- to policies and procedures which address adequately my additional requirements because of impairment (p. 152)
- to a qualified interpreter if I require one (p. 152)
- of access to the criminal process (p. 153)
- to information which acknowledges my requirements within the criminal process (*The Child Witness Pack*: p. 153)
- not to have my evidence discredited just because I'm disabled (p. 153)
- not to be medicalised/made sick/ill just because I'm disabled or have been abused (stigmatised) (p. 154)
- to the acknowledgement that I have suffered oppression on two counts a) because I am disabled b) because I am a child (abused) (p. 154)
- to skilled workers ('therapists') who understand my impairment and can provide an effective survival process.

Disabled children can be abused physically, sexually and emotionally. They can be neglected. Disabled adults themselves have for years been trying to highlight such abuses. The drive for disability rights is a drive for full inclusion in mainstream daily living without prejudice, discrimination or oppression. Challenging the lack of child protection services for disabled children must start a process whereby there will be no second-class citizens and no child citizen left at risk of abuse. 'Let me sort out the normal child first' is a statement that must never to be heard again.

REFERENCES

Brody, P. (1992) 'Developing guidelines for decisions to forgo life – prolonging medical treatment', *Journal of Medical Ethics* (supplement) 18: 8.

Chailey Heritage (1992) *Charter of Children's Rights* (part of guidelines and policies relating to child protection). Child Care Office Chailey Heritage, North Chailey, East Sussex BN8 4EF.

Conte, J. (1989) 'What sexual offenders tell us about prevention strategies', *Child Abuse and Neglect* Vol. 13: 293–301.

Department of Health (1993) *The Child Witness Pack: Helping Children to Cope*, Child-Line, NSPCC and Calouste: Gulbenkian Foundation.

Garbarino, J., Brookhouser, P. and Anthier, K. (1987) *Special Children Special Risks: the Maltreatment of Children with Disabilities* De Gruyter: New York.

Gillon, R. (1993) 'Persistent vegetative state: withdrawal of nutrition and hydration' *Journal of Medical Ethics* Vol. 19: 67.

Jenkins, P. (1993) *Children's Rights: a Participation Exercise for Learning about Children's Rights in England and Wales*, Longman: London.

Kelly, L. (1992) 'The connections between Disability and Child Abuse: A review of the research evidence' *Child Abuse Review* Vol. 1: 157–67.

Kennedy, M. (1993) 'Human Aids to Communication' ABCD Pack, Department of Health.

Kennedy, M. and Gordon, R. (eds) (1993) *Abuse and Children who are Disabled* 'ABCD Pack' Department of Health.

Kennedy, M. and Kelly, L. (1992) 'Inclusion not Exclusion' *Child Abuse Review* Vol. 1 (3): 147–9.

Marchant, R. and Page Marcus (1993) *Bridging the Gap, Child Protection with Children with Multiple Disabilities*, NSPCC: London.

Morris, J. (1991) *Pride against Prejudice, Transforming Attitudes to Disability*, The Women's Press: London.

National Deaf Children's Society (1990) *You Choose*, NDCS: London.

The National Union for The Deaf (1982) *Charter of Rights of the Deaf* part 1, The Rights of the Deaf Child, Guildford.

Proctor, R. (1988) *Racial Hygiene: Medicine under the Nazis*, Harvard University Press: Cambridge MA.

Project 6609–1465 *Study of the Victims*, final report, project 6609–1465 Health & Welfare, Canada.

Senn, C.Y. (1986) *Vulnerable, Sexually Abused and People with Intellectual Handicaps*, G. Allen: Roeher Institute.

Shepherd School, Nottingham (1992) 'Paul Plays Football (and others)' (unpublished paper).

Westcott, H. (1992) *Institutional Abuse of Children – From Research to Policy*, Review, NSPCC: London.

—— (1993) *The Abuse of Disabled Children and Adults*, NSPCC: London.

Wolfensberger, W. (1992) 'A most critical issue: Life or Death', *The Citizen Advocacy Forum* April/June reprinted from *International Journal of Psychology and Psychotherapy* 1990 Vol.8 (1): 63–73.

Part IV

Children's rights: Comparative perspectives

Chapter 12

Children's rights: an American perspective

Cynthia Price Cohen

Although the USA has yet to become a State Party to the United Nations Convention on the Rights of the Child,[1] this should not be taken as an indication of any lack of interest in children's rights. On the contrary, discussions about the rights of children have been taking place actively on the local and national levels for more than twenty-five years[2] and, as is typical in the USA, these discussions have prompted legislative change as well as triggering children's rights law suits that have eventually been argued before the United States Supreme Court.

During the late 1960s and early 1970s, when the Supreme Court was relatively activist,[3] legal cases on behalf of children resulted in them being granted certain Constitutional rights in juvenile justice procedures (see *In re Gault* [1967]); recognition of their right to freedom of speech (see *Tinker* v *Des Moines Independent Community School District* [1969]); and protected from arbitrary school suspension (see *Goss* v *Lopez* [1975]). At the Congressional level, since the early 1970s, children's rights have been the focus of continuing child welfare legislation often aimed at eliminating child abuse.[4] Federal legislation has also been enacted which protects the right of American Indian children to have their tribal affiliation given consideration in foster care and adoption placements.[5] In addition, non-governmental organisations, such as the Children's Defense Fund, have been active in seeking beneficial changes for children, including pressurising Congress to enact financially-based legislation which would improve the living conditions of poor children.

Curiously, in the USA, concern for children's rights seems to progress in waves. The flurry of interest in juvenile delinquency prevention and juvenile justice protections, which characterised the 1960s and 1970s, has been eclipsed by movements to eliminate poverty, control inner city violence, end teenage pregnancy and assist unwed mothers. More recently, headlines have been devoted to the child's right to be heard in custody and adoption cases. Only child abuse prevention has been able to sustain a high profile on the public agenda for more than twenty years.

Policy development often appears to be chaotic and inefficient in such an enormous and diverse country as the USA. Despite appearances, however, change does occur and progress is made, but in a manner which accommodates the

American personality. Unfortunately, because this country must regularly wrestle with a variety of competing interests, the rights of children have been forced to take a back seat. Recent reports from organisations monitoring the situation of children in the USA present a pitiful picture, especially considering that America is one of the richest countries in the world.

According to a recent survey by the American Bar Association (ABA, 1993), poverty is one of the greatest problems faced by children in the USA. The survey points out that poverty affects all aspects of the child's life, including school performance and health. In support of its position, the ABA survey refers to 1991 statistics which indicate that 24 per cent of American pre-school children live in impoverished families. This poverty, moreover, is not confined to inner cities or particular ethnic groups, but can be found in every area of the country. Publicly, child poverty is often blamed on high divorce rates and single parent families. While there may be some support for these allegations, the fact remains that nothing is being done to alleviate the problem. Repeated proposals for the establishment of minimum income benefits to prevent families from falling below the poverty line have never received sufficient support to prompt legislation.

The ABA survey, *America's Children at Risk,* concludes with a list of twenty recommendations urging lawyers to work toward improving the circumstances of American children, both through legal representation and the promotion of supportive legislation and administrative procedures. In addition to confronting child poverty, the ABA urges its members to use their skills as lawyers to represent children and their interests in legal cases concerning education, health, child abuse, foster care and juvenile justice.

Another disturbing report on the situation of American children was released in 1992 by the Children's Defense Fund (CDF). CDF is one of the leading national non-governmental organisations working for children and has been spearheading the drive for USA ratification of the Convention on the Rights of the Child. CDF's report, *America's Children Falling Behind: The USA and the Convention on the Rights of the Child*, was written as an example of the type of report that the USA will have to submit to the Committee on the Rights of the Child, if and when it ratifies the Convention. In its report, CDF highlighted aspects of the American experience of childhood which it believed did not measure up to Convention standards. In addressing America's shortcomings, the CDF cited:

- Fourteen million American children who live in poverty
- The estimated 10,000 children who die each year from the effects of poverty
- The 1991 government report of 2.7 million cases of child abuse which was three times greater than that reported in 1980
- The criminal laws of twenty-four states which allow the execution of juveniles for crimes committed when they were under the age of 18

- The 500,000 children and youths who are deprived of their liberty as the result of juvenile crime
- The 7 million children in the USA who work, including the 2 million who work illegally
- The many children who are rarely given a voice in judicial decisions concerning them in matters of foster care, adoption or custody.

It is important to note that while both the ABA and CDF reports evaluate the situation of children, they are primarily concerned with the child's quality of life, and not with the child's right to be recognised as a person. This distinction is significant for two reasons. First, the traditional view of children's rights, expressed in the 1959 United Nations Declaration of the Rights of the Child, has stressed the need for care and protection of children rather than supporting a child's right to self-expression. Second, as will be explained later, the American view of rights has traditionally emphasised the desirability of 'rights from' rather than 'rights to'. The American understanding of rights can best be described as claims by citizens for protection from undue interference by the State. It does not include claims by citizens for benefits or services.

One explanation for this fractured picture of children's rights is that the USA has no overall children's policy. In fact, there is no single office or bureau within the federal government that is designated to deal with the interests of children, or even of children and families.[6] During the drafting of the Convention on the Rights of the Child, in order to be able to ascertain USA policy on any given set of proposed articles, USA delegates found it necessary to consult with a variety of separate administrative agencies, in addition to conducting a review of Constitutional law.

A second influence on children's rights is the fact that the USA is a notoriously litigious society. As a result, it has a tendency to define its law through litigation. This is also true of rights. In America, rights are definitively upheld only through judicial decisions. This is not surprising, since reliance on judicial interpretation is characteristic of a particular school of American jurisprudence which takes the position that a law has no meaning until it has been interpreted by an authoritative body.[7] Since, from the point of view of judicial interpretation, the subject of children's rights is relatively new, it will undoubtedly be some time before the concept can be fully developed and applied.

CHILDREN'S RIGHTS: THE AMERICAN VIEW

It has become commonplace for histories of children's rights in America to begin with the story of how mid-nineteenth century efforts to protect an abused child required intercession on her/his behalf by the Society for the Prevention of Cruelty to Animals because at that time there was no other organisation or legal process that could come to their aid. Protectors of children, sometimes referred to as 'child savers', brought about considerable changes in favour of children in the latter part of the nineteenth century. These concerned citizens set up orphanages, schools for the blind and deaf and reorganised the criminal justice system so as to provide for the special treatment of juvenile offenders.

The early twentieth century saw this interest in the situation of children change its emphasis from juvenile justice to a concern with eliminating child labour. Throughout this century, there has been a continuing but alternating focus on the needs of children. Unfortunately, as the twentieth century draws to a close, a review of most state statutes will show residual evidence of the concept of 'child as chattel', especially in laws defining the limits of discipline. In most states the parent has absolute control over the child. The state will step in on the side of the child only where there is extreme neglect or bodily injury. Corporal punishment, moreover, is still legal in many states and is the accepted form of school discipline. Supreme Court litigation has brought about a modest amount of recognition of children's rights, but the establishment of full respect for the child's human dignity has yet to be achieved.

To understand fully the status of children's rights in America it is necessary to have at least some comprehension of the American view of rights; a perception which considers them to be virtually 'sacred'. The concept of rights is crucial to American political thought, pre-dates the Revolution and derives much of its content from the sixteenth-century philosophy of John Locke. The significance attached to rights is reflected in the language of the Declaration of Independence which states,

> We hold these truths to be self-evident, that all men are created equal; that they are endowed by their creator with certain inalienable *rights*, among these are life, liberty and the pursuit of happiness. That to secure these *rights* governments are instituted among men, deriving their just powers from the consent of the governed.
>
> (Declaration of Independence, 1776; para. 2, my italic)

Rights were so significant to those who drafted the American Constitution that the concept was one of the main topics of debate at the Constitutional Convention. Participants eventually agreed to the adoption of ten amendments to the Constitution which outlined those rights which the American government must guarantee to its citizens. These amendments have come to be known as the *Bill of Rights*. The rights protected by the first ten amendments are those which are known in international human rights law as *civil and political* rights. They include the right to freedom of speech, freedom of religion, freedom of association and various protections associated with criminal prosecutions. The rights known in international law as economic, social and cultural rights – for example, the right to education, health care, employment and an adequate standard of living – were not included among those in the Bill of Rights[8] and have yet to be given protection under American Constitutional law.[9]

Interpretation and application of the United States Constitution, including amendments, is the responsibility of the United States Supreme Court. This judicial bench, made up of nine Justices, examines significant cases and scrutinises legislation for constitutionality.

Children's rights: supreme court cases

Although the Supreme Court has decided a number of cases which have a bearing on the rights of children and young people, the composite picture of these rights is not entirely consistent. On the one hand, some Supreme Court opinions have recognised the child's right to be treated as an independent, rational individual. On the other hand, there is a line of decisions which continues to hold that the rights of parents are superior to those of the child. This is particularly true of cases which involve the right of the parents to control the child's education. This interest was first addressed by the Court during the 1920s in the cases of *Meyer* v *Nebraska* [1923] and *Pierce* v *The Society of Sisters* [1925]. These precedents remained unchallenged until *Wisconsin* v *Yoder* in 1972. This case concerned the right of Amish parents to prohibit their children from attending public high school, which their religious practices led them to believe would corrupt their children. Even though this opinion came at a time when many of the Court's other decisions were leaning toward recognition of the child's individual rights, here, once again, the Court upheld the right of parents to make educational decisions affecting their children. In a dissenting opinion Mr. Justice William O. Douglas, complained that consideration should also have been given to the preferences of the children.

According to a recent survey, during the period between 1953 and 1992, the Supreme Court decided only forty-seven cases dealing with children's issues.[10] The majority of these fell into four categories: cases dealing with matters relating to illegitimacy; cases addressing the problem of parental control, especially in the area of under-age abortion; cases relating to education and schools, including freedom of expression issues; and cases defining the parameters of juvenile justice standards, including the death penalty. Only a few of these can be said to have achieved 'landmark' status by prompting significant changes to the law. 'Landmark' children's rights cases can be roughly divided into three groups: those which deal with the child in school; those which are related to the juvenile justice process; and those which have to do with other matters, such as the group of privacy cases, which upheld the right of young people to receive information about contraception and abortion and to be able to obtain contraceptives without parental consent.

The first Supreme Court decision to recognise that a child has Constitutional rights was *West Virginia Board of Education* v *Barnette*, in 1943. In its opinion the Court held that a student in school could not be forced to salute the American flag in violation of that child's religious beliefs. Subsequent school-related children's rights cases have been based on constitutional claims protecting freedom of expression, procedural due process, cruel and unusual punishment and freedom from unwarranted searches and seizures. One school-related case that unquestionably achieved 'landmark' status was *Brown* v *Board of Education* [1954].[11] In this decision, the Court put an end to racial segregation in the public schools, stating that 'Segregation of white and colored children in public schools has a detrimental effect upon the colored children,' and that 'in the field of public education, "separate but equal" has no place.'

The Court's holdings in school-related cases were not at all predictable. Of the freedom of expression decisions, the 1969 case of *Tinker* v *Des Moines Independent School District* promised to bring a major change to the Court's interpretation of children's Constitutional rights. For the first time, the Court stated clearly that children were 'persons' within the meaning of the United States Constitution and, therefore, were entitled to Constitutional protection.[12] In *Tinker*, the Court held that school students were Constitutionally entitled to wear black armbands in protest against the Vietnam war. Strangely, the free expression promise of *Tinker* was never realised. A group of cases in the 1980s – which involved such matters as student opposition to the removal of 'objectionable books' from the library, vulgar speech in a student assembly and the removal of questionable material from a student newspaper – were all decided in favour of school authorities. In a similar matter, the Court also supported the right of school administrators to search student's lockers without first obtaining a warrant.

Procedural due process cases, on the other hand, have been reasonably consistent over time. A 1961 decision by the Supreme Court held that a college student could not be expelled without some type of hearing. Fourteen years later, in *Goss* v *Lopez*, the Court applied the same standards to the suspension of a high school student. Ironically, the Court did not find such a hearing to be necessary when the punishment was corporal and did not necessarily require the student be removed from classes for any length of time. Sadly, the Court's *Ingraham* v *Wright* [1977] opinion held that corporal punishment of school children, without a hearing, violated neither the Constitution's due process clause nor its proscription against cruel and unusual punishment, even though this case involved a beating of such severity that the student needed to be hospitalized.

Of all of the children's rights cases, the 'landmark' case of *In re Gault* may be the most well known. Prior to *Gault*, as a result of the child-saving movement of the nineteenth century, juveniles accused of committing a crime were given some sort of informal hearing in a family court setting. *In re Gault* brought an abrupt halt to these inconsistent and unpredictable procedures, by upholding the juvenile's rights to counsel, to prior notice of charges, to remain silent, and to confront and cross-examine witnesses. A subsequent decision added the requirement that proof in juvenile hearings must meet the adult standard of 'proof beyond a reasonable doubt' (*In re Winship* [1970]).

This trend toward granting greater Constitutional protections to juveniles may have had an undesirable side effect. For a number of years, there has been a trend in this country toward granting 'full' adult rights to accused juveniles. In other words, it is becoming commonplace to 'waive' juvenile cases into the adult system and to try juveniles as adult criminals, with adult responsibility and sentencing. While this process is usually limited to those juveniles who have committed very serious crimes, such as murder, the result has been that a large number of young people have received capital sentences and have been executed for crimes they committed while under the age of eighteen. This constitutes a violation of international law.

Although Constitutional litigation can be time-consuming, it was, never-theless, successful when used to establish the rights of black Americans and women. But the above discussion suggests that it may not prove to be the most suitable vehicle for promoting the rights of children. To a certain extent this is because children's rights are such a patchwork quilt, and the claims are so ill-defined. Additionally, many of the rights claims of children, such as the right to an education, are not protected by the Constitution. While children's rights advocates will undoubtedly continue to pursue legal remedies as the only avail-able method for legitimising children's rights at the present time, there is no doubt that many unresolved children's rights issues could be more effectively settled through USA ratification of the Convention on the Rights of the Child.

Children's rights: Convention on the Rights of the Child

Some American children's rights advocates adopt the view that the only way to secure the rights of children is through a Constitutional amendment. They argue that litigation on behalf of black Americans and women would never have succeeded without supportive Constitutional amendments and consequently the same process must be followed on behalf of the child. The problem with this argument is that unless the text of the amendment defines and grants new rights, such an amendment would only extend to children those rights contained in the Bill of Rights, many of which have already been granted through Supreme Court decisions. The fact is, that while it might be beneficial for children to be granted full Constitutional rights, this alone will not solve the problem. Children have special needs which cannot be met simply by treating them as adults. This was one of the lessons of the Convention on the Rights of the Child. Opponents of the Convention asserted that children did not need a special treaty to protect their rights, since, arguably, they were already protected by the International Human Rights Covenants. Yet once the drafting of the Convention got under way, it became quite apparent that the rights of children were more comprehensive and detailed than those recognised by other human rights instruments.

The Convention on the Rights of the Child protects the full range of human rights – civil-political, economic-social-cultural and humanitarian – all of which have been modified to suit the requirements of children. The Convention was drafted in response to the 1979 International Year of the Child and was adopted by the United Nations General Assembly in 1989. What is striking is that those who participated in the Convention's drafting in no way anticipated that the treaty would generate such major interest and enthusiasm among members of the international community. Within a little over two years from the time that it was opened for signature, the Convention had more State Parties than any other international human rights treaty.[13] Clearly, the Convention provides an effective tool for advocating and protecting children's rights.

To the frustration of child advocates, it will not be possible for the Convention to be ratified in order to provide a 'quick fix' for the children's rights picture here in the USA. For one thing, the American treaty ratification process is time-consuming and complicated. First, a treaty must be signed by the President. It is then submitted to the Senate for its Constitutionally mandated 'advice and consent' (see Article VI), where it is thoroughly analysed and debated. This process can take anywhere from several months to (as in the case of the Convention Against Genocide) thirty years! It is only after the Senatorial process has been completed that the treaty can be returned to the President for his final signature before it is sent to the appropriate depository. The ratification process is further complicated by the fact that the USA does not consider human rights treaties to be 'self-executing', which means that the ratification process cannot be completed without the enactment of implementing legislation. Obviously, with such a multi-faceted scenario it is possible for the ratification process to become stalled at any point along the way.

The USA review of the Convention Against Torture and Other Forms of Cruel, Inhuman or Degrading Treatment or Punishment provides an example of this ratification problem. The Torture Convention was approved by the Senate several years ago, but, to date, the ratification process has not been completed because the implementing legislation is not yet in place. President Jimmy Carter's efforts to promote ratification of human rights treaties were similarly frustrated. To his credit he signed four human rights treaties and submitted them to the Senate. As of January 1994, the ratification process had been completed for only one of them: the International Covenant on Civil and Political Rights. The other three still await action by the Senate.[14] The prospects for speedy ratification of the Convention on the Rights of the Child are rather bleak since, lacking the President's signature, as of January 30, 1994, the process of 'advice and consent' has yet to begin.

While it is obvious that the ratification of human rights treaties is never a simple process in America, the Convention on the Rights of the Child presents special difficulties. This is because so many of its rights fall into the category of powers that are reserved to the states. For example, foster care and adoption, juvenile justice, child custody, education and some health care provisions are all administered at the state level, often with greatly differing standards and procedures. As a general rule, the federal government is unwilling to interfere in an area which belongs to state jurisdiction. While this has the potential to derail the Convention's ratification, it is possible that the states rights claim can be minimised by ascertaining the extent to which the laws and regulations of the individual states already meet the standards set by the Convention. In a book of essays, *Children's Rights in America: UN Convention on the Rights of the Child*

Compared with United States Law, a group of American legal scholars concluded that, with the exception of the death penalty, USA legislation regarding children was already in compliance with the Convention's requirements. The only short-coming repeatedly cited by the authors had to do with failure to implement existing legislation (Price Cohen and Davidson, 1990).

The USA's reluctance to sign the Convention on the Rights of the Child is difficult to comprehend when the extent to which this country was involved in the Convention's drafting process is considered. The American delegation was present and participating throughout the entire ten-year period. Numerous Articles in the Convention are there only because of USA support. This is especially true of Articles 12 to 16 (protecting the child's civil and political rights) which were USA initiatives. One not so attractive USA initiative was to lower the age for participation in armed combat to 15 from the Convention's standard of 18 years as the age of majority.

As a general rule, most Americans know very little about international law. They are similarly unfamiliar with the implementation of human rights treaties and they have only minimal knowledge about the UN and its processes. This situation tends to make many Americans very fearful of ratifying human rights treaties and is at least partially responsible for the fact that the USA has ratified so few of them. Nowhere is this disassociation from international legal procedures more noticeable than in the abysmal lack of familiarity with the Convention on the Rights of the Child. Nearly five years after the Convention was adopted by the UN General Assembly, very few American legislators and even fewer lawyers, educators or members of the general public have even heard of the Convention.

Future prospects for children's rights in America

Even though the ratification process has not yet been initiated, those groups which are informed are beginning to take sides for or against the Convention. Those supporting the Convention include not only children's organisations, but also educators, psychologists, pediatricians, legislators, local governments, and lawyers. Those who oppose ratification of the Convention are largely con-servative and/or religious organisations.

Most of the negativism is due to a lack of familiarity with international processes. For example, one group is alleging that if the Convention is ratified, the Committee on the Rights of the Child, which monitors State Party compliance with the Convention, will be able to impose its ideas on the USA government regarding the way American children are to be raised and educated. Rayner, in this volume, shows that the same concerns have been expressed in Australia (see chapter 14). But opponents have failed to grasp the fact that the UN is an organisation of sovereign nations and that any treaty compliance is purely voluntary, since an actual enforcement mechanism does not exist. Some conservative organ-isations are afraid that giving children rights will undermine the family, and they point to such rights as freedom of speech or the right to privacy and say that it is 'unAmerican' for children to have these rights. Ironically, the very Articles which concern them as being 'unAmerican' were drafted and sponsored by the USA – and are based on the Bill of Rights.

At the other end of the spectrum is the National Committee for the Rights of the Child (NCRC), a coalition of organisations that have joined together to promote a general children's rights agenda – in addition to pursuing their individual goals separately. NCRC member organisations' interests are diverse, and as a result, the NCRC's goals cover a wide range of areas. The common thread among NCRC initiatives is the goal of informing and educating the general public about children's rights, and about the Convention on the Rights of the Child in particular. To this end, the NCRC holds conferences and briefings and publishes a newsletter.

One NCRC initiative which is becoming well established, focuses on legal support for the child's right to be heard. The NCRC Legal Action Project provides legal advice and, sometimes, direct assistance to children who are affected by litigation in which the child ought to be able to make his or her wishes known. Typically, these cases have to do with deciding who is to be awarded legal custody of the child as a result of legal actions based on neglect, abuse or divorce and whether the custodian is to be a foster parent, an adoptive parent, one or other of the parents in a divorce case or, perhaps, the grandparents or the Indian tribe. Under current USA practice, which occurs at the state level, the child rarely has a say in the outcome of custody cases. In those situations where the child's opinion is given even marginal consideration, it is usually through an adult representative or 'next friend', not an attorney. George Russ, member of the Board of the NCRC Legal Action Project and adoptive father of 'Gregory K.', the boy who divorced his parents, is himself a lawyer who is ardently pursuing the child's right to be heard. According to Russ:

> If minors' rights are to have any practical significance, minors must be able to protect those rights without being at the mercy of adult willingness to act. Minors must have an independent means of access to the courts to assert their rights, and must be treated as competent to initiate actions when adults fail them.
>
> (Russ, 1993: 365).

A second NCRC initiative involves efforts to secure ratification of the Convention on the Rights of the Child. One aspect of this effort has been the setting up of briefings and informal discussions with members of Congress to teach the uninformed about the Convention. This should not be taken to mean that the Convention has no Congressional support. On the contrary, there have been numerous efforts by both members of the House and the Senate, to pass resolutions urging the President to sign the Convention and submit it for *'advice and consent'*.

Fortunately, the ABA has given its backing to ratification of the Convention on the Rights of the Child. A special Working Group of the ABA was set up to study the Convention and to make recommendations as to possible reservations, understandings and declarations (RUDs), if, and when the Senate begins the process of deliberations over the treaty's ratification. The ABA Working Group produced a report giving a lengthy and detailed Article by Article account of the Convention as it impacts upon the USA legal system. Taking into consideration the Convention's complexities, the effects of the USA federal system and prior USA practice of adding an extensive list of RUDs to human rights treaties, the list of RUDs recommended in the ABA report was surprisingly short. There were only two reservations, four understandings and two declarations.

One reservation has to do with separating juveniles from adults in correctional facilities, which is, of course, impossible if the child is being tried as an adult. The other has to do with limitations on the practice of religion, which would be governed by the law of the USA Constitution. It is a positive indication of growing USA concern for children's rights for this somewhat conservative organisation of American legal scholars and practicing attorneys, aware of prior American practice regarding human rights treaties and RUDs, to complete its study with only two reservations and some minor declarations and understandings. This would seem to bode well for future ratification of the Convention on the Rights of the Child, since it is probably safe to say that no human rights treaty can survive Senate scrutiny without ABA support.

The failure of the USA to sign the Convention on the Rights of the Child remains a puzzle to Americans who are interested in children's rights. The USA took part in the Convention's drafting, and later participated in the 1990 World Summit for Children. President Bush signed the World Summit Declaration which included the Convention's universal ratification among its goals. President Clinton made children a focal point of his election campaign and his wife, Hillary Rodham Clinton, is a recognised children's rights advocate. Yet, nearly five years after the Convention was adopted by the General Assembly, the government continues to drag its feet on children's issues and the Convention's ratification, as it becomes sidetracked by debates over health care, world trade and the economy.

Despite this dismal picture of government inaction, American support for children's rights is growing at grass-roots level. Organisations and groups are beginning to understand that the Convention on the Rights of the Child can be used as a framework on which to base their activities. One of the messages being brought to the public by the NCRC is that implementation of the Convention's standards need not be postponed until the treaty is ratified. Implementation, and the tracking of USA shortcomings should take place *now*, so that when America does become a State Party, the information needed to evaluate its compliance with the Convention will be readily available. The growing efforts by Americans who are conscious of the continuing injustice which the denial of rights to children constitutes, suggests that children in the USA will ultimately be able to have their rights recognised. The exclusion of children from the possession of certain rights is an inexplicable anomaly in a country which takes pride in its democratic heritage.

NOTES

1 At the time of this writing, the USA had yet to become a signatory to the Convention on the Rights of the Child and, as a consequence the ratification process had not even begun. According to Article VI of the USA Constitution, treaties are the supreme law of the land, on a level with federal law and constitutional law and supersede the laws of the states. Under the theory of separation of powers, treaty ratification is a three-step process. First the treaty is signed by the President, then it is sent to the United States Senate for a review known as 'advice and consent', after which it goes back to the President for his final signature.

2 Of course children were the subject of national concern during other periods of American history which resulted in legislation aimed at the protection of their well being. Two significant periods which saw great attention focusing on children were the beginning of the twentieth century and the 1920s. At the turn of the century the focus was on innovative methods of dealing with juvenile delinquents; in the 1920s the emphasis was on the elimination of child labour.

3 In speaking of the Supreme Court, legal analysts usually refer to a particular group of Justices, and the cases they decided by the name of the Chief Justice at that particular time. During certain periods the Court will be known as activist because it has made precedent-breaking decisions and, thus, created new law. For example, during the 1950s and 1970s the Warren Court (under Chief Justice Earl Warren) handed down decisions which greatly broadened civil rights. These rulings covered such topics affecting children as school desegregation, the right to a legal counsel in juvenile cases, and the right of school students to engage in political protest.

   This activism continued into the 1970s under Chief Justice Warren Burger, giving rise to other children's rights rulings which covered such matters as the right to jury trial for accused juveniles, the right to receive information about contraceptive devices and protection against school suspension without benefit of a hearing.

4 Both branches of the USA Congress (Senate and House of Representatives) have special committees which consider matters pertaining to children, youth and families and propose legislation in these areas. See among others, Child Abuse Prevention and Treatment Act (1974).

5 See Indian Child Welfare Act, which challenged the practice of placing Indian children for adoption in non-Indian families.

6 Since the individual states are free to organise their services to citizens in any manner they choose, there are various policy models regarding service delivery at that level which are quite different from those of the federal government.

7 An interesting example of the thinking of the school of jurisprudence known as American Legal Realism can be found in Wendell Holmes, 1907.

8 In fact, the USA has not ratified the International Covenant on Economic, Social and Cultural Rights, and, at meetings of international bodies (such as the Commission on Human Rights), has always taken the position that these are not rights at all, but just good public policy. This is somewhat peculiar, since, during the Great Depression, it was the American President Franklin Delano Roosevelt who urged the drafting of a new Bill of Rights that would create guarantees for such things as 'freedom from want'.

9 While the USA became a State Party to the International Covenant on Civil and Political Rights in 1992, it has yet to ratify the International Covenant on Economic, Social and Cultural Rights and it appears that this is not likely to take place at any time in the near future.

10 Thirty-four of these were between the years of 1969 and 1986, when Warren Burger was Chief Justice. See Gluck Mezey, 1993. Interestingly, Ms. Mezey did not consider *Brown* v *Board of Education* to be a case that fell within her definition of children's rights.

11 This decision brought about the development of a system of bussing to ensure that schools were properly integrated. Almost forty years later, the decision's benefits and after effects are still being debated.

12 It is particularly ironic that the Court ruling granting corporations the status of 'persons' for Constitutional purposes occurred prior to the end of the nineteenth century, while children were not granted similar status until approximately 75 years later.

13 As of January 1994 there were over 150 States Parties.

14 The other three treaties were: the Convention Against All Forms of Racial Discrimination; the International Covenant on Economic, Social and Cultural Rights; and The American Convention on Human Rights.

CASES CITED

Brown v *Board of Education* [1954] 347 US 483
Goss v *Lopez* [1975] 419 US 565
Ingraham v *Wright* [1977] 430 US 361
In re Gault [1967] 387 US 1
In re Winship [1970] 397 US 358
Meyer v *Nebraska* [1923] 262 US 390
Pierce v *The Society of Sisters* [1925] 268 US 510
Tinker v *Des Moines Independent Community School District* [1969] 393 US 503
Wisconsin v *Yoder* [1972] 406 US 205
West Virginia Board of Education v *Barnette* [1943] 319 US 624

REFERENCES

American Bar Association (ABA) (1993) *America's Children at Risk*, ABA: Washington DC.
Children's Defense Fund (CDF) (1992) *America's Children Falling Behind: The United States and the Convention on the Rights of the Child*, CDF: Washington DC.
Gluck Mezey, S. (1993) 'Constitutional Adjudication of Children's Rights Claims in the United States Supreme Court, 1953–92', *Family Law Quarterly* Vol. 27 p. 307.
Price Cohen, C. and Davidson, H. (eds) (1990) *Children's Rights in America; U.N. Convention on the Rights of the Child compared with United States law*, ABA: Washington DC.
Russ, G.H. (1993) 'Through the eyes of a child; "Gregory K"; A child's right to be heard' *Family Law Quarterly* Vol. 27 pp. 365–72.
Wendell Holmes, O. (1907) 'Path of the Law', *Harvard Law Review* 459.

Chapter 13

The Scandinavian experience of children's rights

Målfrid Grude Flekkøy

In 1981 Norway established the world's first Ombudsman for Children. The Ombudsman tradition is a *Scandinavian* tradition, but by 1993 only Norway had established such an office. The precedent prompts an obvious question; why was an Ombudsman for Children established in Norway but not in the other Nordic countries? The anomaly is especially curious given the shared political history and legislative traditions of these countries. Norway was united with Denmark for 400 years until 1814 and with Sweden from 1815 to 1905.

THE CHILD AND NORWEGIAN LEGISLATION

Recognition of children in Norwegian/Danish law goes back 700 years. The penal code (Gulatingsloven and Magnus Lagabøters Rettergangsbot) of the thirteenth century stated that children were not to be punished as harshly as adults. Children (but only those born in wedlock) were acknowledged as heirs to property in the seventeenth century while Church legislation (enacted in 1685 but still valid) recognised children as legal subjects in connection with christening. Magnus Lagabøters Rettergangsbot also asserted the right of an illegitimate child to be provided for – by its mother until the age of three and by its father until the age of seven. Subsequent amendments to the law extended the age-limit for the father's obligation firstly to ten, and then – from 1821 – to fifteen. Even the children of unmarried parents (at least when the liaison was recognised) enjoyed rights to provision as long ago as the thirteenth century, although the entitlement was formulated as an obligation for the adult rather than as a right of the child.

In 1630 the first legislation signalling that public authority might, in certain circumstances supersede parental authority was enacted. Public guardians were appointed in the townships and empowered to assume responsibility for children if after due warning, parents failed to send their children to school or to work in a useful occupation (school was not compulsory at that time). Vagrant children were not tolerated and were sent to institutions which attempted to combine facets of the penal institution with the provision of labour training and 'education'. Following amendments to the law in 1605, 1609 and 1620 'Children's Houses' were established for orphans and children whose parents could not provide a vocation. Discipline was strict and working hours were long, but the children learned a trade as weavers, spinners, or dyers (four hundred boys 'graduated' before the institution was closed in 1650). The creation of this kind of institution indicated an early willingness by the state to assume responsibility for particularly helpless or disadvantaged children.

The first legislation directly concerned with the religious and moral improvement of children (and society) was the Public School Act of 1739. During the 1880s however, several new laws were enacted both in Norway and in Denmark, reflecting a popular belief that children required greater protection which society should provide. Labour legislation was also enacted guaranteeing improvements in health for the growing generation. The belief became widespread that the interests of children and society were synonymous. Social conditions which might give rise to adults becoming a burden on society had to be eradicated and social reforms, including better protection of and provision for illegitimate children, were promoted. Legislation passed in 1892, for example, obliged both parents to provide for the child and required supervision and inspection of the conditions for children in foster homes. But in practice changes were less radical than the law had intended. Many mothers felt unable to request the financial support from the father in the manner which the law required, while the supervision of the foster homes was simply not undertaken.

The next milestone in Norway was the Child Protection Act of 1896. By enacting the law, Parliament squarely established a new principle: care for neglected children was the responsibility of the state. Children encompassed by the law included those who had committed criminal acts, truants from school, children neglected by parents; in summary, guilty, innocent and potentially guilty children. The purpose of the legislation was to remove children from undesirable or unfortunate circumstances and provide them with an upbringing in an orphanage, reform school or other special institution.

A growing understanding of child development, combined with new ideas concerning treatment or rehabilitation rather than merely imprisonment for criminals, led to other reforms – new legislation as well as amendments to existing laws. Legislative changes may, of course, reflect changes in public understanding and attitude, or they may be a factor in accelerating such changes. In some areas of social legislation, changes to the law lagged a long way behind attitudinal changes. Consequently, while the Norwegian Parliament debated the question of 'legitimate' and 'illegitimate' children as early as 1821, amendments to the law to eradicate legal differences between the two groups of children were not finally enacted until 160 years later in the Parents and Children Act 1981. Even after that Act, some distinctions remained. The child's visitation rights following parental separation, for example, depended until recently on whether the parents lived together after the birth of the child. A revision of the law was proposed and debated in 1979, but was only finally changed in 1988, following a proposal from the Ombudsman for Children.

Current Norwegian legislation reflects a general acceptance of the view that the development from childhood to maturity is a gradual process with appropriate responsibilities and rights being attained *en route*. One rather confusing consequence of such a view is the existence of more than 25–30 different age-limits currently operative in Norway. A more recent, but highly significant development, has been the growing tendency to recognise children as legal subjects possessing their own legal rights. The School Act, for example, gives the child the right (and the obligation) to go to school, a right which in many other countries is given to the parents on behalf on the child. A more recent example is the Parents and Children Act which no longer uses the term 'parental authority', but has replaced it with 'parental responsibility'. It is the parents' responsibility to provide for the basic needs of the child. Parents, for example, are responsible for cooperating in order to guarantee the child visiting rights in cases of marital breakdown where parents have separated.

THE NORWEGIAN WELFARE SYSTEM FOR CHILDREN AND PARENTS: A SAFETY-NET WITH HOLES

The principles of the Norwegian welfare system are simple:

- Necessary services should be available to all. The cost should largely be met by public funding, via a personal income tax which reduces differences in income while 'spreading the expenses' over wage-earners' working years.
- The other principle is that most help should be provided to those who need it most; the greater the need the more readily available the service.

The system does not always work according to its own principles, particularly when local and national economic resources are diminishing, and while public social expenditures increase. New sources and methods of funding have been discussed. In the health service there have been proposals for partial payments for some health services and the establishment of private clinics (although supported by public funds), for patients who are able to pay. Nevertheless, services for children and families in Norway, although 'patchy' in many community areas, are provided to a level which surpasses provision in many other countries.

One reason for the establishment of an Ombudsman for Children in Norway, rather than the other Nordic countries however, may be that the Norwegian social welfare system did not place the same degree of emphasis on children which was evident in Swedish and Danish welfare provision. In Norway there are significant gaps at the 'cradle' end of the 'cradle-to-grave' system. There is for example, no maternal and child health division or other 'standard' office focused on children's interests; schools are isolated from other services, and there is no comprehensive family social support system. Consequently, the provision for Norwegian children compares unfavourably to that in other Scandinavian countries when measured by a number of variables. There is also in Norway a tradition of individualism and local control (unlike Sweden), that negates and militates against the centralised or strong state associated with the social welfare tradition (this may offer a partial explanation of why following a referendum of the people in 1972, Norway (now a member of the European Union) did not join the European Common Market when Denmark became a member). The tradition of local control reflects the sparse population of Norway combined with the high number of small, semi-independent municipalities. Norway has 20 counties and 438 municipalities but only 97 municipalities have 10,000 or more inhabitants, while 252 have fewer than 5000 – including approximately 1500 children. Sweden, with twice the national population, has only 270 municipalities.

In summary, while a basic 'safety net' of income support and health programmes is universally available to Norwegian children, their welfare is poorer in some respects than that of children in other Nordic countries, with some gaps in services that are commonly provided even in countries with substantially less commitment to welfare state ideology. An example here is the relative unavailability of pre-school education for Norwegian children compared to their Swedish and Danish counterparts. In the latter countries, where school also starts at seven, 56 per cent and 55 per cent respectively enjoyed pre-school provision in 1987, but in Norway only 30 per cent of children under the age of seven had access to pre-school opportunities, and many of these were in programmes offering only 4–9 hours per week.

Looking more closely at the reasons for these differences, Leira, in comparing the three countries claims:

> Examining the policies concerning mothers' earning and caring commitments, I find the notion of a common Scandinavian 'model' of reproduction policies is exaggerated. The results of policies, particularly as witnessed in Norway, also do not fit well with the 'model' of the Scandinavian welfare states as institutional in their overall design . . . . State-sponsored childcare represents a substantially larger share of the total supply of services in Denmark and Sweden than in Norway. Moreover, the policies of the three countries appear to be grounded in different images of the mother–child relationship, and of the relation of family policy to the economy. In Denmark and Sweden the economy's need for labour was integrated into child policies to an extent not seen in Norway.
>
> (1989: 71)

Leira goes on to point out that in Norway informal child-minding and social network-based arrangements are not included in legislation and are therefore outside the state's sphere of responsibility. The actual provision of day-care by local authorities is not mandatory.

> The welfare state recruits women to the public sector labour market, but the problems of childcare remain the responsibility of the families, particularly the mothers . . . . The welfare state is supposed to take care of those who cannot care for themselves, but care in itself is not esteemed.
>
> (*ibid.*)

The costs of informal and private arrangements are met by the mothers, while only 10 per cent of their taxes go into childcare facilities.

The differences described by Leira concern pre-school children, but the same pattern can be seen with regard to older children. School hours are shorter in Norway, and public care facilities for school-age children were practically non-existent until 1991. In Denmark any child who needed looking after before or after school hours could attend a 'free-time home'. Norwegian schools do not provide meals; Swedish primary and secondary schools serve a hot meal in the middle of the day.

In summary, the relative paucity of welfare provision in Norway compared to Sweden and Denmark, combined with the Norwegian emphasis on individualism and a tradition of political localism, may explain the emergence of an Ombudsman in Norway rather than in any of its Nordic neighbours.

THE CHILD IN A CHANGING SOCIETY

In Norway, as in many industrialised countries, patterns of family life are changing. Few families have more than one or two children; typically both parents work outside the home; the number of single-parent families is increasing; familial support-systems are disappearing. An increasing number of families are living in poverty prompted by unemployment. The influence of these factors on children's lives depends on the extent to which society attempts to compensate children to offset any detrimental effects of such changes.

One consequence of a rapidly changing demography is rarely mentioned: Norway has an aging population. In Norway children currently constitute 25 per cent of the total population but in 20 years time, given a stable birthrate, they will constitute only 15 per cent of the population. The relative declining proportion of total population which children constitute reflects the enormous increase in the population of elderly people. Politicians will become increasingly concerned with the problems of the elderly – not least because the elderly can vote and they can also be elected. Politicians, moreover, have parents who may live to be 80, 90, or even 95 years old. They need care, and politicians are well aware that in the near future they too will form part of the older group in society. The aging character of the Norwegian population and the claims of the elderly for resources and services provides an additional reason in favour of a strong voice for children's claims.

WHY AN OMBUDSMAN FOR CHILDREN?

Children have particular needs and interests which must be respected and which may require special measures to protect and promote them. In addition children constitute a unique group in a democracy in three respects.

First, children have no influence in the choice of persons – or in the composition of institutions – that are responsible for decisions influencing the conditions under which children must live and grow. Children have no way of ensuring that their choice of political party or candidate is elected to serve on municipal, county, state or national governing bodies. Similarly, they have no voice in determining which issues will be on the election agenda.

Second, in contrast to children, adults have the right to vote but also enjoy other means of swaying public opinion. Mass media provide channels through which adults can make their views known and provoke public debate, either as individuals or collectively through pressure groups.

Third, legislation promoting or enforcing the rights of children remains relatively weak compared to legislation governing the rights of adults. The rights of children, for example, are often indirect; the right may be given to an adult (often the parents) to be exercised on the child's behalf. Children's rights are further weakened in that they may be 'conditional' i.e. only valid under certain conditions, for instance that funds are available or that the parents are willing to cooperate to ensure the right of the child.

These were the main reasons for establishing the Ombudsman for Children in Norway in 1981. An Ombudsman for Public Administration had been established in 1962, for Consumer Affairs in 1972, while the Ombudsperson for the Equal Status of Men and Women was appointed in 1979. The first proposal for an Ombudsman for Children appeared in 1968, but gained momentum following the United Nations International Year of the Child in 1979. The Act creating the Ombudsman Office for Children was passed by the *Storting* (Parliament) in March 1981, with a very narrow (5 votes) majority. Three reservations were raised concerning the proposal. First, it was alleged that the Ombudsman would threaten parental authority. Second, that the existence of an Ombudsman might provide an excuse for other organisations and services for children to renege on their responsibilities. Finally, it was suggested that funds allocated to resource and support the office of Ombudsman would be better spent on strengthening existing children's services. These negative arguments are no longer heard in Norway and have long since been confounded by the experience of ombudswork with children, but they are worth reiterating because they are often cited against proposals for similar 'watchdog' mechanisms for children in other countries.

Parliament, by creating the office, gave official recognition to the necessity and legitimacy of child advocacy. The interests of children cover so many areas and prompt consideration of so many issues, that existing offices could neither meet them nor provide an overview of conditions for children.

Unlike the Ombudsman offices for Equal Status of Women or Consumer Affairs, the Ombudsman for Children is not responsible for any single law or sets of laws. The purpose of the office is to 'promote the interests of children *vis à vis* public and private authorities, and to follow the development of conditions under which children grow up' (Act of the Commissioner for Children, Section 3). The only prohibitions on this broad brief relate to the handling of individual conflicts within the family, and cases which have already been brought to court.

As a 'watchdog' guarding children's rights, the Ombudsman must keep an eye on all aspects of society, signal any development that may prove harmful to children's interests, and propose changes designed to improve their condition.

In particular, the Ombudsman must be alert to the potential consequences for children of any part of Norwegian legislation and regulations. The full range of duties and responsibilities of the Ombudsman were laid down in a set of instructions issued in September 1981. The office wields no decision-making power, nor does it have the right to revoke the decisions of other authorities. Advocacy via the spread of information and documented case presentations are therefore its principal weapons. The office seeks to increase public knowledge and change the opinions and attitudes of others in such a way as to improve the situation of children.

Levels of staffing and budget were initially modest. When first established, the office had a total staff of four people and an annual budget of approximately US $300,000, for 1988. This represents roughly one staff member per million Norwegians or one for every 250,000 children at an annual cost of 25 cents per child. An important lesson, therefore, has been that worthwhile results can be achieved even on a low budget. The staff was increased to five and one half in 1990 and currently has eight members. The budget was increased by 25 per cent in 1989 and by a further 25 per cent in 1990 and for the year 1991–2. The expansions in budgets and staffs signal the increasing recognition of the usefulness of the office, the professional status it enjoys and its popular standing with the public. The office handled approximately 2500 complaints annually during the first eight years. About 10 per cent of contacts were initiated by children, who were largely of school age; girls outnumber boys by two to one.

EVALUATION AND RESULTS

There is no doubt that the Ombudsman has been of considerable help in dealing with many individual cases. The first priority, however, was to establish a permanent status and favourable public image for the office. A public opinion poll conducted in November 1989 found that 74 per cent of a random population sample (all over 15 years of age) knew about the office; 83 per cent of these felt that the office was useful and should continue. Only 2 per cent felt that its continued existence was not justified. Between 80 and 90 per cent of voters for parties which initially opposed the office of Ombudsman, now support it. There can be little doubt that the Ombudsman for Children is a permanent, well-known and well established office.

It is impossible, of course, to know precisely what changes might have been implemented in the law relating to children if the Ombudsman had not been established in 1981. By 1989 the role of the Ombudsman in achieving the following measures was publicly acknowledged; each change was achieved, moreover, without any drain on public funds:

1 Legislation prohibiting physical punishment and physical and psychological treatment threatening the physical or pyschological development of children. A prohibition which includes parents

2 Restrictions imposed on the distribution of videogrammes
3 New regulations concerning the rights of hospitalised children
4 Raising the age at which young people can be tried and sentenced by adult courts and imprisoned in adult prisons
5 Improved building regulations for safety and accident prevention in the home
6 Regulations for child safety in cars
7. The establishment of national, governmental guidelines to incorporate the needs of children into all urban and rural planning considerations
8 Recognition in law of children's right to know both their parents, regardless of marital status or whether the parents actually lived together after the child was born.

Other proposals, such as the right of the child to pre-school education or to social welfare benefits have not yet been passed, but nor have they been shelved. But the most important outcome of establishing the Ombudsman is difficult if not impossible to measure: it is simply that children now have a place to go with their opinions and complaints.

The Norwegian Ombudsman for Children combines several functions concerning children's needs and rights. The Ombudsman:

• Receives complaints and requests from individuals (adults and children) who may be helped directly or indirectly by the office
• Receives and distributes information, proposals, referrals to and from the local level services and organisations
• Receives and distributes information to and from the administrative branches at the community, county and national levels
• Communicates information, proposals for changes of procedures, decisions, rules, regulations and legislation to politicians at local and national levels
• Offers advice about the timing and need for new legislation relating to children

In the Norwegian setting there have been evident advantages in fusing these various functions in a single office, but other countries may wish to consider afresh whether these different functions can be usefully and practically combined. In some countries for example, the idea of serving as a direct communication channel between the children themselves and the top-level decision-makers may seem impossible, perhaps because of the prevailing religious law. Leaving out this function deprives children of the possibility to influence decisions directly, but does not mean that children have nowhere to go. A child with a problem may consult parents, relatives, friends or teachers (who may or may not take the problem elsewhere). They may turn to the local services, including organisations, churches or even lower-level courts. But what children may *not* have is a service to turn to when others cannot or will not help.

Ombudswork could be conducted under a variety of organisational formats. In countries where a large number of organisations are already involved in work with children, an 'ombudsman' need not necessarily be established as a statutory office. A non-governmental organisation could be allocated (by parliamentary decision) a special responsibility to work towards establishing and policing the rights of children. In these circumstances, however, it would be very important for public funding (with no strings attached) to be available to guarantee the autonomy of the organisation.

It would also be possible to establish an 'umbrella' organisation enbracing a number of independent groups. Non-governmental organisations would understandably wish to protect their individual identity and commitment to particular causes, but there are many advantages to working cooperatively; similarly, competition can sometimes be detrimental to outcomes and effectiveness. If these constituent organizations could agree to work together, a steering committee could coordinate their work to maximise effect. The steering committee could also propose measures to improve the situation of children and perhaps help monitor the implementation of the Convention on the Rights of the Child.

WHAT ARE THE IMPORTANT LESSONS OF THE NORWEGIAN EXPERIENCE?

Since 1981 public national Ombudsmen for Children have been established in Costa Rica, New Zealand and Sweden. State-level Ombudsmen now exist in Austria and Australia, and local level offices exist in many cities in many countries (see this volume). The adoption of the UN Convention for the Rights of the Child, moreover, has triggered a growing concern to establish structures to monitor the circumstances of children and the policies of governments towards them. Some of the Convention principles are undoubtedly difficult to implement in some countries, where they are perhaps best interpreted as longer-term goals rather than immediate policy prospects. The following is a brief summary of the principles which apply to the Norwegian office and are applicable to similar offices.

The Ombudsman must serve as a voice for children

This should be the fundamental guiding principle of any structure monitoring the fulfilment of children's rights. Serving as a 'voice' or channel of communications between children and the health, welfare and education systems, the judiciary, the local planning boards and any area of government where decisions affecting children are made. The office must transmit the views of children to policy makers, make the needs and rights of children known to the general public, and make sure that the concerns and opinions which children themselves express are taken into account in any decision-making process. It is also important to impart information to children. To make sure, for example, that children are aware of the UN Convention and the requirements it places on government.

The office must be independent of the political administration and other political organisations

The term 'independent' is used very specifically in this context to mean that it should not be possible for the Ombudsman to be manipulated by the government or by political parties. Government officials should not be able to intervene in the work of the office and it should be able to respond honestly to individuals seeking help.

A *public* Ombudsman or Commissioner will necessarily have an administrative link with a branch of government, a clearly specified mandate limiting the scope of his or her activities, and a budget within which to work. But he or she can nonetheless, be 'independent' if the following principles are observed: the Ombudsman must be protected from arbitrary dismissal by government; the Ombudsman must have constitutional support; the office should be based on wide cross-party support rather than springing from the policy of a specific party or government; the Ombudsman requires financial independence. Funding should be guaranteed by the state and not dependent on the party in power. Non-governmental organisations must attain the same level of financial independence, and could do so by having a broad base of financial support.

The office must be accessible to the public including children

Access to the office should be as direct and non-bureaucratic as possible. Children and their families should be able to relate easily to the office by identifying it with a person or, in some situations, with an institution or an organisation which is widely acknowledged to be concerned with children's issues.

The office must be close to decision-making bodies which have an impact on children

One way of bridging the distance between politicians and voters is to provide the public with information about the performance of politicians – which in itself increases the pressure on them to keep their promises and strengthen their commitments.

The office works for and within networks at state and local levels, as well as at the non-governmental level

To be effective, the office must establish close contacts within the community, with departments of state, with schools, professional groups, the media and individuals.

Credibility is one avenue to authority

Ultimately, any office committed to Ombudswork, whether inside or outside the government, will carry weight only if it establishes credibility and is 'legitimated' by the communities and families that it serves. In order to achieve such credibility, it is essential that the office serves only the interests of children; it must never be suspected of having a hidden agenda. Statements must always be based on facts even though valid statistics describing the circumstances of children are not readily available.

Surveying existing Ombudswork offices and similar mechanisms for protecting and promoting children's rights, suggests that a small, homogenous country with a democratic political system and a tradition of using legislation as a tool to improve the conditions of minority groups, are *not* necessarily prerequisites for establishing such an office. A large nation, particularly a federation of states, however, might well need a different kind of organisation, size and/or mandate for the office.

The size of a country, its political system, cultural traditions, governmental structures and the overall position of children within the country, will each influence the choice of organisational structure for monitoring and promoting conditions for children and young people. In some countries this may require the establishment of offices at sub-national levels to be close to the decision-making mechanisms (see chapter 6). In other countries, the office may be constituted by groups of organisations or by a single organisation authorised by the national government to serve as the Ombudsman for Children. But though they can be applied in quite different contexts the principles for successful Ombudswork outlined above are constant.

The Scandinavian experience is spreading. Similar Ombudsman offices have been established in other countries. More significantly, the lessons learned from the Norwegian experience and other similar offices will facilitate the work for children all over the world.

REFERENCES

Barneombudet *Annual Reports 1981–1988* (in Norwegian only) Oslo 1982, 1983, 1984, 1985, 1986, 1987, 1988, 1989.
——— (1987) *Fakta om barn i Norge*, Barneombudet: Oslo.
——— (1988/89) *Fakta om barn i Norge*, 2nd edition Barneombudet: Oslo.
——— (1991) *Facts about Children in Norway*, Barneombudet: Oslo.
Flekkøy, Målfrid Grude (1990) *Working for the Rights of Children*, UNICEF/Firenze (Eng., French, Spanish).
——— (1991a) *A Voice for Children. Speaking out as their Ombudsman* Jessica Kingsley Publishers: London.
——— (1991b) *Models for monitoring the protection of the rights of the child* (mimeo.), UNICEF/Firenze.
——— (1991c) 'Attitudes to children. Their consequences for work for Children' in P. Veerman (ed.) *Ideologies of Children's Rights*, Martinus Nijhoff: Amsterdam.

—— (1992) 'The Future of Child Advocacy on the National and International Levels', conference report, *International Conference on Implementation of the U.N. Convention on the Rights of the Child*, Adelaide.

—— (1993a) *Children's Rights. Reflections on and consequences of the use of developmental psychology in working for the interests of children. The Norwegian Ombudsman for Children: A practical experience* University of Ghent: Belgium.

—— (1993b) 'Children as holders of Rights and Obligations' in D. Gomien (ed.) *Broadening the Frontiers of Human Rights. Essays in Honour of Asbjørn Eide*, Scandinavian University Press: Oslo.

Leira, A.(1985) *Regelmessig barnetilsyn*. Oslo: Institutt for samfunnsforskning, arbeidsnotat 4/85.

—— (1989) *Models of Motherhood. Welfare State Policies and Everyday Practices: The Scandinavian Experience*. Rapport 89: 7, Institutt for samfunnsforskning: Oslo.

Chapter 14

Children's rights in Australia

Moira Rayner

Australia is not a country where rights are universally and equally enjoyed. Many children's lives have been shaped by poverty – affected by Australia's prolonged economic downturn (Harris, 1989, 1990). After decades of economic recession many children belong to a family whose parents are unemployed. They are affected by the sadness and deprivation, the greater risk of disease, accidental injury and death and reduced life opportunities that come with poverty.

Children's social and economic rights – to housing, education, health services, a decent standard of living based on adequate income – are crucial to the realisation of children's rights. The current economic and political climate favours reduction in government activity and the privatisation of its services; children's services are among the first to be reduced when budget cuts have to be made. Government provision of public services such as health, education and welfare is the foundation on which the realisation of children's rights depends. A family without support cannot fulfil the UN Convention's requirement of providing '*an atmosphere of love and understanding*.'

A preoccupation with efficiency and insensitivity to equity claims is often coupled with nostalgia for parental or 'family' discipline and control. There is some evident tension between these calls and the demands placed on Australia by its ratification of the Convention on the Rights of the Child in 1990.

Though Australia was not, as mythology would have it, a convict settlement – only two of the six States began as penal colonies – our political and Constitutional origins do not lie in the age of enlightenment nor the search for religious, political or economic freedom, but in the expansionist ambitions of British land speculators and civil servants. They saw in Australia *terra nullius*, an empty land, conveniently ignoring and overrunning its Aboriginal occupiers. Our colonial history has left Australians somewhat insensitive to the principles and the universality of 'human rights'.

CONSTITUTIONAL AND ADMINISTRATIVE FRAGMENTATION AND THE RIGHTS OF CHILDREN

Australian laws, institutions and policies about children are divided among the original six Australian colonies, now States[1] and two self-governing Territories[2] which are represented in the 'Australian', or Commonwealth, bicameral Parliament in Canberra. Though federated since 1901, each State vigorously guards its sovereignty. Each has its own Governor, written Constitution, Parliament, executive and judiciary. The Australian Constitution (1901) establishes a parallel system of Federal or Commonwealth courts, a Parliament whose upper house (the Senate) provides State representation proportionate to population, and an executive charged with carrying out the business of the Commonwealth government.

The Commonwealth has exclusive legislative powers under the Constitution in some areas – divorce and matrimonial causes, for example, and social security – but it does not have the authority to make laws with respect to children in general. Since the Commonwealth does not have explicit exclusive legislative authority, on occasions when its legislation overrides inconsistent State legislation, the States retain full competence. Most laws, policies and institutions affecting children – welfare and child protection services, health, education, criminal laws – are State based. This has led to a plethora of inconsistent Acts, regulations, practices and institutions across the country. Consequently, the degree to which a child's rights are protected and promoted depends on where the child lives.

One of the most significant, but relatively unused, powers that is exclusive to the Commonwealth is the ability to enter into, and make laws to implement, treaties and international obligations. This has become significant in light of Australia's international commitment to human rights – especially the Convention on the Rights of the Child.[3]

The implementation of these obligations by Commonwealth legislation is somewhat sparing. Much of Australia's public infrastructure is at State (or local) level: State courts and government agencies administer most of the relevant law and policy affecting children, and give effect to its international treaty obligations, so their cooperation is needed and sought. The States are closely involved in the preparation of reports to international bodies on the implementation of treaties.[4] Electorate support for the Commonwealth government is organised on a State and Territory basis. Local issues matter federally.

Many ordinary people were told, during the carefully orchestrated controversy before Australia's ratification of the Convention on the Rights of the Child, that it would mean the loss of parental authority over children to the State, and of Australian sovereignty to the international community represented by the United Nations. Treaties do not become part of Australian law, however, unless they are incorporated into it by statute[5] or by courts interpreting common or statute law. Though the Commonwealth has established a human rights watchdog – the Human Rights and Equal Opportunity Commission (HREOC; established under the Human Rights and Equal Opportunity Commission Act 1986) – this does not necessarily provide a remedy for rights infringements other than for discrimination on particular grounds – sex, race and disability. Each State and Territory (except Tasmania) has also developed its own 'equal opportunity' or anti-discrimination legislation and institutions which co-exist with Commonwealth anti-discrimination laws and remedies. In some cases the statutory officer administers both schemes.[6]

The division of legislative and bureaucratic authority with respect to children has deeply influenced the development of children's law, policy and practice.

The Convention on the Rights of the Child has not been incorporated, legislatively, into federal legislation as other human rights instruments have been.[7] Until very recently there was no uniformity or even complementarity in child custody laws other than where the parties were married, when the (Commonwealth) Family Law Act 1975 applied, among the eight legal systems. Each State and Territory had its own laws and policies with respect to the guardianship and custody of extra-marital children, though 'cross-vesting' provisions now permit courts to exercise jurisdiction over all relevant children affected by disputes before them. Even the laws which prohibit child abuse, or deal with juvenile offending change the moment one crosses State boundaries: the age of criminal responsibility varies from seven in Tasmania; eight in the Australian Capital Territory to ten in most other jurisdictions. Laws prohibiting child pornography, the mechanisms for protecting children from abduction, prostitution and other forms of exploitation or abuse, vary among jurisdictions. Children with special needs are particularly ill-served by the variety of 'child welfare' legislation, bureaucracies, practices and service-delivery across State and Territory borders: there are even different definitions of what constitutes 'child abuse' and requirements for mandatory reporting.[8]

Nor is there any comprehensive national children's policy. This is crucial to the implementation of the Convention on the Rights of the Child. Without a coherent, consistent and permanent voice for children at both national and State level implementation cannot be achieved.

There are examples of national policy leadership, such as the Commonwealth's establishment of the National Child Protection Council in 1991, and the development of the Children's Services Program in 1991–92 (services for disabled children), but there is no national governmental overview of children's policy. Social security benefits may be Commonwealth planned and delivered, but social welfare services such as housing, education, emergency relief, childcare, child protection and family support services are all State-delivered.

There are attempts to achieve a national approach through consultation. In April 1993 the Australian Health Ministers' advisory council endorsed the concept of a National Child and Youth Health Policy. State, Territory and Federal Attorneys General meet regularly, although the standing committee of Attorneys General does not always, or even frequently, agree on uniform or even complementary legislative schemes or reforms, and children's policy is much less a priority than uniform corporations or defamation laws. There is, though, no single Commonwealth portfolio affecting children's policy; this is generally subsumed under 'family' or women's or 'welfare' portfolios.

The Commonwealth's potential to undertake a national role in the development of children's policy, dependent on the agreement of the States and Territories, is limited in 1994 because only one State, Queensland, shares the Federal Australian Labor Party's political platform. It was quite odd to observe that the Commonwealth succeeded in obtaining that consent to its criminalising paedophile activities by Australians overseas, and associated activities within Australia, because of the scandal of Asian 'sex tours'. The irresistible conclusion is that the 'States rights' attitude of our many governments has led to a thoroughly ineffective proliferation of laws, institutions, policies and practices about children within Australia while greater concern is shown for Australia's 'image' in the cities and towns of our Asian trading partners.

THE UN CONVENTION, CHILDREN'S RIGHTS AND THE LAW

Australia's ratification of the Convention on the Rights of the Child could bring about some improvement because Australia has committed itself to implementing a children's rights charter, the key provision of which is Article 12: this gives children the right to participate in decisions which affect them. It is a keystone because it requires that children's views and autonomy be taken seriously.

> *1 States Parties shall assure to the child who is capable of forming his or her own views the right to express those views freely in all matters affecting the child, the views of the child being given due weight in accordance with the age and maturity of the child.*
> *2 For this purpose, the child shall in particular be provided the opportunity to be heard in any judicial and administrative proceedings affecting the child, either directly, or through a representative or an appropriate body, in a manner consistent with the procedural rules of national law.*

Article 12 says what most childcare professionals and good parents say: that a child's views must be valued. To be valued, children must be heard. To be heard, children must be invited to participate, in the decision to be made, in a way they can understand. This puts a duty on adults to understand and involve children. It does not allow adults, or policy-makers, simply to assume the decisions they make about children are proper and 'in their best interests'. The right to be taken seriously is the essence of human dignity, which is fundamental to all human rights.

Needless to say, this is not the rule in Australian child law and practice. Even where the law mandates consultation – for instance, the (Commonwealth) Family Law Act 1975[9] requires a court to give appropriate weight to a child's wishes – there is no means of monitoring its implementation. There is no provision for special training for children's advocates in legal proceedings, despite recommendations from the Commonwealth Family Law Council (1989).

Australian Courts have however begun to use 'rights' language in the interpretation of children's legislation and may also refer to international instruments to resolve ambiguities in domestic Statutes (see *Minister for Foreign Affairs* v *Magno* [1993]). It has not yet been argued, and the argument seems to be open, whether the addition of international instruments into the Schedule of the Human Rights and Equal Opportunity Commission Act 1986 'incorporates' the Convention into Australian law. But the High Court has demonstrated its willingness increasingly to refer to such human rights instruments.[10] Recently the Full Court of the Family Court (in *Murray* v *Director Family Services Act* [1993]) said the court's power to refer to the Hague Convention and the Convention on the Rights of the Child would allow it to fill lacunae in such legislation.

There is also evidence of the independent development of children's participatory rights at common law, particularly in recent cases about children's medical treatment – admittedly unusual ones revolving around child abuse investigations or sterilisation decisions. In some States children have the statutory power to authorise their own medical treatment (see for example the South Australian Consent to Medical and Dental Procedure Act 1985). Otherwise the common law, as expressed in *Gillick* [1986], allows a child to authorise their own medical treatment if they have the intelligence and understanding to comprehend the nature and purpose of what is proposed. The High Court recently addressed this in the 'Marion' case (*Secretary, Department of Health and Community Services* v *JSWB and Anor* [1992]) in stating that no child, not even an intellectually impaired child, should be assumed to lack the legal capacity to consent to their own medical treatment, particularly the sterilisation procedure proposed.

Two judges also dealt with the basis on which adults – and courts – are to make decisions for children who cannot make those choices. Traditionally, courts (and parents) make decisions for their children saying that they are based on their 'best interests'.[11] In this instance Brennan J. said, that to adopt a 'guideline' to the exercise of a discretion to be determined in each set of circumstances of 'best interests', merely leaves the decision to 'an unexaminable discretion'. Instead, he adopted an explicit human rights principle: the measure by which the 'impairment of human dignity' would be affected by the decision.

Common law, however, takes a long and unpredictable time to change through court determinations, but sometimes this is not warranted. Recent developments in two States, Western Australia and Victoria, seem to indicate that if the human rights of children are to be protected, the time has come for the Commonwealth to adopt a pro-active approach. This will take some firmness of resolve. The fundamental reason for the unwillingness of governments to take a global or consistent approach to children's rights is that children's 'rights' are a political hotspot, from which they have all suffered some scorching.

ONE STEP FORWARD, TWO STEPS BACKWARDS?

The resistance to children's rights recognition has become much more evident in the last two years. Good developments have been lost. In South Australia, for example, the path-finding Children's Interests Bureau lost its administrative independence of the State welfare authority in 1993 because of amendments and restructuring; in the same year in Victoria, the independent professional advisory service to the Children's Court was subsumed into the State Department of Health and Community Services, and its child protection workers were authorised to 'represent' children in 'consent' care and protection applications in amendments to the Children and Young Persons Act 1989. Children in need of substitute care also began to suffer under the weight of administrative restructuring and economic cutbacks in that State.

In 1991, shortly after Australia ratified the Convention, the Victorian Equal Opportunity Commissioner commenced an inquiry into claims of serious discrimination against women prisoners detained in a men's prison, Barwon, south of Melbourne. The most serious of the claims were that the 'double confinement' of women in a principally men's maximum security facility prevented their children being with their mothers, most of whom had been metropolitan-based and their primary carers. The Commissioner tried to resolve the issues by negotiation, but without success. The situation deteriorated. In early 1993 it was revealed that new visiting rules required that all visitors, including children, had to be strip-searched (including body cavity searches of infants) before the one hour a week at the weekend, to which their visits were to be restricted. These women prisoners preferred to reject all contact with their children rather than subject them to such procedures.

It was then strongly 'leaked' that it was intended to close Fairlea, the only women's prison in the Melbourne metropolitan area, for economic reasons and to move the prisoners into a maximum security concrete facility, Jika Jika, in Pentridge (men's) prison, described after a fatal fire, as a 'concrete zoo' unfit for human habitation. The Commissioner sought an interim injunction to protect the prisoners' access to their children, pending a hearing. The Victorian government expressed outrage at such 'preemption' of or 'interference' with government policy, but virtually the entire Victorian public was bitterly opposed to the proposal. There is little doubt that the Commissioner's action contributed to the sudden announcement of the abolition of the position of Commissioner for Equal Opportunity exactly three months later.

The trend to cutbacks in children's services and vigorous rejection of children's equity claims in Victoria continued. In sentencing a young stepfather for bashing two year old Daniel Valerio slowly to death, the judge asserted that mandatory reporting of child abuse would have saved him – 25 professionals had seen Daniel in the weeks leading to his death.[12] Weeks later the government did introduce mandatory reporting legislation, to public acclaim. It then slashed the State's provision for early intervention and family support services for such children. Critics of the government's cost-cutting measure on children's rights grounds included Justice Fogarty, a judge of the Family Court of Australia, who had three times reviewed the State's welfare services generally as well as their failure to save this child and recommended mandatory reporting. The cuts, he said, would destroy progress towards an effective child protection service. The judge was personally and publicly attacked by government spokesmen, including the Premier, for his 'political' comment. In Victoria the need for family support had risen dramatically, particularly in areas hard hit by unemployment and the loss of other Government services, where the reporting rate of suspected abuse had risen by more than 40 per cent in six months.

Western Australia's introduction of discriminatory juvenile sentencing legislation in 1992 was a deliberate breach of the Convention. The Crime (Serious and Repeat Offenders) Sentencing Act of 1992 arose as a political response to a perceived crime wave involving stolen vehicles and deadly pursuit in which sixteen people died; five of them were juvenile offenders in that State. The government had established a multi-disciplinary Advisory Committee on Young Offenders, to integrate community responses to juvenile offending. Its recommendations were not accepted and, after Christmas night 1991, became irrelevant. A young pregnant mother and her toddler were killed in a high-speed car chase involving a 14-year-old Aboriginal boy in a stolen car and police. The media turned feral, and the government responded with draconian legislation. The Act provides for mandatory and indeterminate sentencing based on cate-gories of 'prescribed offences'. It overturned the fundamental 'best interests' principle of juvenile sentencing – that detention should be a sentence of last resort, for the shortest appropriate time, not arbitrary, proportionate (which is completely at odds with indeterminacy) and capable of judicial review.[13]

The national outcry from academics, criminologists, religious and human rights advocates led the Commonwealth to criticise the legislation, but it did not attempt to override it as it could have done. It is possible only to infer the pragmatic and political considerations which were at work. The Western Australian legislation discriminated against Aboriginal children – most of the offenders were Aboriginal youths with appalling histories of abuse, exploitation and neglect – in a State somewhat intolerant of Aboriginal youth and possessing the second highest arrest and detention rate for children, particularly Aboriginal children, in the country. The State Labour Government was heading towards what looked like an unwinnable (as it was) State election within the next year, as was the federal Australian Labour Party Government (which was, surprisingly, re-elected). Though it was widely condemned within and outside the State, the legislation was as popular with the Western Australian public as 'Eastern States'' criticism was resented. The legislation was actually broadened in 1993 to cover many other children (Harding, 1993).

The fact that governments deliberately breach human rights standards which they endorse or even overtly support internationally, is not surprising. Adults tend to overlook children's rights at the best of times: the requirement that children suspected of offences should not be questioned by police without a support person or their parent is not reflected in practice. In every mainland State and Territory governments have enacted anti-discrimination laws, then pro-ceeded to breach them. In 1992–93 nearly 35 per cent of the complaints of discrimination received in Victoria were of discrimination by State, Commonwealth and local government.

The imposition of indeterminate, adult sentences on children takes on a more serious aspect if children are also denied advocacy or legal representation. We recognise children's right to express views in disputes between their parents over guardianship and custody – the Family Law Act 1975 (Section 64(1)(b))[14] requires a court to give appropriate weight to a child's wishes and there are other provisions enabling the 'separate representation' of a child.[15] There is provision in various State welfare jurisdictions for a child's views to be expressed. Other than in Victoria there is generally no requirement for legal representation for offending children. Even if there were, there is no provision for specially trained advocates for children or proper government funding for children's specialist legal services.[16] There seems to be little point in recognising a child's right to participation but then denying the means of expressing those or any view.

THE ABUSE OF ABORIGINAL CHILDREN'S RIGHTS

In one area of children's policy the Commonwealth and the States share the responsibility for real human rights abuses: Aboriginal child health and welfare. The wretched position of Aboriginal children was exhaustively documented by the Royal Commission into Aboriginal Deaths in Custody (1991). The gap between the children of the 'haves' and 'have nots' is particularly apparent in Aboriginal families, whose children are three times more likely to die in infancy than non-Aboriginal children, and five times more likely to be hospitalised; whose health problems from upper respiratory tract and middle ear infections (often causing education-disabling deafness), trachoma and intestinal infections have reached crisis proportions in some parts of Australia (Choo, 1990; Health Targets and Implementation Committee, 1988). Many Aboriginal children who commit offences come from appalling social circumstances. The separation of Aboriginal children from their families in earlier generations has left a legacy of mental health problems, and contributes to parenting problems. Aboriginal children face ongoing poverty and lack of appropriate access to education and training and thus to employment, perpetuating that cycle (Harding, 1993). Education is also a means of breaking the cycle.

In December 1992 the Victorian government closed a metropolitan secondary school, Northlands College, for financial reasons (the cost of maintenance to the building). The school had been uniquely successful in encouraging not only Aboriginal, but other deprived and marginalised students, to complete their secondary education and undertake other training. A complaint of race discrimination was made by two Aboriginal children who, without that College, were obliged to meet inappropriate criteria of educational achievement, curricula and teaching methods and to experience racism from other students and some teachers in other schools. They succeeded. The Equal Opportunity Board found that Aboriginal students could not access an education system effectively which was designed for a majority culture insensitive to their cultural heritage and needs, and that the Northlands College was the only secondary school which was appropriate to those needs. It ordered that the school should be re-opened forthwith for the 1994 school year. On the day before that year began the Victorian government won an appeal, on the ground that it was not discriminatory to require Aboriginal students to meet 'white' cultural norms in education. That message, immediately after the International Year of Indigenous Peoples and widespread distress and anger over Aboriginal land entitlements after the Mabo decision (*Mabo* v *Queensland* [1992]), is little short of appalling. So, too, is the evidence that well-intentioned Commonwealth funding policies cannot achieve the desired aim with an intransigent State administration. The Commonwealth provides Aboriginal Education Program funding to ensure access to education on a triennial basis on strategic plans drawn up within each State and Territory. Of what value would it be to Aboriginal students for the education funding to be withdrawn? It could only cause Aboriginal education to deteriorate further.

WHAT IS TO BE DONE?

Advocacy of human rights from the high moral ground is clearly inadequate, and arguably counterproductive, at least in the personal, short-term view. When I was asked to write this chapter I was the Victorian Commissioner for Equal Opportunity, responsible for the administration of Federal and State anti-discrimination law in that State. On 26 October 1993 the Victorian government announced the abolition of the office. Both the powers of the Commission and the rights of complainants will be dramatically diminished (see the Victorian Equal Opportunity (Amendment) Act 1993). There was, and is, enormous support for the work I had been doing. In the months leading up to the announcement, the Commissioner's public profile on government policies which significantly affected children – the closure of schools, particularly Northlands Secondary College; the deprivation of children's access to women in prisons designed for and occupied by men, and the reduction of early intervention and family support services for 'at risk' and abused children – had been very high and much criticised by government as an undue interference with Victorian State government policy. However:

> Services for children cannot . . . be allowed to develop primarily on the economic fluctuations of the nation . . . it is precisely when economic growth falters that attention to the principles of justice is particularly important to ensure that the costs of economic change do not disproportionately affect the life chances of poor children.
>
> (Harris, 1990: 10)

Children's human rights are more than claims of dependence. Human rights are ethical statements about the quality of a human life. Their protection is the reason for our organising into communities. Rights claims are inconvenient, sometimes costly (in monetary terms) and governments do try to avoid them.[17] It is essential to recognise and to speak out for the rights, not the needs, of children, particularly in times of social and economic hardship. At such times there is a greater need, both for an understanding of fundamental human rights and values, and advocacy for those who are unable to claim them for themselves. A 'human right' is a right possessed simply because we are all human beings, and children are people too. As the Preamble to the Convention on the Rights of the Child states:

> *recognition of the inherent dignity and of the equal and inalienable rights of*
> *all members of the human family is the foundation of freedom, justice and*
> *peace in the world.*

There is always a gap between any government's policies about children, and their implementation. In some respects Australia has excelled in its explicit recognition of the special vulnerability of children. The defects in its implementation are remediable.

First, a national plan for children, with ministerial responsibility at both State and Federal levels, should be established. The present *ad hoc* allocation of ministerial responsibility for 'the family' to ministers with 'women's interests' or welfare portfolios is not sufficient nor appropriate. A family is a social construct which ought to provide the environment within which a child will 'grow up in a family environment, in an atmosphere of happiness, love and understanding' so that it can fully assume its responsibilities within the community (Preamble to the UN Convention).

Second, we must change the way in which we respect the rights of children. No country which tolerates some children enjoying what others are excluded from – basic entitlements to a decent standard of living and human rights recognition – can criticise the human rights records of others. To that end Australia should explicitly incorporate the human rights principles it espouses in the Convention in national legislation which can override inconsistent State legislation. Given the lamentable failure of Australia's State and Territory governments to agree to a uniform or even complementary policy base for children's health, education and welfare delivery, the Commonwealth has the duty and the Constitutional and legal authority, to establish a legislative base for the development of national policy for children, based on their human rights, not on the 'rights' of the family or service needs.

Third, Australia must establish independent mechanisms to advise it of its priorities and to monitor its progress on children's rights. Under its external affairs power, the Commonwealth may create the legislative base for a children's charter of rights and an overriding provision for inconsistent State legislation That legislation should also establish a Children's Commissioner with the responsibility for monitoring Australian children's law and practice, with adequate powers to do so, and with the power and the resources to act on complaints of breaches of the rights of children.

Australians know very little about the Convention on the Rights of the Child and the important policy principles that it contains. It is one of the Commonwealth's obligations under the Convention to promote that knowledge. 'Rights' have little meaning if Governments override them because of competing political or economic constraints, or if adults feel they can override them in circumstances that seem special *to them*. The special quality of the human rights of children is that if they are not protected and promoted the damage can never be undone, and will be perpetuated for generations.

NOTES

1 In order of population, New South Wales (capital Sydney); Victoria (Melbourne); Queensland (Brisbane); Western Australia (Perth); South Australia (Adelaide) and Tasmania (Hobart).

2 Formerly 'Commonwealth' territory, but now self-governing: the Northern Territory (capital Darwin) and the Australian Capital Territory (capital Canberra, which is also the national capital).

3 17 December 1990. The ratification was completed only after consultation with and the agreement of the States.

4 This goes part of the way to explain why Australia's first report on its compliance with the *Convention on the Rights of the Child*, due in January 1993, was still incomplete in January 1994: another is the scanty resources devoted by the Commonwealth to compiling that report.

5 This has been done in, for example, the enactment of the (Commonwealth) Racial Discrimination Act 1975 (implementing the Convention on the Elimination of All Forms of Racial Discrimination) and the Sex Discrimination Act (implementing the Convention on the Elimination of all Forms of Discrimination Against Women). Many other international treaties are referred to in the Schedule to the (Commonwealth) Human Rights and Equal Opportunity Commission Act 1986.

6 Western Australia, South Australia, Victoria (at least until 1994), Queensland and the Australian Capital Territory. The grounds, areas and exemptions under each vary significantly.

7 See the (Commonwealth) Sex Discrimination Act 1984 and the Race Discrimination Act 1975. The Convention was incorporated into the Schedule to the Human Rights and Equal Opportunity Commission Act 1986, requiring the HREOC to monitor Australia's compliance with it, during 1993, after Opposition objection based on 'family rights' and 'national sovereignty' arguments.

8 Reporting of suspected abuse is now mandatory in all States except Western Australia.

9 Section 64(1)(b). There is no way of ensuring that a child's views will be expressed without a specific direction from the Court.

10 For instance, in *Mabo* v *Queensland* (1992) 107 ALR 1, 29 (the decision overturning the *terra nullius* principle with respect to 'native title') because of Australia's accession to the First Optional Protocol to the *International Covenant on the Protection of Civil and Political Rights* saying that it 'brings to bear on the common law the powerful influence of the Covenant and the international standards it imports. The common law does not necessarily conform with international law, but international law is a legitimate and important influence on the development of the common law, especially when international law declares the existence of universal human rights.'

11 This is often legislatively required – see, for example, the (Commonwealth) Family Law Act 1975, Section 64(1)(a) (the 'welfare' of the child is the paramount consideration in decisions about custody, guardianship or access).

12 Reporting of suspected abuse was not mandatory in Victoria and Western Australia at the time.

13 The Crime (Serious and Repeat Offenders) Sentencing Act 1992 requires children

who have committed more than a fixed number of prescribed offences to be sentenced according to defined sentencing guidelines which do not include the child's best interests. They are (a) the personal circumstances of any victim of the offence; (b) the circumstances of the offence including any death or injury to a member of the public or any loss or damage resulting from the offence; (c) any disregard by the offender for the interest of public safety; (d) the past record of the offender including attempted rehabilitation and the number of serious offences committed whether prescribed offences or not; the age of the offender; and any remorse or lack of remorse of the offender. Others who committed specific crimes were simply detained indeterminately, with an annual review after the first 18 months.

14 There is no way of ensuring that a child's views will be expressed.

15 See, for example the NSW Children (Care and Protection) Act 1987 Section 12; there is no statutory requirement for children's involvement in care applications in Tasmania or under the Queensland Children's Services Act 1965 though a separate representative has the power to direct 'separate representation' for a child under Section 52; it is mandatory in South Australia under the Child Protection and Young Offenders Act 1979 (Section 12(1a)(b)).

The role of a 'separate representative' of a child (a lawyer) is somewhat problematic, given the lawyer's lack of forensic, psychiatric and relevant skills and training – and the possible conflict between a child's 'best interests' and their instructions: see *Guidelines for Separate Representatives of Children in Appointed Pursuant to Section 65 of the Family Law Act* 1983; In the *Marriage of Lyons and Boseley* [1978] FLC 90-423; *Harris* [1977] FLC 90-276, *Wotherspoon and Cooper* [1981] FLC 91-029, [1993] FLC 92-400 and *P (a child); Separate Representative* [1993] FLC 92-376.

16 The National Children's and Youth Law Centre was established in Sydney by the (private) Australian Youth Foundation in 1993, and OzChild (National Children's Bureau of Australia) has just announced the establishment of a children's legal service in Melbourne; church groups established the Youth Advocacy Centre (Brisbane) and the Youth Legal Service (Perth) and the only specialist legal aid service is to be found in the Western Australian Legal Aid Commission (though good services are found in Victoria and elsewhere).

17 See, for example, the Victorian Education (Amendment) Act 1993, which not only excludes any right of review by the Equal Opportunity Board, but also any kind of judicial review by the Supreme Court, by amending the Victorian Constitution. The latter kind of exemption has become disturbingly commonplace in Victorian legislation since 1992.

CASES CITED

Gillick v *West Norfolk and Wisbech Health Authority* [1986] AC 112
Mabo v *Queensland* [1992] 107 ALR 1
Minister for Foreign Affairs v *Magno* [1993] 112 ALR 529
Murray v *Director Family Services ACT* [1993] FLC 982
Secretary, Department of Health and Community Services v *JSWB and Anor* [1992] 106 ALR 385

REFERENCES

Choo, C. (1990) 'Aboriginal Child Poverty' in *Child Poverty Policy Review* Brotherhood of St Laurence: Melbourne.
Family Law Council (1989) *Representation of Children in Family Law Proceedings*.

Harding, R.W. (ed.) (1993) *Repeat Juvenile Offenders; The Failure of Selective Incapacitation in Western Australia* Research Report no. 10, November, The University of Western Australia Crime Research Centre.

Harris, P. (1989) 'Child Poverty, Inequality and Social Justice' in *Child Poverty Policy Review* Brotherhood of St Laurence: Melbourne.

—— (1990) 'All Our Children' in *Child Poverty Policy Review* Brotherhood of St Laurence: Melbourne.

Health Targets and Implementation Committee (1988) *Health For All Australians* Australian Government Printing Service: Canberra.

Chapter 15

Outside childhood: street children's rights

Judith Ennew

In February 1993 UNICEF hosted 34 experts from 20 countries at the *Spedale degli Innocenti* in Florence, to take part in the 4th Global Seminar of the International Child Development Centre (ICDC) usually referred to as the 'Innocenti Centre'. It is a building designed by Brunelleschi, constructed between 1419 and 1424 in order to care for the orphaned and abandoned children of the city state. It is an extraordinarily beautiful building. Above the loggia runs a series of medallions by Della Robbia, each depicting a baby, described by E.M. Forster in *A Room with a View*, as 'those divine babies whom no cheap reproduction can ever stale . . . with their shining limbs bursting from the garments of charity, and their strong white arms extended against circles of heaven' (Forster, 1978: 39). Patricia Light, the Information Officer at ICDC, who passes through the archways of the loggia every day on her way to work believes that these babies gave Eglantyne Jebb the idea for the emblem of the first five-point Declaration on the Rights of the Child and the original logo of agencies such as Save the Children. The experts who met in February 1993 may have paid these divine babies only a passing glance. Their discussions concerned children with a different kind of visibility, who have also come to be a kind of modern icon – street children.

Later that same year, I stood at the opposite side of the Piazza to the loggia of the Innocenti in the early morning before another meeting about working children, taking a few moments to watch the developing November light bring the dull terracotta to life. Under the archways a heap of rugs and blankets began to stir. A girl emerged from a sleeping bag and methodically began to pack her belongings into a bundle. Within moments she was ready and had left the Piazza. I estimated that she was about 14 years old. The Florentines crossing the square to work or to bring their well-wrapped toddlers to the nursery school that now operates in the Innocenti did not seem to see her.

The contrast between children inside buildings and inside families with those who are outside both, is, like Brunelleschi's building, a modern phenomenon. Until the beginning of the eighteenth century, family life was lived far more in the public domain. The streets were the location for commerce, social life and socialisation. Children were less separated from adults and private life was not confined to a special domestic sphere, inside houses and nuclear families (Aries, 1979). As Patricia Holland points out, the defining characteristics of modern, Western childhood are dependency and powerlessness, the idea of the unhappy child completes the concept. The unhappy child does not have an adult to depend on – to be powerful on its behalf or, if it needs to be rescued, to put it back into childhood which, in ideological terms, stands for happiness, play, innocence and some kind of essential goodness in human nature. Child victims, of which street children are the most obvious in visual reproductions, have also come to stand for the dependency and powerlessness of the developing world: 'In the act of looking at these presentations, viewers recognise themselves as both adult and Western, as individuals with the ability to change a child's life for the better without changing their own for the worse' (Holland, 1992: 150). In contrast, child workers 'have rarely found a place in available imagery'. But street children have a particular image problem, 'it needs only a slight shift of perspective to see the child on the streets as an undesirable vagrant' (ibid.: 161) or, as in the case of the girl sleeping outside the Innocenti, not to see her at all.

It is no coincidence, I would claim, that the Convention on the Rights of the Child was drafted during the same decade as an unprecedented increase in interest in groups of children called 'street children'. Both the Convention and a number of initiatives for these children sprang from the same source, in activities connected with the United Nations International Year of the Child in 1979. In the juxtaposition of the Convention and the image of the street child the entire discourse of children's rights stands revealed. The Convention, in the drafting process, the resulting text and in its implementation, takes as its starting point Western, modern childhood, which has been 'globalised' first through colonialism and then through the imperialism of international aid (Detrick, 1992; Fyfe, 1989; Boyden, 1990).

One of the most crucial aspects of this nation of childhood is domesticity. The place for childhood to take place is inside – inside society, inside a family, inside a private dwelling. This means that street children are society's ultimate outlaws. As children are increasingly conceptualised as vulnerable and in danger from influences outside the private world of the family so they are increasingly banished from the streets. In the Western world they have lost the freedom to explore the world of peer group relationships and the geography of their community. Modern streets are for the circulation of traffic and pedestrians, they are no longer the locus of social life and socialisation. Modern streets, particularly at night, have come to be thought of, particularly in North America and Northern Europe as morally dangerous, especially for children (Boyden, 1990). Children who join police, prostitutes and adult vagrants on this arena at night are not only outside society, they are also outside childhood.

STREET CHILDREN AND THE CONVENTION ON THE RIGHTS OF THE CHILD

A number of Articles of the UN Convention on the Rights of the Child affect street and working children jointly and severally most days of their lives.

Article 2:
Protection against discrimination is denied to street children who are stigmatised by the street children image, which causes the public and state agents such as the police to view them as asocial and amoral. In Brazil, for example, they are blamed for the majority of street crime despite statistical evidence to the contrary (Ennew and Milne, 1989). In extreme cases this leads to their violent deaths at the hands of police and vigilantes (Dimenstein, 1991).

Article 3:
With very few exceptions, state provision for street children is undertaken less in their best interests and more in the interest of cleansing the streets of their presence. Far from being placed in situations of care under the supervision of competent staff with adequate standards of safety and health, many are placed in adult prisons, in violent and overcrowded reformatories, or in orphanages staffed by unqualified and often abusive personnel where pitifully inadequate resources make a mockery of any attempts to provide reasonable care.

Article 4:
Article 4 of the Convention states that countries must provide for children 'to the maximum extent of their available resources'. In the words of Thomas Hammarberg, one of the members of the Committee on the Rights of the Child, this means that 'it is not sufficient to give children what remains when the needs of other groups have been satisfied' (in Ennew and Milne, 1993: 5). Hammarberg's comment applies to an even greater extent to children outside childhood, already marginalised by society and not in receipt of any welfare provision, either from families of from the state.

Article 6:
The child's 'inherent right to life' and to 'survival and development' is denied to those street children who are gunned down in Brazil, Guatemala and South Africa, as well as to children who die or are permanently disabled as the result of working in hazardous conditions, like the explosion in a fireworks factory in Meenapatti, Sivakasi, on 12 July 1991, in which over 40 children died (Bhima Sangha, 1991).

Articles 7 and 8:
The rights to name, nationality and identity that are enshrined in these Articles are denied to many street children. Like so many disadvantaged children in developing

countries they are born to families so marginalised that their births are never registered. In essence they have no existence, which means they cannot later register for school, work or welfare. This underscores their outlaw status.

Articles 9, 10, 18, 20, 21 and 27:
All the provisions of Articles dealing with separation from parents, family reunification and adoption apply with particular force to street children. Moreover, as a visible group of children needing to be rescued from the street, they are an especially handy target for middle-class concern. This means that they are frequently in danger of being taken off the streets and either placed in institutions or for adoption without attempts being made to trace their natal families and perhaps support a reunification process. Their lack of documents reinforces this process. There is often an assumption that the family is 'a structure they have never known', despite the evidence that they not only have experienced family life but also often have some contact with parents or other kin (see for example Aptekar, 1988; Swart, 1990; Tyler *et al.*, 1992).

The principle in Article 18 that parents have 'the primary responsibility for the upbringing and development of the child' is accompanied by the state's responsibility to 'render appropriate assistance' to them in this task, which is also implied in Article 27. The lack or inadequacy of welfare provision, childcare facilities and other appropriate supports to parents fosters the conditions in which children are obliged to work to ensure family survival, or may leave home because of intolerable conditions. What is amazing is that so many marginalised families manage to hold together and care for their dependent children in situations of dire poverty. If they did not perform this superhuman task so well there would be many more children of the street.

Article 20:
Street children are frequently the product of abusive or neglectful parenting. Society has already failed to protect them from that. What is more, they are also both abused and neglected on the street. Programmes to rehabilitate them are almost always under-resourced and there have been few attempts to systematise or evaluate the work that is carried out, mostly by non-governmental organisations.

Article 22:
Refugee children, especially when they are unaccompanied by adults, often become street children whose legal status is particularly insecure. This can be compounded by other disadvantaging factors, as in the case of the Portuguese-speaking children from Mozambique who are now trying to scrape a living on the streets of Zimbabwe's capital, Harare.

Article 23:
Some children find themselves on the streets because they have an impairment. In the absence of adequate social support, families may find it impossible to cope

with severe physical, mental or behavioural problems experienced by their children. It may seem that there is no future for disabled family members apart from a lifetime of begging. In other cases children become disabled as a result of life on the streets. Traffic accidents, violence and drug use all have greater capacity for damaging the young and entail more peril for children than they do for adults.

Article 24:
Life on the streets can be particularly unhealthy and unhygienic, as can be seen from the following catalogue of the health problems suffered by a 15-year-old during seven years of living on the streets: scabies, lice, fleas, conjunctivitis, impetigo, amoebic dysentery, giardiasis, ascaris and gonorrhoea. More recently, he was infected with HIV (Connolly, 1990). A further problem for street children is accessing medical care. Because of their appearance and the stigma surrounding their existence they are often chased away from hospitals and clinics.

Article 26:
The inadequacy of social security systems for marginalised populations as a whole has adverse affects on the vast majority of the world's children. The fact that children have to seek a living on the streets and that their families are unable to provide sufficient overall support to keep them from living on the streets is an extreme symptom of this widespread social neglect of the most vulnerable groups. A further irony is that the type of work that children do on the street, in the informal sector, is not subject to the social insurance schemes that could provide a measure of protection. Likewise, children who work in the formal sector tend to do so illegally, below the minimum age for work. That is one of the reasons why they are employed: it keeps down the wage bill to employers. This amounts to a double disadvantage for street and working children. Because they are outside the family they cannot receive the benefits of social security. Despite the fact that they are workers, they are ineligible for social insurance because they are outside the formal sphere of work.

Articles 28, 29, 31 and 32:
As all street children work for survival it is axiomatic that they are not protected from economic exploitation. Moreover, child labour laws are seldom implemented and may even work to the detriment of child workers by expelling them from the formal labour market and obliging them to seek an income in casual, poorly-paid, exploitative and hazardous activities.

There are those who claim that the provision of compulsory education is all that is required to eliminate child labour (see for example Weiner, 1991). But education alone cannot do this unless children are freed from the necessity of working to survive. Moreover more children would attend schools if the education was relevant to their lives, experiences and aspirations in content and more interactive and respectful in its methods.

Article 33:
Not all street children are drug addicts, although some of the more lurid literature implies this and is thus connected to the stigmatisation of and discrimination against these children. However, drugs (particularly solvents) are easy and cheap to acquire and many children resort to regular use. Although there are some rehabilitation intervention programmes there is no consistent policy either at a national or international level that specifically aims to protect children from drug abuse.

Articles 34, 35 and 36:
Sensational accounts of street children often state or imply that they are all involved in prostitution. The truth is less exciting and more sordid. Many children, both male and female, sell sex at some time during their lives on the streets, but they are not all prostitutes; many who are would rather not be and sell sex only as a last resort. Many others do not sell sex at all. However, street children are increasingly suffering from a further discrimination because of the spread of HIV infection amongst them. Sexually transmitted diseases are a common health hazard, not only because of prostitution, but also because of the sexual relationships many have with each other, which some experience as warm and caring.

Far from being lucrative child sex is cheap. That is one of the most insufferable features of its essential tragedy. Children have no power to ask for a high fee from adult customers.

The highest profits in child sexual exploitation are not made from the sexual transaction itself but from the secondary exploitation of those who deal in prurient stories about it. This is not confined to the media. It is quite clear that some NGO activity has a voyeuristic element, not only in advocacy about child sexual exploitation but also in the glamorisation of street children as a group. Street children themselves often feel this acutely. Some do not wish to be given the label at all (see for example de Oliveira, 1989). Others complain about the failure of media exposures to produce tangible improvements in their situation (Reddy, 1992).

Articles 37 and 40:
All too often street children are deprived of their liberty, which may reflect the common assumption of their criminality. Even if they are not incarcerated in jails or reformatories they are institutionalised in orphanages and children's homes where the regime may be harsh or abusive and experienced as a form of imprisonment (Reddy, 1992). In many cases, after summary justice, they are confined in adult prisons, where they suffer ill-treatment at the hands of both staff and other prisoners. The effects can be traumatic: 'Giovanni had been beaten and abused while in prison. He was crudely tattooed all over his body, leaving names scrawled in blue ink, carved into his skin. The wounds were infected . . . . The emotional scars were even deeper' (in Rocky, 1990: 5).

STREET CHILDREN AND PARTICIPATORY RIGHTS

In a recent work, Roger Hart described his ladder of participation which lists the steps in so-called child participation from the false rungs of manipulation, decoration and tokenism to what he suggests is the ideal: activities that are initiated by children but in which decisions are shared with adults (Hart, 1992). Since the early 1980s, some street children projects have claimed to involve them as participants in planning and implementing projects, and also in political action and campaigning on their own and society's behalf. If they are outside society then they bring a new force to bear on changing society – or so the story goes. One of the political participation models most frequently cited is also examined by Hart, the Brazilian Movement of Street Children (or 'for' Street Children – translations interestingly cannot agree!).

The Brazilian Movement was established in 1985, with its roots in UNICEF's Alternatives for Street Children project work with the popular movement. Anthony Swift's account of its history tells us that 'The emerging leaders were securely linked with grass-roots communities and eager to build up an ability to represent their interests at national level. *With its greater experience of power structures and processes*, UNICEF provided valuable counselling' (Swift, 1991: 17, my emphasis). The popular programmes established first local, and then state commissions. In 1985 the state commissions organised and elected the first National Commission of the National Movement for Street Boys and Girls.

Between 26 and 28 May 1986, the first national meeting for street children was held in Brasilia, bringing together 432 street children aged 8 to 16 years from different parts of Brazil selected by ballot from among their peers. Only a few adults were invited to the conference, which discussed the themes of work, education, violence, family, political organisation and health – chosen by the children themselves in a series of preparatory meetings throughout the country. Their conclusions were presented through drama at the closing ceremony. The conference was well covered by the media 'with over 15 pages in newspapers and magazines, an hour on TV and innumerable radio items and wire service stories that found their way to Europe' (Fyfe, 1989: 112). The meeting had been a public success, but political effects were less clear. The bulletin of the non-governmental organisation Childhope states that:

> When the movement first met . . . almost no government officials came to hear the children. However, some press did come . . . and noted the absence of government officials. Consequently, the President of Brazil met with an official delegation of street children following the meeting to assure them that his government was concerned and interested.
>
> (*Esperanza*, 1990: 1)

Subsequently, the Movement was among NGO members of the National Commission on the Child and the Constitution, which led to legislative changes, including the Statute on the Child (Swift, 1991). Later work includes centres for training street educators and campaigns against violence towards street children (which, nevertheless, continues unabated) (*ibid.*).

Of the 1986 meeting, Hart says:

> The original goal of the event was simply to develop solidarity between the many separate groups of street children, although the choice of Brasilia as a location was designed to sensitize the authorities. However, because the children were so organised and articulate during the debates, the press responded with enormous enthusiasm and the congress became a landmark event in creating public awareness about the lives of street children.
>
> (Hart, 1992: 31)

He suggests that this happened at that time because of a coincidence between the return to democracy and the role of street educators in the popular movement. He describes the way in which street educators work with street children:

> the children raise the themes, develop the activities, and construct the rules for their own functioning, with the street educator working only as a facilitator. The children elect those educators to work with them with whom they feel most comfortable.
>
> (*ibid.*: 32)

By implication, Hart feels that this is high on his 'ladder of participation', far from the 'manipulation', 'decoration' and 'tokenism' that usually characterise the physical presence of children in 'political' events in the name of participation (*ibid.*: 8–10). The most common forms of child participation in adult political activities is limited window dressing, in which children wear appropriate T-shirts, march in adult-regulated processions, sing a sentimental song or present prepared testimony for which they are enthusiastically (even ecstatically) applauded.

The Brazilian Movement has notched up some victories. The discussion of the 1986 Meeting,

> as reported in extensive press coverage, was both painful and liberating. Since the conference, exposure of the conditions of street children has become widely disseminated . . . [the Movement] has brought international attention to the problems of street children and thereby jolted the authorities into action.
>
> (Hewitt, 1992: 57)

Since 1986, in addition to the Statute on the Child, there have been many enquiries and legislative changes in Brazil. These are good signs, but one wonders about the extent to which the activities are actually child-initiated, given that all the prominent coordinators and spokespersons nationally are adults (see for example Dimenstein, 1991). For negotiating with police it is arguable that this may be necessary. Moreover, there is no doubt that the Brazilian activities have led to some child involvement at levels previously unexplored. For example:

> Local committees for street and working children, which are found throughout

Brazil, offer opportunities for dialogue between the children, government
agencies, and non-government organisations . . . [in which] there has been a
steadily growing participation by children . . . as they become more confident
in speaking.

(Hart, 1992: 32)

At national level, however, a tendency towards tokenism and decoration remains.
The second meeting in Brasilia in September 1989 shows a Movement that had
increased in size. No fewer than 750 street children gathered from 26 states,
sponsored by the Movement and by the Brazilian Institute of Social and Economic Analysis. Forty organisations were represented, both international and
national, with street children and adults from other Latin American countries. The
event is described in various Childhope publications: the children 'played the
guitar and danced. They smoked and discussed politics without fear of being
shoved into a cell or prodded toward yet another shelter' (Childhope, 1989: 5).
The meeting 'featured many activities such as games, singing, puppet-making,
and cultural presentations in addition to children's testimonies, and talks on
contraception and sexually transmitted diseases' (*ibid.*), thus providing a fairly
typical mix of adult supervised recreation, recitation and learning. There was an
element of spectacle. One 11-year-old boy is mentioned by name as 'one of the
great attractions' of the meeting; there was a march in the streets to the National
Congress that was felt by some observers to be 'a political initiative to gain public
support for certain candidates running for president in the November 15 election'
(*ibid.*). Certainly there was more political interest, the politicians 'jockeyed for
position next to the children when the press was taking pictures and filming the
event!' (*Esperanza*, 1990: 1). Most of these descriptions read like fairly accurate
accounts of decoration and tokenism.

Current organised child participation in meetings of experts discussing child
affairs takes three forms: parallel conference, performance and testimony. All
three occurred in 1992 at the Second International Conference on Street Children
(Health Rights and Actions) in Rio de Janeiro, which was part-sponsored by the
Movement. The parallel conference was exactly that – it reported back on the last
day, but apart from this the two lines never met. There was no dialogue. Performance occurred at several points but principally during lunchtime on the second
day, when delegates were treated to a display of street dancing. The street child
performers wore conference badges and many photographs were taken. The
security guard round the university conference hall where sessions took place
visibly doubled. Testimony was rather more dramatic than usual. In most street
child conference testimony children are given the microphone and asked to talk
about their lives on the street. Many are highly articulate and often give moving
accounts. On this occasion in Rio the main street child testimony occurred during
the opening session. Delegates were first welcomed by Benedito Dos Santos. The
street children, six teenage girls, made a theatrical entrance from the rear of the
hall, with their heads swathed in cloths that hid their features so that they could

not be identified but which gave them the stigmatising image of terrorists. Seated on the platform surrounded by press flashguns and the smaller flares of participants' automatic cameras, they gave testimony about the harsh treatment they had received the previous night in a park called Praca Saenz Pena. With their voices sometimes raised to a shout, often angry, sometimes edged with hysteria, they told how the police had thrown them to the ground, kicked and punched them and threatened to kill them. One 14-year-old, very pregnant, broke down and sobbed into the microphone. As they left to take part in newspaper interviews and more photographs the audience applauded and cheered.

What was the point of this, when all the participants were already fully aware of violence against street children in Brazil and many other countries? In a country in which shame is an important cultural motivator, a small political advantage was gained by the fact that the newspapers reported the majority of the audience to be foreigners (*O Globo*, 4 September, 1992). The girls received no direct benefit, and even the political point does not justify exploiting them in this kind of theatre. This was not participation, it was spectacle. Once they had left, the waters of the Conference closed over them.

At the 1993 meeting of the Movement for Street Children there was some lasting controversy about the fact that children from Recife had been taken over and were being used by the popular organisation. With this and other indications in mind, it seems true to say that children have little release from adult supervision, even when they are outside childhood and the name of the game is participation. In the words of a sceptical observer of the children's rights movement, 'Post-modern paternalism no longer says "Shut up kids, I know what is good for you" but prefers to say "Speak up kids, I am your voice"' (Théry, 1991: 105, my translation).

THE UNWRITTEN RIGHTS OF STREET CHILDREN

As this review of Articles of the Convention on the Rights of the Child reveals, street children do not enjoy rights of protection and provision. Indeed, this very non-enjoyment makes them appear to be unnatural children. As far as participatory rights are concerned, their status remains ambiguous. But what about the people that they are, these young people who work for themselves, care for each other and do not, in fact, ask society to rescue them? Do they have any specific rights that challenge the hegemony of Northern childhood? I would suggest that children in exceptionally difficult conditions, such as street children, may need special rights, or special consideration within the rights as written in the UN Convention. These might include some of the following.

The right not to be labelled:
This not only implies that the stigmatising category 'street child' leads to unfair and sometimes abusive discrimination against certain children, but also that many of the characteristics typically ascribed to children who live and work on the

streets are incorrect. They are not abandoned, they usually do have families, not all are drug addicts, prostitutes or criminals. Many such children reject the label because of its negative connotations.

The right to be correctly described, researched and counted:
It follows from the right not to be labelled that children on the street have a right to expect correct information to be collected from them and disseminated about them. This means a commitment on the part of the research community to make sure that scientific and ethical methods of data collection are used. It means not using hasty, badly constructed questionnaires, for which most street children are adept at providing equivocal information. It entails careful observation, the use of triangulation, control groups and participatory data collection techniques in which children are informed about the purpose of the research and to which they give their consent. It is particularly important to avoid exaggerating numbers through guesstimates, and the use of anecdotal case study material to illustrate (and therefore 'prove') the hypotheses of well-meaning service providers.

The right to work, and to do so in fair conditions and for fair wages:
Until such time as welfare provision reaches a level at which children do not have to work to provide for themselves and their families, they have a right to be active in the labour market. It is crucial that they should be protected from hazardous conditions, given security of employment and equal wages when they perform the same or similar tasks to adults. Special considerations for childhood are necessary to make sure that children have particular protection from hazards that have a greater or more harmful effect on developing bodies, minds and emotions than they do on those who have grown to adulthood. This means that they have a right to expect the medical and public health communities to know about harmful impacts at different ages and stages of growth, which information is currently not available. It also becomes a duty of health professionals and employers to ensure that the effects of working are monitored.

In addition, children who work must not be denied access to education. This means flexibility of both working and schooling schedules as well as appropriate methods and materials in the education process.

The right to have their own support systems respected:
Emphasis on the importance of families in the Convention on the Rights of the Child is based on the modern conception of families as private arenas for the correct performance of childhood. There is no provision in the Convention for respect and support to be paid to children's own friendships and support networks. Given the privileged position of the peer group in the psychology of both pre-pubertal and adolescent children this is curious. In the case of street children, who usually belong to and contribute to a supportive group of children, this gives a potentially harmful edge to rehabilitation programmes. The friendships and close relationships in these groups are important for the emotional and physical

well-being of members. They are strengths to be built on, rather than ties to be broken (Ennew, 1992).

The right to appropriate and relevant services:
Many service provision projects for street children are inappropriate. Middle-class adults do not necessarily know what is in the best interest of street children. They arrive with food for children who are well-fed, and bundles of clothes for children who have nowhere to keep spare garments. Research comparing different groups of children in Nepal shows that street children have a better nutritional status than children living in slums, or children in impoverished rural areas (Baker, 1993). Inappropriate service provision not only fails to address the children's most pressing needs, it is also a waste of valuable resources and often serves only to provide the donor with a 'feel good' factor. Many street children do not take up the services provided for them because they are inappropriate. In Nairobi, for example, despite suffering from the types of diseases mentioned in the dicussion of Article 24 above children did not attend a free health clinic. One reason was that it offered curative rather then preventative treatment. The other was that the opening hours were inconvenient. They might have been convenient for the health workers but they clashed with the children's work opportunities (Dallape, 1988).

The right to control their own sexuality:
Street children often have sex for money or with each other. But sexual activity is forbidden within childhood. This means that children who are taken off the street for rehabilitation are assumed to be rescued from sexual activity until they become adults. In the rehabilitation process they may be taught that their sexual experiences were bad and should be forgotten and rejected. But their sexual experiences were real and a part of their developing identity. The close relationship with another street child may have been meaningful and powerful, more important than any other relationship thus far. Children have a right to expect that their relationships will be addressed with respect by adults.

The right to be protected from secondary exploitation:
In Latin America people refer to the 'Pornography of Misery'. Media, human rights activists, and fundraising departments of development NGOs are all guilty of exploiting the histories of children in stories that emphasise children's vulnerability, exaggerate their weaknesses and turn them into victims. The comments of children from Bangalore and Honduras show that this is unacceptable to them. Street children are not just handy targets for any passing photographer or journalist who wants to make a quick buck from selling an image or an anecdote. Children have a right to their privacy and to respect for their individuality.

The right to be protected from harm inflicted by 'caring' social agencies:
Unfortunately, street children not only suffer from inadequate provision from

society, and inappropriate provision from well-meaning intervention projects. They are also frequently subject to physical, sexual and emotional abuse from staff and volunteers within projects whom society has empowered to care for them. This is inexcusable harm. They have a right to expect that the staff of all projects and programmes set up for their benefit are properly recruited, trained, managed and supported. This means a duty on the part of society to set standards for work with this particular group of children to ensure the accountability of all programmes working on their behalf. Too often the attitude prevails that anything that cleans children off the streets must be good. If no one asks questions about the appropriateness of the staff and methods being used, children are placed even further outside the law than they were on the streets.

CONCLUSION

The Convention on the Rights of the Child was drafted with a particular type of childhood in mind, and treats children outside this model as marginal. This means that children's rights as a concept within the human rights field does not fully engage with the whole range of human beings who are defined as children. A number of Articles target children – such as street children – for particular attention, with respect to child labour and sexual exploitation for example, but this in itself can be seen as a marginalising process. These and other Articles may be ambiguous or contradictory in the face of the real experiences of these children. They may suffer from discrimination because they are labelled and targeted. This may have life-long effects. If they are to have special consideration this should take account of their individuality – not merely the 'difficult' category to which they have been assigned.

REFERENCES

Aptekar, L. (1988) *Street Children of Cali*, Durham and London: Duke University Press.
Aries, P. (1979) *Centuries of Childhood*, London, translation Jonathan Cape Ltd., Harmondsworth, Penguin.
Baker, R. (1993) 'Street Children: What do we assume?' Unpublished BA dissertation, Dept. of Anthropology, University of Durham.
Bhima Sangha (1991) A Bhima Sangha Enquiry Committee Report on Blast in Fireworks Factory, Meenampatti, July–October 1991, mimeo, Bangalore: The Concerned for Working Children.
Boyden, J. (1990) 'Childhood and the Policy Makers: a comparative perspective on the globalisation of childhood', in A. James and A. Prout (eds) *Constructing and Deconstructing Childhood: Contemporary Issues in the Sociological Study of Childhood*, London, New York, Philadelphia: The Falmer Press.
Childhope (1989) *Our Child Our Hope* 1 (4) November: 5.
Connolly, M. (1990) 'Surviving the Streets', *AIDS Action*, August, Issue 11, London: AHRTAG: 1–2.
Dallape, F. (1988) *An Experience with Street Children*, Nairobi: Undugu Society of Kenya.
Detrick, S. (1992) *The United Nations Convention on the Rights of the Child: A Guide to the Travaux Préparatoires*, Dordrecht, Boston, London: Martinus Nijhoff Publishers.

Dimenstein, G. (1991) *Brazil: War on Children*, London: Latin America Bureau.

Ennew, J. (1992) 'Parentless friends: a cross-cultural examination of networks among street children and street youth', paper presented at the Symposium of the Sonderforschungbereicht 227 Praevention und Intervention im Kines und Jungendalter, University of Bielfeld, 'Social Networks and Social Support in Childhood and Adolescence', 7 October, 1992.

Ennew, J. and Milne, B. (1989) *The Next Generation: Lives of Third World Children*, London: Zed Press.

—— (1993) 'If Children had a Voice they would Protect' in *Towards Freedom* Vol. 42 (7) pp. 4–7.

Forster, E.M. (1978) *A Room with a View*, Harmondsworth: Penguin.

Fyfe, A. (1989) *Child Labour*, Cambridge: Polity Press.

Hart, R. (1992) *Children's participation: from tokenism to citizenship*, Innocenti Essays No. 4, Florence: UNICEF.

Hewitt, T. (1992) 'Children, abandonment and public action', in M. Wuyts, M. Mackintosh and T. Hewitt (eds.) *Development Policy and Public Action*, Milton Keynes: Open University Press.

Holland, P. (1992) *What is a Child? Popular Images of Childhood*, London: Virago Press.

Oliveira, W.F. de (1989) Street Kids in Brazil: an exploratory study of medical status, health knowledge and the self, MPH dissertation, University of Minnesota.

Reddy, N. (1992) *Street Children of Bangalore*, New Delhi: UNICEF.

Rocky, M. (1990) 'Whose child is this?', *Esperanza*, New York: Childhope USA.

Swart, J. (1990) *Malunde: the street children of Hillbrow*, Johannesburg: Witwatersrand University Press.

Swift, A. (1991) *Brazil: the fight for childhood in the city*, Innocenti Studies, Florence: UNICEF.

Tyler, F.B., Tyler, S.L., Tomasello, A., and Connolly, M.R. (1992) 'Huckleberry Finn and street youth everywhere: an approach to primary prevention' in G.W. Albee, L.A. Bond and T.V. Cook Munsey *Global Perspectives on Prevention: Primary Prevention of Psychopathology*, Vol. XLV, Sage Publications: 200–12.

Théry, I. (1991) 'La Convenzione Onu sui diritti del bambino: nascita di una nuova ideologia', *Politiche Sociali per L'Infanzia e L'Adolescenza*, Milan: Edizioni Unicopli.

Weiner, M. (1991) *The Child and the State in India: Child Labour and Education Policy in Comparative Perspective*, Princeton: Princeton University Press.

Chapter 16

Respecting children's right to physical integrity
'What the world might be like . . .'

Peter Newell

There is no more obvious sign of the low status which children still enjoy in most societies around the world than the readiness of adults to defend smacking, slapping and beating them. Adults' right to physical integrity – to protection from all forms of inter-personal violence – is upheld by the law and by prevailing social attitudes in most if not all societies. But as yet that right has not been extended to cover children except in a handful of countries.

Extreme forms of violence and humiliation affecting children – serious physical and sexual abuse, pornography and prostitution, the murder of street children and the effects of armed conflict on children – are increasingly acknowledged and universally condemned. But undoubtedly the most common experience of inter-personal violence for most children in most societies is that of physical punishment at the hands of their parents or other carers. The significance of the issue lies in the way in which this particular form of inter-personal violence is uniquely defended (often passionately defended) in complete contrast to pre-vailing attitudes of condemnation of all other forms of inter-personal violence. The defence reflects persisting concepts of parental 'ownership' of children, of children as objects, less than people.

This chapter documents the gradual emergence and current growth of a movement aiming to extend to children the right to physical and personal integrity, to freedom from all forms of inter-personal violence and humiliation – a right which adults tend to take for granted. There is a great deal of evidence to suggest that achieving this aim will assert children's status as people, help to give their claims a higher political priority in all societies, as well as reducing the immeasurable load of pain and injury inflicted daily on children in the name of punishment. Over time it will reduce levels of all forms of violence in human societies – for violence is a learned response, and most of it is learned in childhood. As Alice Miller has written:

> We are still barely conscious of how harmful it is to treat children in a degrading manner. . . . We don't yet know, above all, what the world might be like if children were to grow up without being subjected to humiliation, if parents would respect them and take them seriously as persons.
>
> (Miller, 1987: 65)

In the UK, child psychologists John and Elizabeth Newson, who have been studying British childrearing habits for more than 40 years, concluded in 1989: 'The majority of British parents we have interviewed seem to believe that physical punishment is an inevitable and probably necessary aspect of ordinary child upbringing'. In 1985, they found almost two-thirds of a large sample of mothers admitting that they already smacked their 1-year-old children. Earlier, they had found that 22 per cent of seven-year-olds had already been hit with an implement, and a further 53 per cent of seven-year-olds had been threatened with an implement (Newson and Newson, 1989).

Worldwide, although the research is fairly scanty, it seems that the use of physical punishment has tended to follow enslavement, colonisation, military occupation and certain religious teaching. In some cultures not subject to such influences, notably small-scale hunter-gatherer societies, the use of inter-personal violence or pain in childrearing is unusual. In some societies, physical punishment is still commonly used in the penal system on adults too (although international human rights instruments do not accept its use). Even where it is accepted throughout a culture however, it is important to emphasise that its use discriminates against children because of their greater physical vulnerability and the imperatives of their growth and development.

PREVALENCE

Parental physical punishment

Studies on levels of violence to children in countries in all continents find high levels of physical punishment by parents. EPOCH-WORLDWIDE, an informal alliance of organisations and individuals around the world which share the aim of ending all physical punishment and deliberate humiliation of children through legal reforms and education, is aiming to collect information on the degree to which children's right to physical integrity is breached in every country. In 1992 EPOCH-WORLDWIDE circulated a questionnaire to governmental and non-governmental bodies in more than 100 countries. The following summaries reflect research findings so far collected (see EPOCH-WORLDWIDE, 1993).

Australia: a 1987 study of primary school children revealed that 81 per cent of boys and 74 per cent of girls had been hit by their mother, and 76 per cent of boys and 63 per cent of girls by their father.

Barbados: a 1987 survey found 70 per cent of respondents 'generally approving' of parental physical punishment; of these 76 per cent endorsed beating children with belts or straps.

India: physical punishment is a common disciplinary practice in many communities in India. A survey of university students in 1991 found 91 per cent of males and 86 per cent of females had been physically punished in their childhood.

Korea: a 1982 survey by the Child Protection Association found that 97 per cent of interviewed children had been physically punished, many severely.

New Zealand: a 1993 opinion poll found 87 per cent of respondents agreeing that there were circumstances when it was all right for parents to smack a child, but only 3 per cent believing there were circumstances in which it was all right for a parent to 'thrash' a child. Twice as many men as women endorsed hitting teenagers or thrashing a child in certain circumstances.

Romania: a survey in 1992 found that 84 per cent of a sample of parents regarded spanking as a normal method of childrearing and 96 per cent did not regard it as humiliating.

USA: a 1985 survey of a representative sample of over 3,000 families with children under 17 found that 89 per cent of parents had hit their 3-year-old child during the previous year; about a third of 15- to 17-year-olds had been hit.

School corporal punishment

There has been significant progress towards ending physical punishment of children in schools and other childcare institutions in all continents. The UK became the last country in Europe, east and west, to end corporal punishment in state-supported education in 1987 (abolition does not cover pupils of fee-paying parents in private schools). The Education Act 1993 declared it illegal for any school to dispense inhuman or degrading punishments. But government seemed equivocal, with the then Minister of Education John Patten, expressing regret in a radio interview that corporal punishment had become illegal (BBC *Today Programme* 4 January 1993). On 16 March 1994, a High Court judge upheld the right of childminder Anne Davis to 'smack' children in her care despite Article 19 of the UN Convention (see chapter 5). The judgment overturned an earlier decision in favour of Sutton Council endorsing the local authority's refusal to register any childminder who inflicted physical punishment on children.

Poland ended school corporal punishment in 1783. It is still used commonly in school systems in half the states of the USA (where, for example, in 1990 one in ten of all school students in the State of Mississippi received corporal punishment), in India, in some states of Canada and Australia, in South Africa and many other African countries. In South Africa surveys in the mid-1980s found 12 per cent of the school population, and 30 per cent of black pupils reporting being beaten once a day. In contrast, in 1992 the Supreme Court of Namibia declared corporal punishment unconstitutional in the school and penal systems. In Botswana it is not permitted but is apparently still common, and in Burkino Faso it was prohibited by decree in 1965.

Physical punishment in penal systems for young offenders

Physical punishment is still available as a sentence of the courts, and also 'as a punishment for children and young people in penal institutions in some countries. Within Africa, courts in The Gambia can sentence children to be whipped; also children from the age of seven who are deemed to be guilty of an offence can be caned summarily with authorisation from a senior police officer. In Zimbabwe, a Supreme Court decision which outlawed judicial whipping of juveniles in 1989 has been overruled by legislation re-introducing the penalty in 1992. In Sudan whipping is still used on juveniles as young as ten. In Guyana whipping is available as a sentence for boys under 14 years old (a maximum of 12 strokes); males over 14 may be whipped and flogged to a maximum of 24 strokes. Girls may not be whipped or flogged but may be sentenced to solitary confinement. Whipping is also permitted as a punishment in training schools for young offenders (EPOCH-WORLDWIDE survey 1993).

This adds up to a momentous catalogue of pain and humiliation – suffered by children at the hands of parents, teachers and other adults, acting generally with legal authority and supported in most countries by prevailing social attitudes.

WORLDWIDE PROGRESS TO PROTECT CHILDREN

But there is light at the end of the tunnel. There has certainly been accelerating progress to end physical punishment and deliberate humiliation of children in institutional settings. More significantly, in the last 15 years in a handful of countries growing respect for human rights and a belated realisation that children are human too have led to major reforms which extend to children fully the right to protection from all forms of physical and mental violence.

It was in 1979, International Year of the Child, that Sweden became the first country to prohibit all physical punishment and humiliating treatment of children. Traditional rights of parents to hit their children existed unchallenged in Sweden until 1949. In that year, when a new Parenthood and Guardianship Code was introduced, there was discussion about limiting severe physical punishment. Parents right to 'punish' was amended to a right to 'reprimand'. Abolition of school corporal punishment came into effect in 1958, and in all other Swedish childcare institutions in 1960. In 1967 the criminal law on assault was changed to remove the provision which excused parents who caused minor injuries through physical punishment. In 1977 the Swedish Parliament set up a Children's Rights Commission. Its first proposal was that an explicit ban on subjecting children to physical punishment or other degrading treatment should be added to the Parenthood and Guardianship Code. Consultation found little opposition, and early in 1979 a Bill was passed by a majority of 259 to 6. The law now reads:

> Children are entitled to care, security and a good upbringing. Children are to be treated with respect for their person and individuality and may not be subjected to physical punishment or any other humiliating treatment.
>
> (Parenthood and Guardianship Code, Amended 1983, Chapter 6, Section 1)

Implementation of the new law in Sweden was accompanied by a substantial education campaign. Milk cartons arriving on Swedish breakfast tables carried a cartoon of a girl saying 'I'll never ever hit my own children', and an explanation of the law. The Ministry of Justice circulated 600,000 copies of a pamphlet entitled *Can you bring up children successfully without smacking and spanking?* which was translated into ten minority languages including (probably most importantly) English. The pamphlet emphasises:

> while the purpose of the new legislation is indeed to make it quite clear that spanking and beating are no longer allowed, it does not aim at having more parents punished than hitherto. . . . The law . . . now forbids all forms of physical punishment of children, including smacking etc., although it goes without saying that you can still snatch a child away from a hot stove or open window if there is risk of its injuring itself. Should physical chastisement meted out to a child cause bodily injury or pain which is more than of very temporary duration, it is classified as assault and is an offence punishable under the Criminal Code. In theory at least, this was still true before the new Bill came into force, although it was not generally known. However the advent of the new law has swept all doubt aside, although as before trivial offences will remain unpunished, either because they cannot be classified as assault or because an action is not brought.
>
> (Ministry of Justice, 1979)

One of the many 'red herring' arguments produced by adults to ridicule the idea of legal reform against physical punishment is that it seeks to 'criminalise little smacks'. But this predictably misses the point. The proposal is not for a new law but simply to extend existing laws on assault – which in theory protect adults from all assaults however trivial – to protect children too. Trivial assaults of adults by adults do not get to court, and for exactly the same reasons, trivial assaults of children would not either. At the moment the law defends not just trivial assaults of children, but gross invasions of their physical integrity, in-cluding beatings with sticks, belts, and slippers. In Sweden, in the 14 years since the law came into effect, there has been one and only one prosecution of a parent for what might be regarded in the UK as 'ordinary' physical punishment. An 11-year-old boy reported his father to the police for spanking him, and the father was fined 100 Kroner (about £9) for assault under the criminal law.

Swedish children were a major target for the education campaign: the Bill was used to teach pupils the process of law-making in Parliament, so that they learnt its content too, and it was built into other parts of the curriculum, including child development.

Since the 1960s when legal reforms against physical punishment started, there is evidence of a dramatic change in the attitudes of Swedish parents. Public opinion polls carried out between 1965 and 1981 showed a doubling of the proportion of parents who believed that children should be raised without corporal punishment (from 35 per cent to 71 per cent – 74 per cent of women and 68 per cent of men); over the same period the proportion believing that corporal punishment was 'sometimes necessary' halved from 53 per cent to 26 per cent, and the 'don't knows' reduced from 12 per cent to 3 per cent (SIFO (a Swedish polling agency): 1981).

Research into the effects of the Swedish law was carried out in 1981 and 1988 by Professor Adrienne Haeuser. Her conclusions were entirely positive:

> The law has dramatically reduced physical punishment and commitment to it. It has broken the inter-generational transmission of the practice. It has helped to reduce serious child-battering . . . Professionals in particular have welcomed having a 'clear line' to transmit to parents.
>
> (Haeuser, 1988: 93)

In the UK there has been some attempt to misrepresent the effects of the Swedish law, with scaremongering suggestions of thousands of children being taken into compulsory state care as a result of the new law: in fact the proportion of children in compulsory care in Sweden is very significantly lower than in the UK, and is steadily decreasing (Newell, 1989).

The only serious challenge to the Swedish reform came from some parents who were members of a fundamentalist religious group. They made an application to the European Commission of Human Rights alleging that the new law breached their rights, guaranteed under the European Convention on Human Rights, to respect for family life. Their case, as reported by the Commission, was that they believed in 'traditional' ways of raising their children 'and in particular, as an aspect of their religious doctrine, they believed in the necessity of physical punishment of their children, which they justify by reference to Biblical texts and doctrinal works . . .'. The Commission rejected the application, concluding that 'the actual effects of the law are to encourage a positive review of the punishment of children by their parents, to discourage abuse and prevent excesses which could properly be described as violence against children'. The Commission described the Swedish criminal law on assault as 'a normal measure for the control of violence . . . its extension to apply to the ordinary physical chastisement of children by their parents is intended to protect potentially weak and vulnerable members of society'. Thus the European human rights machinery has confirmed that the state can legitimately interfere in family life with the objective of promoting children's rights and protecting them from violence (European Commission of Human Rights, 1982). As an official of the Swedish Ministry of Justice emphasised:

> By the prohibition of physical punishment, the legislator wanted to show that

a child is an independent individual who can command full respect for his or her person, and who should thus have the same protection against physical punishment or violence as we adults see as being totally natural for ourselves.

(Ekdhal, 1989)

Other Scandinavian countries pursued similar reforms: in Finland, a major overhaul of children's law led to the inclusion of general principles for child-rearing:

The objects of custody are to ensure the well-being and the well-balanced development of a child according to his individual needs and wishes, and to ensure for a child close and affectionate human relationships in particular between a child and his parents. A child shall be ensured good care and upbringing as well as the supervision and protection appropriate to his age and stage of development. A child should be brought up in a secure and stimulating environment and should receive an education that corresponds to his wishes, inclinations and talents.

A child shall be brought up in a spirit of understanding, security and love. He shall not be subdued, corporally punished or otherwise humiliated. His growth towards independence, responsibility and adulthood shall be encouraged, supported and assisted.

(Child Custody and Right of Access Act 1983: Section 1)

Significantly, this Finnish Act also obliges custodial parents before they make any decision 'relating to the person of the child' to, where possible 'discuss the matter with the child taking into account the child's age and maturity and the nature of the matter. In making the decision, the custodian shall give due consideration to the child's feelings, opinions and wishes' (*ibid.*: Section 4). In Finland as in Sweden, opinion polls have shown a significant drop in support for physical punishment. A major survey of the experiences and views of 15- and 16-year-old teenagers, carried out by the Central Union for Child Welfare in 1989, found that 19 per cent had experienced mild violence from their parents and 5 per cent severe violence during the year of the survey. These children were already at least 10 years old when the law came into effect. Asked whether they believed they would use physical punishment in the upbringing of their own children in the future, only five per cent said 'yes' (Sariola, 1992: 28–9).

Two more Scandinavian countries, Denmark (in 1986) and Norway (in 1987) quickly followed with similar legal reforms. On 15 March 1989 the Austrian Parliament voted to amend its Family Law and Youth Welfare Act to state explicitly that in bringing up children 'Using violence and inflicting physical or mental suffering is unlawful'.

THE UNITED NATIONS CONVENTION – A NEW ERA FOR CHILDREN'S RIGHTS

1989 also saw the tentative dawn of a new era for the world's children: the United

Nations General Assembly adopted the UN Convention on the Rights of the Child (see chapters 5 and 8, this volume). The Convention provides for the first time new principles and detailed standards for treatment of the world's children. And its Articles provide a very clear confirmation of the child's right to physical integrity.

The Preamble refers to the 'equal and inalienable rights of all members of the human family', as well as to children's rights to 'special care and assistance'.

It is Article 19 which asserts the child's right to protection from 'all forms of physical or mental violence':

1 States Parties shall take all appropriate legislative, administrative, social and educational measures to protect the child from all forms of physical or mental violence, injury or abuse, neglect or negligent treatment, maltreatment or exploitation including sexual abuse, while in the care of parent(s), legal guardian(s) or any other person who has the care of the child.

2 Such protective measures should, as appropriate, include effective procedures for the establishment of social programmes to provide necessary support for the child and for those who have the care of the child, as well as for other forms of prevention and for identification, reporting, referral, investigation, treatment and follow-up of instances of child maltreatment described heretofore, and, as appropriate, for judicial involvement.

Thus Article 19, while including protection from what is commonly defined as 'abuse' goes further in covering 'all forms of physical or mental violence'. It also goes beyond the prohibition in Article 37, that 'No child shall be subjected to torture or other cruel, inhuman or degrading treatment or punishment', which reflects provisions in other international instruments, including the European Convention on Human Rights. There will no doubt be some who will argue that 'smacking is not violent', in line with the hypocrisy and double standards that still characterise many adults' attitudes to violence directed at children. Consider what is involved in physical punishment – a large person deliberately inflicting a degree of pain on a smaller, often very much smaller person, sometimes with the hand or foot, often with implements including shoes, sticks, belts, wooden spoons, and hairbrushes. In what other context would such conduct not be regarded as 'violent'?

Article 2 insists that the rights in the Convention must be available

without discrimination of any kind, irrespective of the child's or his or her parent's or legal guardian's race, colour, sex, language, religion, political or other opinion, national, ethnic or social origin, property, disability, birth or other status.

Read together with Article 19, this emphasises that there can be no dilution of children's right to physical integrity, to protection from all forms of violence, on grounds of religion, race or culture. No longer can selective quotations from the Bible ('Spare the rod and spoil the child' etc.) and pleas of cultural childrearing traditions be used in defence of physical punishment.

If taken seriously and implemented fully, the Convention could indeed transform the lives of children. These are of course very big 'ifs', given adults' traditional treatment of children. The Convention has certainly achieved very rapid recognition; by 1993 147 countries had ratified it i.e. accepted its provisions and committed themselves to implementation. The UK ratified in December 1991. The Convention is not enforceable in the same way as the European Convention on Human Rights: individual children cannot make applications alleging breaches. But it does set up a system for monitoring implementation. A ten-member UN Committee on the Rights of the Child has been elected by ratifying states. Within two years of ratification, and from then every five years, each state must submit a report to the Committee setting out progress towards full implementation, and state representatives are invited to a formal public session of the Committee to be interrogated about their report. The process of considering country reports has begun, and already the Committee has indicated that it does not believe corporal punishment of children is compatible with the Convention (UN Committee on The Rights of the Child 27 January 1993).

ACCELERATING REFORMS

Over time, the reconsideration of laws, policies and above all attitudes to children which is demanded by the Convention must lead adults to respect children's status as people with the same fundamental right to physical integrity as we take for granted. Beyond the five countries that have already acted to ensure their laws give equal protection to children's physical and personal integrity, there is also evidence of change in Germany, Switzerland and Scotland.

It is significant that where recognition of children's rights has led to the establishment of formal structures to represent children's interests at government level, advocacy to end social and legal acceptance of physical punishment has almost invariably been adopted as a high priority. Thus as indicated above, in Sweden it was the Children's Rights Commission that proposed the 1979 law. In Norway, the world's first children's ombudsperson, Målfrid Flekkøy, was instrumental in convincing the government to adopt a similar legal reform (see chapter 13, this volume). In Germany, the KinderKommission has recommended legal reform (echoing a recommendation from a governmental commission set up to consider ways of reducing all forms of inter-personal violence in society). In New Zealand in 1993 the Commissioner for Children challenged the government to remove the statutory confirmation of parents' rights to use physical punishment, and launched his own education campaign, including booklets entitled *Think about it: is hitting your child a good idea?* and *Hitting children is unjust.* And the South Australian Children's Interests Bureau has also publicly challenged physical punishment.

Several countries in Europe are poised on the verge of reform: in Germany in 1992, following the recommendations from two governmental commissions and pressure from non-governmental organisations, the Minister of Justice announced that a prohibition of physical punishment would be introduced within two years. In Poland, a governmental commission has recommended a ban in the context of constitutional reform. In Switzerland a Working Group on Child Abuse, set up by the Federal Department for Internal Affairs recommended that the Constitution should be revised to prohibit corporal punishment and degrading treatment of children explicitly – both within and outside the family (Federal Department for Internal Affairs, 1992). In the UK, the governmental Scottish Law Commission proposed in a report on reform of family law presented to Parliament in 1992 that it should become a criminal offence to hit a child with an implement or in a way which causes or could cause injury or significant pain or discomfort lasting more than a very short time. The Commission however failed to advocate children's equal right to physical integrity, proposing that what it termed the 'safe disciplinary smack' should remain within the law (Scottish Law Commission, 1992).

Beyond Europe, in Canada in July 1993 the Federal Ministry of Justice announced that it would repeal the statutory confirmation of parents' and others' physical punishment rights, and launch a public information campaign on positive alternatives. In Bolivia the Commission on Children and Youth is reviewing child protection laws in the light of ratification of the UN Convention, and in Guatemala, the law is being revised with a view to eradicating all forms of ill-treatment.

In September 1993 more than 600 participants from 15 African countries assembled in Capetown for the Second African Congress on Child Abuse. They unanimously adopted a resolution supporting moves to eliminate all physical punishment of children through legal reform and education. A year previously, Article 5 of a Charter adopted by the Children's Summit of South Africa (drafted by a representative group of children and young people) read:

> All children have the right to be protected from all types of violence including: physical, emotional, verbal, psychological, sexual, state, political, gang, do-mestic, school, township, community, street, racial, self-destructive and all other forms of violence.
>
> All children have the right to freedom from corporal punishment at school, from the police and in prisons, and at home.
>
> (Children's Summit of South Africa, 1 June 1992)

BEYOND CHILDREN'S RIGHTS – OTHER REASONS FOR NOT HITTING CHILDREN

Alongside the growing movement to respect the rights of children world-wide, there has been a growth in understanding of the immense damage done both to individual children and to the growth of human societies by adult cruelty to children. While the basic human rights argument provides the moral imperative for fully respecting children's right to physical integrity, there are plenty of supporting arguments. First, physical punishment teaches children nothing positive, nothing whatever about the behaviour we want from them. It is in fact a telling lesson in bad behaviour – someone you hopefully love and respect believes that using a degree of violence is a useful way of sorting out a conflict.

Second, much serious injury to children could be avoided: children are frequently 'accidentally' injured quite seriously as a result of even minor physical punishments (dodged or misplaced blows can cause falls and head injuries, boxed ears can burst ear drums, shaking babies and small children can cause concussion, brain damage and even death).

Third, and most significantly for the development of future human societies, the many volumes of research into determinant factors in the growth of violent attitudes and violent actions in childhood and later adult life – bullying, domestic violence, child abuse, violent crime etc. – invariably highlight physical punishment and other humiliating treatment as a significant factor. It is this evidence that has been reviewed recently by commissions in various countries, set up because of concern at escalating levels of all forms of inter-personal violence, and seeking strategies for prevention. In each case they have proposed as a priority ending physical punishment of children. As the Australian commission concluded: 'The greatest chance we have to prevent violence in society is to raise children who reject violence as a method of problem-solving, who believe in the right of the individual to grow in a safe environment' (National Committee on Violence, 1989).

This is, above all, a very personal issue. People's own experiences as children and as parents get in the way of compassionate and logical consideration of the arguments. If it were simply an intellectual matter, we would have given up hitting and humiliating children decades if not centuries ago. If we can quickly do so now, we could indeed transform our world.

REFERENCES

Charter of Children's Summit of South Africa 1 June 1992.

Ekdhal, B. (1980) *The Ombudsman and Child Maltreatment*, report of an international seminar organised by Radda Barnen.

EPOCH-WORLDWIDE (1993) *Survey of Behaviour Towards Children in 100 Countries*. Further information from EPOCH-WORLDWIDE 77 Holloway Road, London N7 8JZ.

European Commission of Human Rights (1982) *Seven Individuals v Sweden: Decision on Admissibility of Application 8811/79*, 13 May.

Federal Department for Internal Affairs (1992) *Child Abuse in Switzerland*, Report to the Head of the Federal Department of Internal Affairs, Berne, June.

Haeuser, A. (1988) *Reducing Violence to US Children: Transferring Positive Innovations from Sweden*, Summary. University of Wisconsin School of Social Welfare: Milwaukee.

Miller, A. (1987) *For Your Own Good: the Roots of Violence in Child-rearing*, Virago: London.

Ministry of Justice (1979) *Can you bring up children successfully without smacking and spanking?* Ministry of Justice: Stockholm.

National Committee on Violence (1988) Announcement of the establishment of the Committee by the Federal Minister of Justice, October.

Newell, P. (1989) *Children are people too; The Case Against Physical Punishment*, Bedford Square Press: London.

Newson, E. and Newson, J. (1989) *The Extent of Parental Physical Punishment in the UK*, Approach Ltd: London.

Office of the Commissioner for Children (1993) *Think about it: Is hitting your child a good idea?* and *Hitting children is unjust*, Office of the Commissioner for Children: Wellington, New Zealand.

Sariola, H. (1992) 'Results of banning physical punishment in Poland' in *Ending Physical Punishment of European Children*, report of an international seminar organised by Radda Barnen and held in London in March 1992.

Scottish Law Commission (1992) *Report on Family Law*, HMSO: Edinburgh.

SIFO (1981) *Physical Punishment and Child Abuse*, Stockholm.

United Nations Committee on the Rights of the Child (1993) consideration of an initial report from Sudan. Press release HR/3298, 27 January.

Chapter 17

Russian children's rights

Judith Harwin

INTRODUCTION

The Soviet Union signed the UN Convention on the Rights of the Child on 13 June 1990 and it was ratified three months later. Within a year the Soviet Union had collapsed and with it went the whole political and economic framework that had prevailed for seven decades. Undoubtedly the transition to a market economy and democratic pluralist society are the two most significant factors influencing how children's rights in Russia are conceptualised and implemented at the present time. The political restructuring has firmly re-established the entitlement to freedom of belief and expression, unfettered by the ideological beliefs of the State. Economic restructuring has undermined the former basic tenet of socialism that the State should aim to protect all its members equally. The new philosophy asserts that the State cannot and should not protect all its citizens to the same degree.

This fundamental restructuring creates both opportunities and risks for children. The new entitlements to freedom of belief bring major opportunities to strengthen children's autonomy rights, but economic shifts remove the guarantee of a welfare safety net that socialism provided to protect all its children. Two years after signing the Convention, the Russian Federation submitted a lengthy and thorough report to the UN on its progress and difficulties in meeting the standards laid down in the Convention on the Rights of the Child (Russian Federation, 1992). This report provides a rich source of data on programmes and policies for the promotion and safeguarding of Russian children's rights. These data, supplemented and updated by my own research into childcare before and after the failed coup in 1991, provide the main informational sources for this chapter. The chapter focuses on two key themes in the study of children's rights; rights to self-determination and rights to protection.

RIGHTS TO AUTONOMY: A VOICE FOR CHILDREN OR PARENTS?

In virtually all societies children's rights to determine their upbringing are extremely limited, particularly in the case of young children. But socialism imposed much greater restrictions on the upbringing a child was likely to receive. These restrictions were primarily placed on parents but they inevitably affected the opportunities available to children. Under socialism the State had always maintained a clear entitlement to define the political obligations of parents in child-rearing. The Fundamentals of Family Law never attempted to set out a specific list of parental obligations in any other area of upbringing, but in the sphere of political ideology, it required parents to nurture a love of the Mother-land and a respect for socialism in their children. Parents were required to bring up their children, 'in the spirit of devotion to the motherland, to inculcate a communist attitude towards labour and train children to actively contribute to building a communist society' (USSR Fundamental Principles of Law and Marriage and the Family, 1968, Art. 18). Parents, moreover, were not allowed to raise their children with any religious beliefs. If they did, legislation was in place which legitimated compulsory removal of the child from the parental home. Statistics have never been available to indicate how frequently this provision was used, but there is some evidence that Jewish and Baptist children were placed in State care on this ground in the 1960s. Anecdotal accounts suggest that by the 1970s the provision had largely fallen into disuse, yet it remained in statute as late as 1990 even though the family code was substantially amended in May of that year. The 1990 Act also contained another striking anomaly. It left intact the requirement to bring up children according to socialist beliefs (USSR Law, 1990a).

It is hard to explain this curious missed opportunity in family law which is at odds with other legislation passed later in the same year. In October 1990, for example, Gorbachev enacted new legislation which lifted the ban on religious organisations and gave the go-ahead for the establishment of Sunday Schools (USSR Law, 1990b). Later that month further legislation guaranteed freedom of belief for individuals (Russian Federation Law, 1990).

Since the failed coup in 1991, the momentum to widen parental choice has continued. Major legislation on education has established parental rights to choose non-State schooling, fee-paying and religious schooling (Russian Federation Law, 1992). New opportunities have also opened up for non-Russian parents to send children to schools where tuition is conducted in their mother tongue with greater emphasis placed on ethnic tradition and custom. Clearly these develop-ments are congruent with the UN Convention's requirements to take into account culture and tradition and, more broadly, to give recognition to basic human rights such as freedom of thought, conscience and religion.

Children have undoubtedly benefited from these changes, but the concept of child, as opposed to parental, empowerment has been very poorly articulated. It might have been anticipated that the human rights movement in Russia would have been accompanied by a broad-ranging debate on ways of giving children and young people a much clearer voice in society. Indeed there was some evidence that this was beginning in the Gorbachev years. Opinion polls of young people began to be conducted concerning their political beliefs, personal hopes and aspirations. An important law enacted in April 1991, moreover, enabled children for the first time to initiate judicial action if teachers exceeded their powers by attempting to interfere in children's personal lives (USSR Law, 1991). This was a measure of some significance, but was never put into operation because of the collapse of the USSR. Formerly, teachers had the right and duty to visit the parental home to carry out a family assessment and could require parents to participate in school-provided counselling if there was evidence of unsatisfactory parenting. Teachers could also compel young people to take part in crop harvests and threaten them with sanctions, such as blocking their enrolment in higher education, if they refused to participate.

Gorbachev's initiatives to promote children's autonomy rights have not, however, made significant progress since the failed coup. Although the Education Act of 1992 affirms children's freedom of belief and expression, it is not as radical as French law, for example, which provides for children's representation in school government.

An important proposal which would undoubtedly have had wide significance for children's autonomy rights was contained in a 1992 draft law on 'the protection of the family, motherhood, fatherhood and childhood'. It established children's rights to be heard in any legal or administrative or any other kind of proceedings affecting their welfare, provided that the child was of sufficient age and understanding and could freely express his/her views. But this law, for reasons totally unconnected with this particular provision, failed to satisfy Parliament and has been shelved for the time being. There is then a significant lacuna where children have only limited rights to be consulted in decisions affecting their welfare. In adoption proceedings, for example, there is a duty to take into consideration the wishes and feelings of any child aged 10 or over, but children under that age are left without legal entitlement to be consulted. In childcare decision-making outside the court arena, there are no mechanisms to enable participation by the child – such as regular review or access to complaints procedures.

Finally, a draft law on children's rights prepared by the children's charity the Children's Fund, was also thrown out by Parliament. This law had been widely criticised by child law specialists on the grounds that it was largely declaratory and lacked implementation and enforcement mechanisms.

None of these measures failed because they were child liberationist, but their failure nevertheless leaves a gap in the child empowerment movement, and given that Article 12 lays down such a clear benchmark on the importance of taking the child's views into account, this gap demands an explanation. The most obvious reason is probably the most important. Protection rights are being prioritised over participation rights. The authorities are being totally overwhelmed by the urgency of measures needed to protect children and help safeguard their survival and development needs. Indeed, as we shall see later, the government has been very active in trying to implement a childcare and protection strategy. Accusations of a *laissez-faire* policy would be entirely misplaced. The urgency of unmet child protection needs is probably not the whole story however. To this must be added the legacy of Soviet socialism, which through the whole range of socialisation mechanisms tended to value obedience rather than promoting critique and self-determination. Finally, increasing children's autonomy rights seems to be one of the most difficult objectives to achieve in all societies. In England it is only with the recent 1989 Children Act that children have gained new rights, for example, to initiate court proceedings and withhold consent to medical examinations and treatments. Yet as recent test cases have demonstrated, if the price of autonomy is the child's safety, empowerment becomes the subordinate principle (see chapter 3, this volume).

CHILDREN'S NEEDS FOR PROTECTION

The size and nature of the problem

The experience of Eastern European bloc countries which embarked on transition before Russia has some depressing lessons on the short-term effects of economic and political restructuring (Cornia and Sipos, 1991). All have met with difficulties in safeguarding children's basic survival needs. Shortages of suitable nutrition and difficulties in obtaining medical supplies have been common as the former exchange suppliers dried up. The picture in Russia amply confirms this general trend. In 1992, Lakhova – the presidential adviser on the family – declared that 'children are the most unprotected group in society' (Lakhora, 1992). With 40 million children below the age of 18 living in the Russian Federation on 1 January 1992 the statistics highlight a problem on a scale difficult to conceive in a small country such as England where the total population is only approximately 58 million.

The presidential adviser's account was stark and is fleshed out in detail in the report to the UN which catalogues a whole array of health and social problems among children. Infant mortality had been steadily rising and in 1991 the number of deaths of children under one year of age had reached 17.8 per 1000. By 1993 it had reached 19.3 according to official estimates, although Unicef believes that the real rate is much closer to 30 per 1,000 – much higher than the European average (British Medical Journal, 1994). The report went on to detail an acute shortage of children's food, especially milk products. It also noted an overall decline in nutritional standards as families consumed more starchy foods and less meat, vegetables and fruit due to falling incomes and rising prices.

The growth of social problems highlighted in the report is no less acute. Delinquency was reported to have risen by 50 per cent over the last five years while female crime had doubled. Truancy also had risen by more than 2.5 times. Existing institutions, moreover, were unable to meet the needs of the most vulnerable children. Only 6,400 of the 8–9,000 children suffering from cerebral palsy could be accommodated. Many children are in State care: 100,000 children, of whom 90 per cent have living parents, had simply been abandoned to State care. And statistics from the Ministry of Internal Affairs paint a grim picture of life in care. In 1992, 20,000 children ran away from children's homes and State boarding-schools to escape beatings and psychological abuse from staff. Finally, 55,000 of the 332,000 refugees in Russia in 1992 were children.

To describe this situation as little other than disastrous, both in the short and long term, is not to resort to hyperbole. The acknowledgement raises a central question – how is the government trying to meet the acute needs of children for care and protection? The remainder of the chapter focuses on two particular areas of government policy; income maintenance and child welfare programmes.

Income maintenance

In the early post-Revolutionary era of Soviet socialism an ambitious and wide-ranging social security system was established which not only contrasted very favourably with Tsarist schemes, but was very much in advance of many European countries. Central to this system was the official commitment to the family, which eventually came to be placed under the protection of the State in the revised Constitution of 1977. By the late 1980s, however, many gaps in provision for families with children were evident. In particular, one parent families, families on low incomes and those with several children, were particularly vulnerable and suffered from very low living standards (George, 1992). Thus in 1988 'of the approximately 40 million people living below the poverty line, approximately half are members of large families (three or more children) while about 20 per cent are pensioners, most of whom live alone. The remaining 30 per cent . . . is accounted for by mainly single parent and young families with one or two children' (Shcherbakov, 1990). In other words 80 per cent of those officially recognised as being poor were families with children. One of the root causes of the problem was that benefits were fixed so that their value fell over time. Consequently, although a number of incremental changes were introduced in the late 1980s such as better cash grants to children in poor families (1986–87) and grants for the first time to disabled children, their value was not protected against inflation.

Gorbachev's first commitment was to cushion the family against the shift to market principle while at the same time making profound alterations to the social security system. In a useful review article on social security changes, Liu notes that one of Gorbachev's major achievements was to establish a link between family allowances and the minimum wage by April 1991 (Liu, 1993). At the same time entitlement to benefits was widened to include payments to *all* families with children; previously benefits had only been available to families with two children or according to a means-test. Gorbachev also introduced special protection for disadvantaged families which incorporated a wide range of categories. Families whose per capita income was less than four times the minimum wages were paid quarterly cost-of-living allowances until the child reached the age of 18 as well as a monthly child benefit. Working mothers' entitlement to paid maternity leave was extended until the child reached 18 months, with further protected leave up to the child's third birthday. Special single parent monthly payments were introduced along with payments for children whose parents were evading maintenance. Payments to children in orphanages and children's homes and those who had contracted AIDS and were under the age of 16, were also introduced.

Yeltsin reiterated the linkage between family allowances and the minimum wage and throughout 1992 continued to try to protect families. Family benefits were raised three times and special supplementary flat-rate payments were paid twice (Liu, 1993). Disability allowances and benefits for orphans also were increased. But the evidence is that all these family allowances failed to keep pace with inflation and fell below minimum subsistence standards of living. With inflation running at 20–25 per cent per month, it is hardly surprising that government ambitions to protect families from poverty outstripped their capacity to do so. This failure obviously creates a very dangerous situation and is a clear breeding ground for both personal and political discontent. Given the severe financial hardship currently being experienced by so many families, combined with the evidence of privations contained in the report to the UN, it is perhaps unsurprising that the December 1993 elections gave the Liberal Democrats under Zhirinovsky such gains and undermined Yeltsin's capacity to push through his own reform programme.

Family Support Programmes to protect children

A new philosophy

The developments currently taking place in the creation of a system of personal social services constitute nothing short of a revolution. The Yeltsin administration has always recognised that the psycho-social repercussions of 'marketisation' would require an entirely new type of personal service to the nation, which could help promote self-reliance and family health. The idea came not from Yeltsin's policy-makers, but from Gorbachev and his staff, who saw the development of a network of psycho-social and socio-legal personal services as a key element in his strategy to imbue socialism with a human face. In the socialist era, assistance to vulnerable families came largely through the workplace, schools, Trade Unions and a range of politico-social organisations. Assistance tended to be practical, commonsense based and lacked any theoretical or professional underpinning. This was no casual oversight. In the early days of socialism, political ideology emphasised societal reorganisation as the way of overcoming individual human suffering. Later, it was simply an area of low priority (Madison, 1978). As there was no public debate or information available on the extent of unmet need it was easy to pretend the problems did not exist. By the late 1980s the myth had exploded as glasnost forced into public view the absence of services for children with disabilities, and the plight of children in care who were unknown to society and forgotten both by society and their own parents (Harwin, 1988, 1994). Scandals came to light describing the conditions in care and the helplessness of children to fight regimes which were brutal or kept them incarcerated using false diagnoses. The spate of *ad hoc* measures adopted in the mid to late 1980s to improve childcare services as well as the creation of a new Children's Fund were a start in the right direction. But these developments fell far short of the restructuring currently taking place which alters radically the direction of childcare policy and practice.

The UN Convention emphasises the importance of children being brought up in their own family. This principle is the driving force behind the new developments. Present government strategy rests on several key points.

1   Families should be supported to look after their own children through the provision of a range of community-based psycho-social services.
2   There should be a range of specialist services for children and families to be provided by a mixture of government and non-government organisations which should be available at every tier of administration.
3   These services should be provided by a cadre of specially trained professional staff.
4   Services should be targeted to those most in need.
5   Children who are disabled should wherever possible be integrated into mainstream society according to normalisation principles.
6   Every effort should be made to find homes for children in institutional care.

In this way the child rescue orientation which dominated practice in the socialist years, when relatives were unable or unwilling to assist, has been replaced. Childcare strategy has now been firmly tethered to the broader framework of family support.

Progress in implementation

Considerable progress has already been made in many of these areas. By August 1993 there were already approximately 500 social-service type facilities for children and families (Panov, 1993). These included children and family centres operating at territorial level, as well as centres providing psycho-pedagogical assistance, social rehabilitation centres for young offenders and shelters and refuges for handicapped children, runaways and for women and children. By the year 2000 it is hoped that there will be 3000 centres. Of the 500 centres already in existence, 200 are run by the Ministry of Social Protection, some have been developed by voluntary organisations, while others operate on an inter-agency basis, with joint funding.

There have also been significant developments in social work education and training. The green light to the development of social work as a professional paid activity came in the last days of Gorbachev in 1991 (USSR Law, 1991) and, by the end of 1991, more than 50 higher education institutions began social work courses (Panov, 1993). By mid-1993 more than 1000 social workers had received their professional qualifications.

Russia has every reason to be immensely proud of these developments which have been achieved over a very short time and in the face of profound difficulties in society. Three factors have facilitated these achievements. First, there has been a clear political will to achieve change in child and family policy and the development of an overall strategy to achieve it – reflected in the Presidential Decree of June 1992 'On measures to achieve the World Declaration to safeguard the survival, protection and development of children in the 1990s'. That political will has found practical expression through the development of new initiatives at central government level. Yeltsin has appointed an Adviser on the Family, who is also in charge of coordinating inter-departmental policy-making. Second, a new Ministry – the Ministry of Social Protection (formerly the Ministry of Social Security) – has been given a lead role. Formerly it was only concerned with pensions and services for disabled children and adults. The Ministry of Social Protection has widened its remit to include all vulnerable groups and has a separate department exclusively concerned with policy development and implementation in respect of children and family services. This Ministry has no history of intervention in this area, and is therefore better able to bring a fresh approach. Finally there have been a number of specific programmes at Republic and federal level such as the Children of Russia programme which has adopted a targeting approach to identify priority areas for action.

FUTURE THREATS AND OBSTACLES

These developments are impressive, but there are a number of serious obstacles which may weaken future policy-making and service development for children and families. Some of these obstacles will prove easier to overcome than others. At present, for example, the new services have no statutory authorisation in law. Progress in this area is already under way. A resolution adopted by the College of the Ministry of Social Protection made arrangements for the necessary work to be done by the end of December 1993, so that proposals could be placed with the Council of Ministers in 1994.

Other problems may be far harder to resolve. First, despite the political will to introduce reform demonstrated so far, there has been confusion and uncertainty at Parliamentary level which has undermined service development. During 1993 there were proposals to relocate all children and family services from the Ministry of Social Protection and Ministry of Education (which has a major responsibility for child protection) to an entirely new Commission on Guardianship and Adoption (Dzugaeva, personal communication 1993).[1] The rationale for this proposal was unclear, and both Ministries strongly opposed the initiative which was eventually dropped. It nevertheless demonstrated the vulnerability of existing Ministries to reorganisation. There has also been major uncertainty, for the last eighteen months, over the future of the Children's Inspectorate within the Ministry of Education which has statutory responsibilities to intervene when parents are unable or unwilling to look after their children. There have been proposals to absorb the Inspectorate into the Ministry of Social

Protection which would create a far more coherent, unified framework for family and child policy, practice and service delivery than exists at present. No decisions have been made however, with the resultant demoralising of an important group of staff, who at present have skills in the sharp end of child protection not shared by others.

Funding problems must be added to these difficulties. When the Ministry of Social Protection was established it expected to receive substantial transfers from Communist Party funds, but these never materialised. The Ministry was also placed in charge of the administration of a Fund for the Social Support of the Population, set up in 1991 by Presidential decree. It was to act as a top-up fund for vulnerable groups and to provide assistance to single mothers, children, social rehabilitation centres and children's homes. The State committed itself to providing the money for this fund in its first year of operation at the federal level, expecting the Fund to be able to find alternative budgetary sources thereafter. These sources did not materialise however, with the result that in 1993 the Fund operated without any official financial support. Efforts to enlist the support of the Ministry of Finance have so far proved unsuccessful. The experience of this Fund is only one example of the difficulties in finding revenue from outside state funds. While the commercial sector is potentially the richest source of funding for social support, tax allowances currently provide very few incentives to enterprises to invest their money in this way.

Other clear areas of difficulty have emerged. Difficulties in understanding the needs and objectives of the new children and family services have hindered their development in some areas of the Federation and resulted in patchy provision. This uncertainty over the nature and purposes of social work needs to be taken extremely seriously. There have already been reports of a mismatch between training programmes and social work practice, resulting in disillusionment and costly staff wastage. Social work has been developing at a tremendous pace and at present there exists a worrying euphoria over its potential, and a tendency to regard the new social workers as the future saviours of society. It is easy to see why social work, which emphasises the individual, should be so attractive to a society which for so long suppressed the 'personal' in service provision. But if social work fails then the new saviours will become the new scapegoats. To avoid this there must be an energetic attempt to tether social work intervention to specific legal powers and duties and thereby set boundaries on its scope. This will also require a fundamental review of existing childcare law.[2] Without this there is a real danger that the new protectors of children will become the source of their disillusionment.

Finally, present political developments – the growth of right-wing forces and nationalism – make it seem less certain than even a year ago, that the new democracy can be secured and be able to push through its ambitious reform programme.

CONCLUSIONS

It should come as no surprise that child protection needs have taken precedence over children's participatory rights. The need for child protection is undoubtedly the most urgent. Real progess has been made, but the advances should not be exaggerated. The new structures are rudimentary and fragile and it would be precocious to talk of the existence of a real infrastructure for the delivery of child and family services. More generally, demand for services will undoubtedly outstrip supply in the foreseeable future. The gap between provision and need will widen as the effects of poverty and unemployment – the latter still officially very low – bite harder in the next few years.

It has never been the government's intention, of course, to be the sole provider of social services to children and families. The voluntary sector has been growing from a nil base over the last few years, but similarly confronts major difficulties. Relationships between State and voluntary sector are problematic and characterised by a lack of coordination. Above all there is a shortage of services. To these difficulties must be added the decline of childcare provision under socialism. Nursery provision, for example, previously available for well over 50 per cent of the population, has substantially declined. It is not just State nurseries which have closed, but enterprises formerly very active in this field have also been beating a retreat. It is too costly for both state and private enterprises to continue providing nursery care which conflicts with their new market-driven economic goals.

In short, welfare provision for Russian children and families under marketisation is likely to follow the experience of Western social service agencies, and find that it can meet the needs of only the most deprived and disadvantaged. This may prove even more true in Russia because of the very weak material base. The evident tragedy is that Russian aspirations are on such a grand scale. Policy makers wish to establish a comprehensive range of services encompassing psycho-social, legal and pedagogical assistance. If these cannnot evolve fast enough the Russian people may well look back nostalgically to the socialist era. Some are already questioning whether the new regime has really brought empowerment to parents and their childen, or could do so in the future.

NOTES

1 A. Dzugaeva is Chief Specialist, Department for Rehabilitation and Special Education, Ministry of Education of the Russian Federation.
2 A new review of family law is now underway, which includes an examination of childcare provisions.

CASES CITED

Re K, W and H [1993] 1 FLR 854
Re R [1991] 4 All ER 177
Re W [1992] 4 All ER 627

REFERENCES

British Medical Journal (1994) 'Life expectancy in Russia falls' *British Medical Journal* Vol. 308, p. 553.

Cornia, G.A. and Sipos, S. (1991) *Children and the Transition to the Market Economy*, Avebury: Aldershot.

George, V. (1992) 'Social Security in the USSR', *International Social Security Review*, No. 4.

Harwin, J. (1988) 'Glasnost children' 6 April, p. 23.

—— (1994) 'The Impact of Economic and Political Change on Russian Child Protection Policy' in S. Ringen and C. Wallace (eds) *Societies in Transition: East Central Europe Today* Vol. 1, pp. 105–27, Avebury: Aldershot.

Lakhora (1992) 'What kind of generation are we raising?' *Russian Gazette*, March.

Liu, L. (1993) 'Income security in transition for the aged and children in the Soviet Union and in the Russian Federation', *Social Security Bulletin*, Vol. 56 (1).

Madison, B. (1978) 'Social Services for women: problems and priorities' in D. Atkinson, A. Dallin and G.W. Lapidus (eds) *Women in Russia* The Harvester Press.

Panov, A. (1993) Unpublished briefing document to the College of the Ministry of Social Protection of the Russian Federation on measures for the development of social services for women and children. Panov is the first Deputy Director of the Department of Problems of the Family, Women and Children, Ministry of Social Protection.

Pozdnyakova, Larisa Stepanovna, Head of Department of Economics and Finance, Ministry of Social Protection. Interview, 25 October 1994.

Rassmotrenie dokladov, predstavlennykh gosudarstavami-uchastnikami v sootvetstvii so stat'ei 44 Konventsii, Pervonachal'nye doklady . . . v 1992 gody. Report to the UN by the Russian Federation, October 1992. (In Russian only.)

Shcherbakov, V. (1990) 'Social protection measures under market conditions' *The Current Digest of the Soviet Press* Vol. XLII, No. 32, pp. 1–2.

Russian Federation Law (1990) 'O svobode veroispovedanii'.

—— (1992) 'Ob obrazovanii'.

USSR Law (1990a) 'O vnesenii izmenenii i dopolnenii . . . po voprisam, kasayushchimsya zhenshchin, sem'i i detstva.

—— (1990b) 'O svobode sovesti i religioznykh organizatsiyakh'.

—— (1991) 'Ob obshchikh nachalakh gosudarstvennoi molodezhnoi politiki v SSSR. (This law was the first to make provision for the development of social work as a paid profession.)

Name index

Subject index